EA

Birthdays of

the Rich and

Famous™

Book One: *Entertainment*

The birthdays of more than 12,000 people from all parts of the entertainment world, arranged by categories

Compiled & Edited by
Alan Romanoff

Darco Press
Cleveland

To Maureen and the kids,
who put up with a lot

Birthdays of the Rich and Famous™
Published by Darco Press

Published by:
Darco Press
P O Box 5553
Cleveland OH 44101

ISBN 1-887320-00-8
Library of Congress Catalog
Card Number 95-068813

Printed in USA by
Brown Business Graphics
Cleveland OH

TABLE OF CONTENTS

PREFACE

Our goal was to make this a truly unique book. How?

First, we concentrated on just one field---entertainment---in all its forms and phases: from vaudeville and silent movies to TV talk shows and rock videos; from Broadway musicals and opera to country music and rap; from actors and comedians to directors and newscasters.

Then, we expanded our coverage to include not only those who appear in the spotlight, but also the talented and creative people who work behind the scenes. You will find all the stars, of course, and many supporting players as well.

Last, we placed limits of *time* and *place* on those who would be listed. So, while we pay tribute to legendary performers, and include many foreign stars whose careers brought them to the United States, the emphasis is on American entertainers of the last half century.

Performers are listed by major fields---Actors, Dancers, Comedians, Singers and so on---and there are also many interesting sub-categories. For example, under the main heading *Singers & Musicians* is *Country & Western Music;* and that is further divided into such topics as *Bluegrass* and *Western Swing.* Members of popular groups such as *Alabama* are also listed separately.

Hundreds of books were consulted to obtain the material in this one volume. Dates were double-checked whenever possible. When conflicting dates arose-- and this was not unusual--we used the one that seemed most reliable. Still, mistakes are inevitable in a project of this scope. We apologize for this, and will correct any brought to our attention in a future edition.

We trust you will find this a source of much useful information; but it is also intended as a book that will encourage browsing just for fun, and we hope it serves that purpose, too.

(This book is planned as part of a series, with each volume covering different fields of endeavor. We invite your comments, so that future volumes will be as valuable as possible.)

SILENT FILMS ACTORS

Adams Claire	9-24-00
Adoree Renee	9-30-1898
Allison May	6-14-1895
Alvarado Don	11-4-00
Arliss George	4-10-1868
Ayres Agnes	9-4-1896
Baggot King	1874
Bancroft George	9-30-1882
Banky Vilma	1-9-1898
Bara Theda	7-20-1890
Barriscale Bessie	1884
Barthelmess Richard	5-9-1895
Bayne Beverly	11-11-1894
Bellamy Madge	6-30-00
Bennett Belle	10-21-1892
Blackwell Carlyle	4-21-1888
Blythe Betty	9-1-1893
Boardman Eleanor	8-19-1898
Booth Edwina	9-13-09
Bosworth Hobart	8-11-1867
Bow Clara	8-6-05
Bowers John	12-25-1899
Brent Evelyn	10-20-1899
Brian Mary	2-17-08
Bronson Betty	11-17-06
Brooks Louise	11-14-06
Burke Billie	8-7-1885
Busch Mae	1-20-1897
Bushman Francis X	1-10-1883
Calvert Catherine	4-20-1890
Chadwick Helene	11-25-1897
Chaney Lon	4-1-1883
Clark Marguerite	2-22-1883
Clayton Ethel	1884
Clayton Marguerite	1896
Cody Lew	2-22-1884
Collier William Jr	2-12-02
Compson Betty	3-18-1897
Coogan Jackie	10-26-14
Cortez Ricardo	9-19-1899
Costello Dolores	9-17-1905
Costello Helene	6-21-03
Costello Maurice	2-2-1877
Craig Nell	1891
Crisp Donald	7-27-1880

D'Arcy Roy	2-10-1894
Dalton Dorothy	9-22-1893
Dana Viola	6-28-1897
Dane Karl	10-12-1886
Daniels Bebe	1-14-01
Davies Marion	1-3-1897
Dean Priscilla	1896
DeCordoba Pedro	9-28-1881
DeLaMotte Marguerite	6-22-02
Desmond William	5-21-1878
Dexter Elliott	9-11-1870
Doro Marie	2-4-1882
Dove Billie	5-14-00
Dresser Louise	10-5-1878
Durfee Minta	1897
Eagels Jeanne	6-26-1894
Edeson Robert	1-23-1868
Fairbanks Douglas	5-23-1883
Farnum Dustin	5-27-1874
Farnum William	7-4-1876
Farrell Charles	8-9-01
Fawcett George	8-25-1860
Faye Julia	9-24-1896
Ferguson Elsie	8-19-1883
Ferguson Helen	7-23-01
Finch Flora	2-11-1869
Fischer Margarita	2-11-1886
Ford Harrison	3-16-1892
Frederick Pauline	8-12-1883
Gardner Helen	1885
Garon Pauline	9-9-01
Gaynor Janet	10-6-06
Gilbert John	7-10-1895
Gillingwater Claude	8-2-1870
Gish Dorothy	3-11-1898
Gish Lillian	10-14-1896
Gordon Vera	6-11-1886
Gordon Julia Swayne	1879
Gordon Robert	1895
Goudal Jetta	7-18-1898
Graves Ralph	1-23-00
Gray Lawrence	7-28-1898
Griffith Corinne	11-24-1896
Haines William	1-1-00
Hale Creighton	5-14-1882
Hall James	10-22-00

Hamilton Mahlon	1883
Hamilton Neil	9-9-1899
Hampton Hope	1901
Hanson Lars	7-26-1886
Harlan Kenneth	7-26-1895
Harris Mildred	11-29-01
Harron Bobby	4-24-1894
Haver Phyllis	1-6-1899
Hawley Wanda	7-30-1895
Hayakawa Sessue	6-10-1889
Holding Thomas	1-25-1880
Holmes Stuart	3-10-1887
Howes Reed	7-5-00
Hughes Gareth	8-23-1894
Hughes Lloyd	10-21-1897
Jannings Emil	7-23-1884
Johnson Arthur V	2-2-1876
Joy Leatrice	11-7-1896
Joyce Alice	10-1-1890
Kellermann Annette	7-6-1887
Kennedy Madge	8-1-1892
Kenyon Doris	9-5-1897
Kerrigan J Warren	7-25-1889
Kerry Norman	6-16-1889
Kingston Winifred	1895
Kosloff Theodore	4-5-1882
LaBadie Florence	1893
LaMarr Barbara	7-28-1896
Landis Cullen	7-19-1898
LaPlante Laura	11-1-04
Larkin George	11-11-1888
LaRocque Rod	11-29-1896
LaVerne Lucille	11-8-1872
Lawrence Florence	1888
Lee Lila	7-25-01
Leonard Marion	1880
Lewis Ralph	1872
Lincoln Elmo	6-14-1899
Lockwood Harold	4-12-1887
Logan Jacqueline	11-30-01
Long Walter	3-5-1879
Love Bessie	9-10-1898
Love Montagu	1877
MacDermott Marc	1881
MacDonald J Farrell	6-6-1875
Mack Charles Emmett	1900

Mackaill Dorothy	3-4-03
MacLean Douglas	1-14-1890
Madison Cleo	1883
Mansfield Martha	1900
Markey Enid	2-22-1896
Marlowe June	11-6-03
Marmont Percy	11-25-1883
Marsh Mae	11-9-1895
Marshall Tully	4-13-1864
Mason Shirley	6-6-01
McAvoy May	9-18-01
McGregor Malcolm	10-13-1892
McKim Robert	8-26-1887
Meighan Thomas	4-9-1879
Miller Patsy Ruth	6-22-05
Miller Walter	3-9-1892
Minter Mary Miles	4-1-02
Moore Colleen	8-19-00
Moore Matt	1-8-1888
Moore Owen	12-12-1886
Moore Tom	11-14-1884
Moran Lois	3-1-08
Moreno Antonio	9-26-1887
Morrison James	11-15-1888
Mulhall Jack	10-7-1887
Murray Mae	5-10-1885
Myers Carmel	4-4-1889
Myers Harry C	1882
Nagel Conrad	3-16-1897
Naldi Nita	4-1-1891
Nazimova (Alla)	6-4-1879
Negri Pola	12-31-1894
Nielsen Asta	9-11-1893
Nilsson Anna Q	3-3-1890
Nissen Greta	1-30-06
Novarro Ramon	2-6-1899
Novello Ivor	1-15-1893
O'Brien Eugene	11-14-1882
O'Malley Pat	9-3-1891
O'Neil Sally	10-23-08
Oakman Wheeler	1890
Ogle Charles	6-5-1865
Ovey George	12-13-1870
Owen Seena	1896
Pearson Virginia	3-7-1888
Percy Eileen	8-1-1899

Periolat George	1876	Stewart Anita	2-7-1895
Peters House	3-12-1880	Stonehouse Ruth	10-24-1893
Philbin Mary	7-16-03	Storey Edith	3-18-1892
Phillips Dorothy	10-30-1889	Swanson Gloria	3-27-1897
Pickford Jack	8-18-1896	Sweet Blanche	6-18-1895
Pickford Mary	4-8-1894	Taliaferro Mabel	5-21-1889
Pitts Zasu	1-3-1898	Talmadge Constance	4-19-00
Polo Eddie	1875	Talmadge Norma	5-26-1897
Post Guy Bates	9-22-1875	Talmadge Richard	12-3-1896
Potel Victor	1889	Taylor Estelle	5-20-1899
Powell David	1885	Tearle Conway	5-17-1878
Power Tyrone Sr	5-2-1869	Tellegen Lou	11-26-1881
Prevost Marie	11-8-1898	Terry Alice	7-24-1899
Price Kate	2-13-1872	Thomas Olive	10-29-1884
Prim Suzy	1-11-1895	Thurman Mary	4-27-1894
Pringle Aileen	7-23-1895	Torrence Ernest	6-26-1878
Purviance Edna	10-21-1894	Torres Raquel	11-11-08
Quirk Billy	1881	Travers Richard C	4-15-1890
Ralston Esther	9-17-02	Truex Ernest	9-19-1890
Ralston Jobyna	11-24-02	Tryon Glenn	9-14-1894
Randolph Anders	12-18-1876	Tucker Richard	1884
Rawlinson Herbert	11-15-1885	Turner Florence	1885
Ray Charles	3-15-1891	Ulric Lenore	7-21-1892
Reid Wallace	4-15-1891	Valentino Rudolph	5-6-1895
Reynolds Vera	11-25-00	Valli Virginia	6-10-1895
Rhodes Billie	1895	Varconi Victor	3-31-1896
Rich Irene	10-13-1891	Vidor Florence	7-23-1895
Rich Vivian	1893	VonEltz Theodore	1894
Richman Charles	1-12-1865	Walker Charlotte	12-29-1878
Roberts Florence	3-16-1861	Walker Johnnie	1896
Roberts Theodore	10-2-1861	Walker Lillian	4-21-1888
Robson May	4-19-1858	Walsh George	3-16-1889
Rogers Charles 'Buddy'	8-13-04	Walthall Henry B	3-16-1878
Roland Ruth	8-26-1892	Warner H B	10-26-1876
Roscoe Alan	8-23-1887	Warwick Robert	10-9-1878
Rubens Alma	2-8-1897	Washburn Bryant	4-28-1889
Russell William	4-12-1886	Welch Niles	7-29-1895
Salisbury Monroe	1876	White Alice	8-28-07
Santschi Thomas	10-14-1878	White Pearl	3-4-1889
Sedgwick Eileen & Josie	1895	Williams Earle	2-28-1880
Sills Milton	1-12-1882	Williams Kathlyn	5-31-1888
Smalley Phillips	8-7-1875	Wilson Lois	6-28-1896
Snow Marguerite	9-9-1889	Windsor Claire	4-14-1897
Stanley Forrest	8-21-1889	Wolheim Louis	3-28-1880
Starke Pauline	1-10-00	Wong Anna May	1-3-07
Stedman Myrtle	3-3-1889	Young Clara Kimball	1890

FILM ACTORS

Abbott Philip	3-20-24
Ackland Joss	2-29-28
Acquanetta	7-17-20
Adams Brooke	2-8-49
Adams Julie	10-17-26
Adams Maud	2-12-45
Adjani Isabelle	6-27-55
Adler Luther	5-4-03
Adrian Iris	5-29-12
Agar John	1-31-21
Agutter Jenny	12-20-52
Aherne Brian	5-2-02
Ahn Philip	3-29-11
Aiello Danny	6-20-33
Aimee Anouk	4-27-32
Albert Eddie	4-22-08
Albertson Frank	2-2-09
Aldon Mari	11-17-29
Alexander Ross	7-27-07
Allan Elizabeth	4-9-08
Allbright Hardie	12-16-03
Allbritton Louise	7-3-20
Allen Karen	10-5-51
Allen Nancy	6-24-50
Allen Patrick	3-17-27
Allwyn Astrid	11-27-09
Allyson June	10-7-17
Alonso Maria Conchita	6-29-57
Alvarado Trini	1-10-67
Ames Adrienne	8-3-07
Ames Leon	1-20-03
Amis Suzi	1-5-58
Anderson Warner	3-10-11
Andersson Bibi	11-11-35
Andersson Harriet	1-14-32
Andress Ursula	3-19-36
Andrews Dana	1-1-09
Andrews Edward	10-9-14
Angel Heather	2-9-09
Angeli Pier	6-19-32
Ankers Evelyn	8-17-18
Ann-Margret	4-28-41
Annabella	7-14-09
Arbus Allan	2-15-18
Archer Anne	8-25-47

Archer John	5-8-15
Arkin Alan	3-26-34
Arlen Richard	9-1-00
Armendariz Pedro	5-9-12
Armstrong R G	4-7-17
Armstrong Robert	11-20-1890
Arnold Edward	2-18-1890
Arnoul Francoise	6-3-31
Arquette Rosanna	8-10-59
Arthur Jean	10-17-05
Arthur Robert	6-18-25
Asher Jane	4-5-46
Ashley Elizabeth	8-30-39
Ashley John	12-25-34
Aslan Gregoire	3-28-08
Astor Mary	5-3-06
Atwill Lionel	3-1-1885
Audran Stephane	11-8-32
Auer Mischa	11-17-05
Auger Claudine	4-26-42
Aulin Ewa	2-14-49
Aumont Jean Pierre	1-5-09
Austin Charlotte	11-2-33
Avery Val	7-14-24
Ayres Lew	12-28-08
Bacall Lauren	9-16-24
Bach Barbara	8-27-49
Bacon Irving	9-6-1893
Bacon Kevin	7-8-58
Baddeley Hermione	11-13-06
Badel Alan	9-11-23
Bainter Fay	12-7-1891
Baker Carroll	5-28-31
Baker Diane	2-25-38
Baker Joe Don	2-12-36
Baker Stanley	2-28-28
Bakewell William	5-2-08
Baldwin Alec	4-3-58
Baldwin William	1963
Balin Ina	11-12-37
Balsam Martin	11-4-19
Bancroft Anne	9-17-31
Banderas Antonio	1960
Bannen Ian	6-29-28
Bardot Brigitte	9-28-34
Bari Lynn	12-18-13

****

Barker Lex	5-8-19
Barkin Ellen	4-16-55
Barnes Binnie	3-25-05
Barnett Vince	7-4-02
Barrie Mona	12-18-09
Barrie Wendy	4-18-12
Barrymore Diana	3-3-21
Barrymore Drew	2-22-75
Barrymore Ethel	8-15-1879
Barrymore John	2-15-1882
Barrymore John Drew	6-4-32
Barrymore Lionel	4-28-1878
Bartok Eva	6-18-29
Barty Billy	10-25-24
Basehart Richard	8-31-14
Basinger Kim	12-8-53
Bass Alfie	4-8-21
Bassett Angela	8-16-58
Bates Alan	2-17-34
Bates Barbara	8-6-25
Bates Kathy	6-28-48
Bauer Steven	12-2-56
Baxter Anne	5-7-23
Baxter Warner	3-29-1889
Baye Nathalie	7-6-48
Beal John	8-13-09
Beals Jennifer	12-19-63
Beatty Ned	7-6-37
Beatty Robert	10-9-09
Beatty Warren	3-30-37
Bedelia Bonnie	3-25-48
Beery Noah	1-17-1884
Beery Wallace	4-1-1885
Bell James	12-1-1891
Bellamy Ralph	6-17-04
Belmondo Jean-Paul	4-9-33
Belushi Jim	6-15-54
Benben Brian	6-18-56
Bendix William	1-14-06
Bening Annette	5-5-58
Benjamin Richard	5-22-38
Bennett Bruce	5-19-06
Bennett Constance	10-22-04
Bennett Joan	2-27-10
Benson Robby	1-21-57
Bentley John	12-2-16

****

****

Berenger Tom	5-31-50
Berenson Marisa	2-15-47
Bergen Polly	7-14-30
Berger Senta	5-13-41
Bergerac Jacques	5-26-27
Bergin Patrick	2-4-51
Bergman Ingrid	8-29-15
Berlin Jeannie	11-1-49
Berry Halle	8-14-68
Best Willie	5-27-16
Beswick Martine	1941
Bettger Lyle	2-13-15
Bey Turhan	3-30-20
Beymer Richard	2-21-39
Bice Robert	3-4-14
Bickford Charles	1-1-1889
Bikel Theodore	5-2-24
Bill Tony	8-23-40
Bing Herman	3-30-1889
Birkin Jane	12-14-46
Bishop Julie	8-30-14
Bissell Whit	10-25-09
Bisset Jacqueline	9-13-44
Black Karen	7-1-42
Blackman Honor	8-22-25
Blair Betsy	12-11-23
Blair Janet	4-23-21
Blair Linda	1-22-59
Blake Marie	8-21-1896
Blakely Colin	9-23-30
Blakely Susan	9-7-48
Blakeney Olive	8-21-1894
Blakiston Caroline	2-13-33
Blakley Ronee	1946
Blanchard Mari	4-13-27
Blondell Joan	8-30-09
Bloom Claire	2-15-31
Bloom Verna	8-7-39
Blore Eric	12-23-1887
Blyth Ann	8-16-28
Bochner Hart	10-3-56
Bogarde Dirk	3-28-20
Bogart Humphrey	12-25-1899
Bogosian Eric	4-24-53
Boles John	10-27-1895
Bolkan Florinda	2-15-41

****

* *

Bolling Tiffany	2-6-47
Bologna Joseph	12-30-38
Bond Lillian	1-18-10
Bond Ward	4-9-04
Bondi Beulah	5-3-1892
Bonham-Carter Helena	5-26-66
Booth James	12-19-30
Borchers Cornell	3-16-25
Borg Veda Ann	1-11-15
Borgnine Ernest	1-24-17
Bostwick Barry	2-24-45
Bouchet Barbara	8-15-43
Bowman Lee	12-28-14
Boyd Stephen	7-4-28
Boyer Charles	8-28-1897
Boyle Peter	10-18-33
Bracco Lorraine	10-2-50
Bracken Eddie	2-7-15
Bradley Grace	9-21-13
Brady Scott	9-13-24
Braga Sonia	6-8-50
Branagh Kenneth	12-10-60
Brandauer Klaus Maria	6-22-44
Brando Jocelyn	11-18-19
Brando Marlon	4-3-24
Brasselle Keefe	2-7-23
Brazzi Rossano	9-18-16
Bremer Lucille	2-21-22
Brennan Eileen	9-3-35
Brennan Walter	7-25-1894
Brent George	3-15-04
Brian David	8-5-14
Bridges Beau	12-9-41
Bridges Jeff	12-4-49
Bridges Lloyd	1-15-13
Brinckerhoff Burt	10-25-36
Britt May	3-22-33
Britton Barbara	9-26-19
Broderick Matthew	3-21-62
Brodie Steve	11-25-19
Bromberg J Edward	12-25-03
Bronson Charles	11-3-21
Brook Clive	6-1-1887
Brooke Hillary	9-8-14
Brooks Geraldine	10-29-25
Brooks Jean	12-23-16

* *

Brooks Phyllis	7-18-14
Brooks Rand	9-21-18
Brophy Edward	2-27-1895
Brown Blair	4-23-47
Brown Bryan	6-23-47
Brown Georgia	10-21-33
Brown James L	3-22-20
Brown Tom	1-6-13
Brown Vanessa	3-24-28
Browne Coral	7-23-13
Browne Roscoe Lee	5-2-25
Bruce Nigel	2-4-1895
Bruce Virginia	9-29-10
Brynner Yul	7-11-20
Buchholz Horst	12-4-33
Bujold Genevieve	7-1-42
Bull Peter	3-21-12
Bullock Sandra	7-26-65
Buono Victor	2-3-38
Burgess Dorothy	3-4-07
Burstyn Ellen	12-7-32
Burton Richard	11-10-25
Busey Gary	6-29-44
Butterworth Charles	7-26-1897
Byington Spring	10-17-1886
Byrd Ralph	4-22-09
Byrne Gabriel	5-12-50
Caan James	3-26-39
Cabot Bruce	4-20-04
Cabot Sebastian	7-6-18
Cabot Susan	7-9-27
Caesar Harry	2-18-28
Cage Nicolas	1-7-64
Cagney James	7-17-1899
Caine Michael	3-14-33
Calder-Marshall Anna	1-11-47
Calhern Louis	2-16-1895
Calvert Phyllis	2-18-15
Calvet Corinne	4-30-26
Campbell Bill	7-7-59
Canale Gianna Maria	9-12-27
Cannon Dyan	1-4-37
Capucine	1-6-35
Cardinale Claudia	4-15-38
Carere Christine	7-27-30
Carlisle Mary	2-3-12

* *

****

Carlson Richard	4-29-12
Carol Martine	5-16-22
Carr Darleen	12-12-50
Carradine John	2-5-06
Carradine Keith	8-8-49
Carradine Robert	3-24-54
Carrera Barbara	12-31-45
Carroll John	7-17-05
Carroll Leo G	10-18-1892
Carroll Madeleine	2-26-09
Carter Helena	8-24-23
Carter Janis	10-10-17
Cash Rosalind	12-31-38
Castellano Richard	9-4-34
Castle Peggie	12-22-27
Cates Phoebe	7-16-63
Catlett Walter	2-4-1889
Cattrall Kim	8-21-56
Caulfield Joan	6-1-22
Caulfield Maxwell	11-23-59
Chakiris George	9-16-32
Chandler Chick	1-18-05
Chandler George	6-20-02
Chandler Helen	2-1-06
Chandler Jeff	12-15-18
Chaney Lon Jr	2-10-06
Channing Stockard	2-13-44
Chaplin Geraldine	7-31-44
Chapman Marguerite	3-9-20
Charleson Ian	8-11-49
Chen Joan	4-26-61
Chong Rae Dawn	2-28-61
Christian Linda	11-13-23
Christie Julie	4-14-40
Christopher Jordan	10-23-40
Christy Dorothy	5-26-06
Churchill Marguerite	12-25-09
Cilento Diane	10-5-33
Clark Dane	2-18-13
Clarke Mae	8-16-07
Clayburgh Jill	4-30-44
Clift Montgomery	10-17-20
Clive Colin	1-20-1898
Close Glenn	3-19-47
Clyde June	12-2-09
Cobb Lee J	12-9-11

****

****

Coburn Charles	6-19-1877
Coburn James	8-31-28
Cochran Steve	5-25-17
Coe Barry	11-26-34
Colbert Claudette	9-13-03
Colby Anita	8-5-14
Colicos John	12-10-28
Collier Lois	3-21-19
Collyer June	8-19-07
Colman Ronald	2-9-1891
Comer Anjanette	8-7-42
Comingore Dorothy	8-24-13
Compton Joyce	1-27-07
Connery Sean	8-25-30
Constantine Eddie	10-29-17
Conte Richard	3-24-14
Conti Tom	11-22-41
Conway Morgan	3-16-03
Conway Tom	9-15-04
Cook Donald	9-26-00
Cook Elisha Jr	12-26-06
Cooper Gary	5-7-01
Cooper Jackie	9-15-22
Coote Robert	2-4-09
Corday Mara	1-3-32
Corey Jeff	8-10-14
Corey Wendell	3-20-14
Corri Adrienne	11-13-33
Corrigan Lloyd	10-16-00
Corsaro Frank	12-22-25
Cort Bud	3-29-50
Cortesa Valentina	1-1-25
Costner Kevin	1-18-55
Cotten Joseph	5-15-05
Coulouris George	10-1-03
Court Hazel	2-10-26
Courtenay Tom	2-25-37
Courtland Jerome	12-27-26
Cowan Jerome	10-6-1897
Coyote Peter	10-10-42
Craig James	2-4-12
Crain Jeanne	5-25-25
Crane Richard	6-6-18
Crawford Broderick	12-9-11
Crawford Joan	3-23-04
Cregar Laird	7-28-16

****

Crews Laura Hope	12-12-1879
Cromwell Richard	1-8-10
Cronyn Tandy	11-27-45
Crosby Kathryn Grant	11-25-33
Cross Ben	12-16-48
Cruise Tom	7-3-62
Culver Roland	8-31-00
Cummings Constance	5-15-10
Cummings Robert	6-9-08
Cummins Peggy	12-18-26
Currie Flinlay	1-20-1878
Curry Tim	4-19-46
Curtis Alan	7-24-09
Curtis Jamie Lee	11-22-58
Curtis Tony	6-3-25
Cusack Cyril	11-26-10
Cusack Joan	10-11-62
Cusack John	6-28-66
Cushing Peter	5-26-13
D'abo Maryann	12-27-60
D'abo Olivia	1-22-67
D'Angelo Beverly	11-15-52
Dafoe Willem	7-22-55
Dahl Arlene	8-11-27
Dahlbeck Eva	3-8-20
Dale Esther	11-10-1885
Dallesandro Joe	12-31-48
Dalton Audrey	1-21-34
Dalton Timothy	3-21-44
Damita Lili	7-19-01
Damon Mark	4-22-33
Dandridge Dorothy	11-9-22
Daniell Henry	3-5-1894
Daniels Jeff	2-19-55
Danner Blythe	2-3-43
Dantine Helmut	10-7-17
Danton Ray	9-19-31
Darby Kim	7-8-48
Darc Mireille	5-15-38
Darcel Denise	9-8-25
Darnell Linda	10-16-21
Darrieux Danielle	5-1-17
Darro Frankie	12-22-17
Darrow Henry	9-15-33
Darrow John	7-17-07
Darvi Bella	10-23-29

Darwell Jane	10-15-1879
Dauphin Claude	8-19-03
Davenport Harry	1-19-1866
Davenport Nigel	5-23-28
Davidovich Lolita	7-15-51
Davis Bette	4-5-08
Davis Brad	11-6-49
Davis Geena	1-21-57
Davis Judy	4-23-55
Davis Ossie	12-18-17
Davis-Reagan Nancy	7-6-21
Davison Bruce	6-28-46
Day Laraine	10-13-20
Day-Lewis Daniel	4-29-57
Dean James	2-8-31
DeCordova Arturo	5-8-08
Dee Frances	11-26-07
Dee Ruby	10-27-24
Dee Sandra	4-23-42
DeHaven Gloria	7-23-25
DeHavilland Olivia	7-1-16
Dekker Albert	12-20-05
Dell Claudia	1-10-10
Dell Myrna	3-5-24
Delon Alain	11-8-35
Delorme Daniele	10-9-27
DelRio Dolores	8-3-05
DeMille Katherine	6-29-11
Demongeot Mylene	9-28-36
DeMornay Rebecca	8-29-61
DeMunn Jeffrey	4-25-47
Dench Judi	12-9-34
Deneuve Catherine	10-22-43
DeNiro Robert	8-17-43
Denner Charles	5-29-26
Denny Reginald	11-20-1891
Depardieu Gerard	12-27-48
Depp Johnny	6-9-63
Derek Bo	11-20-56
Derek John	8-12-26
Dern Bruce	6-4-36
Dern Laura	2-10-67
Derr Richard	6-15-17
DeSica Vittorio	7-7-01
Dewhurst Colleen	6-3-26
Dexter Anthony	1-19-19

****

Dexter Brad	4-9-17
Diaz Cameron	8-30-72
DiCaprio Leonardo	11-11-74
Dick Douglas	11-20-20
Dickson Gloria	8-13-16
Dietrich Marlene	12-27-01
Diffring Anton	10-20-18
Dillman Bradford	4-14-30
Dillon Matt	2-18-64
Dillon Melinda	10-31-39
Dix Richard	7-18-1894
Dixon Jean	7-14-1896
Dobson Tamara	5-14-47
Dodd Claire	12-29-08
Domergue Faith	6-16-25
Donahue Troy	1-27-37
Donald James	5-18-17
Donat Robert	3-18-05
Donath Ludwig	3-5-00
Donlevy Brian	2-9-1899
Donnelly Ruth	5-17-1896
Doran Ann	7-28-13
Dorleac Francoise	3-21-42
Dorn Philip	9-30-01
Dors Diana	10-23-31
Dotrice Roy	5-26-23
Douglas Kirk	12-9-16
Douglas Melvyn	4-5-01
Douglas Michael	9-25-44
Douglas Paul	4-11-07
Douglas Robert	11-9-09
Dourif Brad	3-18-50
Dow Peggy	3-18-28
Downey Robert Jr	4-4-65
Drake Betsy	9-11-23
Drake Charles	10-2-14
Drake Frances	10-22-08
Drake Tom	8-5-18
Dressler Marie	11-9-1869
Drew Ellen	11-23-15
Drexler Rosalyn	11-25-26
Dreyfuss Richard	10-29-47
Dru Joanne	1-31-23
Dullea Keir	5-30-36
Dumbrille Douglas	10-13-1890
Dumont Margaret	10-20-1889

****

****

Duna Steffi	7-4-14
Dunaway Faye	1-14-41
Dunn James	11-2-05
Dunne Griffin	6-8-55
Dunne Irene	12-20-1898
Dunnock Mildred	1-25-04
Duprez June	5-14-18
Duryea Dan	1-23-07
Dusay Marj	2-20-36
Duvall Robert	1-5-30
Duvall Shelley	7-7-49
Dvorak Ann	8-2-12
Eastwood Clint	5-31-30
Eaton Shirley	1936
Edwards Bill	9-14-18
Egan Richard	7-29-23
Eggar Samantha	3-5-39
Eichhorn Lisa	2-4-52
Eilers Sally	12-11-08
Ekberg Anita	9-29-31
Ekland Britt	10-6-42
Elam Jack	11-13-16
Elliott Denholm	5-31-22
Ellis Patricia	5-20-16
Elsom Isobel	3-16-1893
Elwes Cary	10-26-62
Emerson Faye	7-8-17
Emerson Hope	10-29-1898
Erdman Richard	6-1-25
Erickson Leif	10-27-11
Errol Leon	7-3-1881
Erwin Stuart	2-14-02
Esmond Carl	6-14-05
Esmond Jill	1-26-08
Estevez Emilio	5-12-62
Evans Gene	7-11-24
Evans Joan	7-18-34
Evans Madge	7-1-09
Evelyn Judith	3-20-13
Ewell Tom	4-29-09
Eythe William	4-7-18
Fairbanks Douglas Jr	12-9-09
Farmer Frances	9-19-13
Farr Felicia	10-4-32
Farrell Glenda	6-30-04
Farrow Mia	2-9-45

****

Feld Fritz	10-15-00
Fellows Edith	5-20-23
Ferrer Jose	1-8-09
Ferrer Mel	8-25-17
Ferris Barbara	10-3-40
Fetchit Stepin	5-30-1892
Field Betty	2-8-18
Field Sally	11-6-46
Field Shirley Ann	6-27-38
Field Virginia	11-4-17
Finch Peter	9-28-16
Finkel Fyvush	10-9-22
Finlay Frank	8-6-26
Finney Albert	5-9-36
Fiorentino Linda	3-9-60
Firestone Eddie	12-11-20
Firth Peter	10-27-53
Fishburne Laurence	7-30-61
Fisher Carrie	10-21-56
Fitzgerald Barry	3-10-1888
Fitzgerald Geraldine	11-24-14
Fix Paul	3-13-02
Flanders Michael	3-1-22
Flavin James	5-14-06
Fleming Rhonda	8-10-23
Flemyng Robert	1-3-12
Fletcher Louise	7-22-34
Flippen Jay C	3-6-1898
Flynn Errol	6-20-09
Flynn Miriam	6-18-52
Foch Nina	4-20-24
Fonda Bridget	1-27-64
Fonda Henry	5-16-05
Fonda Jane	12-21-37
Fonda Peter	2-23-39
Fontaine Joan	10-22-17
Forbes Ralph	9-30-02
Ford Glenn	5-1-16
Ford Harrison	7-13-42
Ford Wallace	2-12-1898
Forrest Frederic	12-23-38
Forrest Sally	5-28-28
Forsyth Rosemary	7-6-44
Fossey Brigitte	3-11-46
Foster Jodie	11-19-62
Foster Preston	8-24-02

Fox Edward	4-13-37
Fox James	5-19-39
Francis Kay	1-13-1899
Franklin Pamela	2-4-50
Franz Arthur	2-29-20
Franz Eduard	10-31-02
Fraser Ronald	4-11-30
Freeman Mona	6-9-26
Freeman Morgan	6-1-37
Frey Leonard	9-4-38
Frobe Gert	2-25-13
Frye Dwight	2-22-1899
Gabel Martin	6-19-12
Gabin Jean	5-17-04
Gable Clark	2-1-01
Gabor Zsa Zsa	2-6-16
Gahagan Helen	11-25-00
Gam Rita	4-2-28
Ganzel Teresa	3-23-57
Garbo Greta	9-18-05
Garcia Andy	4-12-56
Gardenia Vincent	1-7-22
Gardiner Reginald	2-27-03
Gardner Ava	12-24-22
Garfield Allen	11-22-39
Garfield John	3-4-12
Gargan William	7-17-05
Garner James	4-7-28
Garr Teri	12-11-44
Garson Greer	9-29-08
Gassman Vittorio	9-1-22
Gates Nancy	2-1-24
Gavin John	4-8-28
Gaynes George	5-16-17
Gazzara Ben	8-28-30
Gazzo Michael V	4-5-23
Geeson Judy	9-10-48
Gelin Daniel	5-19-21
George Susan	7-26-50
Gere Richard	8-31-49
Giannini Giancarlo	8-1-42
Gibson Mel	1-31-51
Gibson Virginia	4-9-28
Gilbert Billy	9-12-1894
Gilchrist Connie	2-2-01
Gilmore Virginia	7-26-19

Girardot Annie	10-25-31
Glaser Vaughn	1882
Gleason James	5-23-1882
Gleason Lucille	2-6-1886
Gleason Russell	2-6-08
Glenn Scott	1-26-42
Glover Crispin	9-20-64
Glover Danny	7-22-47
Glover Julian	3-27-35
Goddard Paulette	6-3-11
Goldberg Whoopi	11-13-49
Goldblum Jeff	10-22-52
Goldwyn Tony	5-20-60
Gomez Thomas	7-10-05
Gooding Cuba Jr	9-2-68
Goring Marius	5-23-12
Gortner Marjoe	1-14-41
Gould Elliott	8-29-38
Grahame Gloria	11-28-25
Granger Farley	7-1-25
Granger Stewart	5-6-13
Grant Cary	1-18-04
Grant Hugh	9-9-60
Grant Lee	10-31-27
Grant Rodney	1960
Granville Bonita	2-2-23
Grapewin Charley	12-20-1875
Gray Coleen	10-23-22
Greene Graham	6-22-52
Greene Richard	8-25-18
Greenstreet Sydney	12-27-1879
Greenwood Joan	3-4-21
Greer Jane	9-9-24
Gregson John	3-15-19
Grey Jennifer	3-36-60
Grey Nan	7-25-18
Grey Virginia	3-22-17
Grier Pam	5-26-49
Grier Roosevelt	7-14-32
Griffith Hugh	5-30-12
Griffith Melanie	8-9-57
Grimes Gary	6-2-55
Grizzard George	4-1-28
Grodin Charles	4-21-35
Guardino Harry	12-23-25
Guild Nancy	10-11-25

Guinness Alec	4-2-14
Gunn Moses	10-2-29
Gurie Sigrid	5-18-11
Guttenberg Steve	8-24-58
Gwenn Edmund	9-26-1875
Gwynne Anne	12-10-18
Haas Hugo	2-19-01
Haas Lukas	4-16-76
Hackett Joan	3-1-42
Hackman Gene	1-30-31
Haden Sara	1897
Hagerty Julie	6-15-55
Haim Corey	12-23-72
Hale Alan	2-10-1892
Hale Jonathan	1891
Hall Jon	2-26-13
Hamill Mark	9-25-52
Hamilton George	8-12-39
Hamilton Linda	9-26-56
Hamilton Lynn	4-25-30
Hamilton Margaret	9-12-02
Hamilton Murray	3-24-23
Hanks Tom	7-9-56
Hannah Daryl	12-3-60
Harding Ann	8-7-01
Harlow Jean	3-3-11
Harper Tess	8-15-50
Harris Ed	11-28-50
Harris Richard	10-1-30
Harris Rosemary	9-19-30
Harrison Linda	7-26-46
Harrison Rex	3-5-08
Hart Dolores	10-20-38
Hartman Elizabeth	12-23-41
Harvey Laurence	10-1-28
Hassett Marilyn	12-17-47
Hasso Signe	8-15-10
Hatfield Hurd	12-7-18
Hauer Rutger	1-23-44
Havoc June	11-8-16
Hawke Ethan	11-6-70
Hawkins Jack	9-14-10
Hawn Goldie	11-21-45
Haworth Jill	8-15-45
Hay Alexandra	7-24-48
Hayden Sterling	3-26-16

Hayes Allison	3-6-30
Hayward Brooke	7-5-37
Hayward Louis	3-19-09
Hayward Susan	6-30-18
Hayworth Rita	10-17-18
Headley Glenne	3-13-55
Heard John	3-7-45
Heckart Eileen	3-29-19
Hedren Tippi	1-19-35
Heflin Van	12-13-10
Helm Anne	9-12-38
Helmore Tom	1-4-12
Hemingway Margaux	2-19-55
Hemingway Mariel	11-22-61
Hemmings David	11-18-41
Hendrix Wanda	11-3-28
Hendry Ian	1-13-31
Henreid Paul	1-10-08
Henry Charlotte	3-3-13
Hepburn Audrey	5-4-29
Hepburn Katharine	5-12-07
Herrmann Edward	7-21-43
Hershey Barbara	2-5-48
Hervey Irene	7-11-10
Heston Charlton	10-4-22
Heywood Anne	12-11-37
Hillaire Marcel	4-23-08
Hiller Wendy	8-15-12
Hingle Pat	7-19-23
Hobart Rose	5-1-06
Hobson Valerie	4-14-17
Hodiak John	4-16-14
Hoey Dennis	3-30-1893
Hoffman Dustin	8-8-37
Hofmann Isabella	12-11-57
Hogan Paul	10-8-39
Holden Fay	9-26-1895
Holden Gloria	9-5-08
Holden William	4-17-18
Holliday Judy	6-21-22
Holloway Sterling	1-4-05
Holm Celeste	4-29-19
Holm Ian	9-12-31
Holmes Phillips	7-22-09
Holmes Taylor	5-16-1878
Homeier Skip	10-5-30

Homolka Oscar	8-12-03
Hopkins Anthony	12-31-37
Hopkins Miriam	10-18-02
Hopper Dennis	5-17-36
Horton Edward Everett	3-18-1886
Hoskins Bob	10-26-42
Houghton Katharine	3-10-45
Houston Donald	11-6-23
Howard John	4-14-13
Howard Leslie	4-3-1893
Howard Ronald	4-7-18
Howard Trevor	9-29-16
Hubbard John	4-14-23
Hudson Rochelle	3-6-15
Hudson Rock	11-17-25
Huffman David	5-10-45
Hughes Mary Beth	11-13-19
Hulce Tom	12-6-53
Hull Henry	10-3-1890
Hume Benita	10-14-06
Hunnicut Arthur	2-17-11
Hunnicutt Gayle	2-6-43
Hunt Linda	4-2-45
Hunt Marsha	10-17-17
Hunter Holly	3-20-58
Hunter Ian	6-13-00
Hunter Jeffrey	11-25-25
Hunter Kim	11-12-22
Hunter Tab	7-11-31
Huppert Isabelle	3-16-55
Hurt John	1-22-40
Hurt William	3-20-50
Hussey Olivia	4-17-51
Hussey Ruth	10-30-14
Huston Anjelica	7-8-51
Huston Walter	4-6-1884
Hutchinson Josephine	10-12-16
Hutton Robert	6-11-20
Hutton Timothy	8-16-60
Hyams Leila	5-1-05
Hyde-White Wilfrid	5-12-03
Hyer Martha	4-10-24
Iglesias Eugene	12-3-26
Ingalls Joyce	1-14-50
Ireland Jill	4-24-36
Ireland John	1-30-15

****

*Irons Jeremy	9-19-48
Irving Amy	9-10-53
Ivey Judith	9-4-51
Jackson Anne	9-3-25
Jackson Frieda	12-29-09
Jackson Glenda	5-9-36
Jackson Samuel L	12-21-48
Jacobi Lou	12-28-13
Jacobsson Ulla	5-23-29
Jagger Dean	11-7-03
Jason Sybil	11-23-29
Jayston Michael	10-29-36
Jeffries Lionel	1926
Jenkins Allen	4-9-1890
Jenks Frank	1902
Jens Salome	5-8-35
Jergens Adele	11-26-17
Jewell Isabel	7-19-09
Johann Zita	7-14-04
Johns Glynis	10-5-23
Johnson Celia	12-18-08
Johnson Kay	11-29-04
Johnson Richard	7-30-27
Johnson Rita	8-13-12
Johnson Van	8-25-16
Jones Dean	1-25-31
Jones James Earl	1-17-31
Jones Jennifer	3-2-19
Jones L Q	8-19-27
Jones Tommy Lee	9-15-46
Jordan Dorothy	8-9-08
Jory Victor	11-23-02
Joslyn Allyn	7-21-05
Jourdan Louis	6-19-19
Joyce Brenda	2-25-15
Judd Edward	10-4-32
Judge Arline	2-21-12
Julia Raul	3-9-40
Jurado Katy	1-16-27
Jurgens Curt	12-13-12
Justice James Robertson	6-15-05
Justin John	11-24-17
Kahn Madeline	9-29-42
Kapoor Raj	12-4-24
Karina Anna	9-22-40
Karloff Boris	11-23-1887

****

****

Kashfi Anna	9-30-35
Kasznar Kurt	8-13-13
Kaufmann Christine	1-11-45
Keaton Diane	1-5-46
Keaton Michael	9-9-51
Kedrova Lila	10-9-18
Keitel Harvey	5-13-39
Keith David	5-8-54
Keith Ian	2-27-1899
Keith Robert	2-10-1898
Kellaway Cecil	8-22-1893
Keller Marthe	1-28-45
Kellerman Sally	6-2-37
Kelly Grace	11-12-29
Kelly Nancy	3-25-21
Kelly Paul	8-9-1899
Kemp Jeremy	2-3-35
Kendal Felicity	9-25-46
Kendall Kay	5-21-26
Kendall Suzy	1944
Kennedy Arthur	2-17-14
Kennedy Merna	9-7-08
Kensit Patsy	3-4-68
Kent Barbara	12-16-06
Kent Jean	6-21-21
Kerr Deborah	9-30-21
Kerr John	11-15-31
Keyes Evelyn	11-20-19
Khambatta Persis	10-2-50
Kibbee Guy	3-6-1882
Kidder Margot	10-17-48
Kidman Nicole	6-20-67
Kiel Richard	9-13-39
Kilbride Percy	7-16-1888
Kiley Richard	3-31-22
Kilian Victor	3-6-1891
Kilmer Val	12-31-59
Kincaid Aron	6-15-43
King Andrea	2-1-15
Kingsford Walter	9-20-1882
Kingsley Ben	12-31-43
Kinskey Leonid	4-18-03
Kinski Klaus	10-18-25
Kinski Nastassia	1-24-60
Kirkland Sally	10-31-44
Kjellin Alf	2-28-20

****

****

Kline Kevin	10-24-47
Knapp Evalyn	6-17-08
Knight Esmond	5-4-06
Knight Shirley	7-5-36
Knowles Patric	11-11-11
Knox Alexander	1-16-07
Knox Elyse	12-14-17
Kohner Susan	11-11-36
Korvin Charles	11-21-07
Koscina Sylva	8-22-33
Kovack Nancy	3-11-35
Kreuger Kurt	7-23-16
Kristel Sylvia	9-28-52
Kruger Alma	9-13-1868
Kruger Hardy	4-12-28
Kruger Otto	9-6-1885
Kwan Nancy	5-19-39
Kyo Machiko	3-25-24
Ladd Alan	9-3-13
Ladd David	2-5-47
Ladd Diane	11-29-32
Lafont Bernadette	10-26-38
Lahti Christine	4-4-50
Lake Arthur	4-17-05
Lake Veronica	11-15-19
Lamarr Hedy	11-9-13
Lamas Fernando	1-9-15
Lambert Christopher	3-29-57
Lancaster Burt	11-2-13
Lanchester Elsa	10-28-02
Landi Elissa	12-6-04
Landis Carole	1-1-19
Landis Jesse Royce	11-25-04
Lane Diane	1-22-63
Lane Lola	5-21-06
Lane Priscilla	6-12-17
Lane Richard	1899
Lane Rosemary	4-4-13
Lang June	5-5-15
Langan Glenn	7-8-17
Lange Hope	11-28-33
Lange Jessica	4-20-49
Langella Frank	1-1-40
Langenkamp Heather	7-17-64
LaPaglia Anthony	1-31-59
LaRue Jack	5-3-02

****

Latell Lyle	4-9-05
Latimore Frank	9-28-25
Laughton Charles	7-1-1899
Laurie Piper	1-22-32
Law John Philip	9-7-37
Lawford Peter	9-7-23
Lawrance Jody	10-19-30
Lawrence Barbara	2-24-30
Lawrence Marc	2-17-10
Lawton Frank	9-30-04
Lederer Francis	11-6-06
Lee Belinda	6-15-35
Lee Bernard	1-10-08
Lee Canada	5-3-07
Lee Christopher	5-27-22
Lee Jason Scott	1967
Leeds Andrea	8-18-14
Leibman Ron	10-11-37
Leigh Janet	7-6-27
Leigh Jennifer Jason	2-5-62
Leigh Suzanna	7-26-45
Leigh Vivien	11-5-13
Leighton Margaret	2-26-22
LeMat Paul	9-22-45
Lemmon Jack	2-8-25
Leonard Sheldon	2-22-07
Leslie Joan	1-26-25
Levene Sam	8-28-05
Lewis Fiona	9-28-46
Lewis Juliette	6-21-73
Linden Eric	9-15-09
Lindfors Viveca	12-29-20
Lindsay Margaret	9-19-10
Liotta Ray	12-18-55
Lisi Virna	8-11-37
Lister Moira	8-6-23
Lithgow John	10-19-45
Little Cleavon	6-1-39
Littlefield Lucien	8-16-1895
Livesey Roger	6-25-06
Locke Sondra	5-28-47
Lockhart Gene	7-25-1892
Lockwood Margaret	9-15-16
Loden Barbara	7-8-34
Loder John	1-3-1898
Loggia Robert	1-3-30

****

Lollobrigida Gina	7-4-27
Lom Herbert	1-19-17
Lombard Carole	10-6-08
Lone John	10-13-52
Loren Sophia	9-20-34
Lorre Peter	6-26-04
Lorring Joan	4-17-26
Louise Anita	1-9-15
Lowe Chad	1-15-68
Lowe Edmund	3-3-1892
Lowe Rob	3-17-64
Loy Myrna	8-2-05
Lualdi Antonella	7-6-31
Lugosi Bela	10-20-1882
Lukas Paul	5-26-1891
Luke Keye	6-18-04
Luna Barbara	3-2-37
Lund Art	4-1-20
Lund John	2-6-13
Lundgren Dolph	11-3-59
Lundigan William	6-12-14
Lupino Ida	2-4-18
Lydon Jimmy	5-30-23
Lynley Carol	2-13-42
Lynn Diana	10-7-26
Lynn Jeffrey	2-16-09
Lyon Ben	2-6-01
Lyon Sue	7-10-46
Lytell Bert	2-24-1885
MacDowell Andie	4-21-58
MacGraw Ali	4-1-39
Mack Helen	11-13-13
MacKenzie Joyce	10-13-29
MacLane Barton	12-25-02
MacLaine Shirley	4-24-34
MacMahon Aline	5-3-1899
MacMurray Fred	8-30-08
Macready George	8-29-09
Madigan Amy	9-11-60
Magee Patrick	1924
Magnani Anna	3-7-09
Mahan Billy	7-9-30
Main Marjorie	2-24-1890
Mako	12-10-33
Malden Karl	3-22-12
Malkovich John	12-9-53

Mallory Boots	10-22-13
Malone Dorothy	1-30-25
Malone Nancy	3-19-35
Mander Miles	5-14-1888
Mangano Silvana	4-21-30
Manners David	4-30-01
Mano D Keith	2-12-42
Mansfield Jayne	4-19-32
Mantegna Joe	11-13-47
Mara Adele	4-28-23
Marais Jean	12-11-13
March Fredric	8-31-1897
Marchal Georges	1-10-20
Marchand Corinne	12-4-37
Margo	5-10-17
Margolin Janet	7-25-43
Maritza Sari	3-17-10
Marley John	10-17-14
Marly Florence	6-2-18
Marquand Christian	3-15-27
Marsh Joan	7-10-13
Marsh Marian	10-17-13
Marshal Alan	1-20-09
Marshall Brenda	9-29-15
Marshall Herbert	5-23-1890
Marshall Trudy	2-14-22
Marshall William	10-2-17
Marshall William	8-19-24
Martin Dewey	12-8-23
Martin Nan	7-15-27
Martin Strother	3-26-19
Martinelli Elsa	8-3-33
Marvin Lee	2-19-24
Masina Giulietta	3-22-20
Mason James	5-15-09
Mason Marsha	4-3-42
Mason Pamela	3-10-18
Massen Osa	1-13-16
Massey Anna	8-11-37
Massey Daniel	10-10-33
Massey Ilona	6-16-10
Massey Raymond	8-30-1896
Masters Ben	5-6-47
Masterson Mary Stuart	6-28-66
Mastrantonio Mary Elizabeth	11-17-58
Mastroianni Marcello	9-28-23

Matheson Murray	7-1-12
Mathews Kerwin	1-8-26
Matlin Marlee	8-24-65
Matthau Walter	10-1-20
Mature Victor	1-29-15
Maura Carmen	9-15-45
Maxwell Lois	2-14-27
Maxwell Marilyn	8-3-21
Mayo Virginia	11-30-20
Mazurki Mike	12-25-09
McCallister Lon	4-17-23
McCarthy Andrew	11-29-62
McCarthy Kevin	2-15-14
McCowen Alec	5-26-26
McDaniel Hattie	6-10-1895
McDevitt Ruth	9-13-1895
McDonald Marie	1923
McDonnell Mary	4-28-52
McDowall Roddy	9-17-28
McDowell Malcolm	6-13-43
McEnery Peter	2-21-40
McGee Vonetta	1-14-48
McGillis Kelly	7-9-57
McGovern Elizabeth	7-18-61
McGraw Charles	5-10-14
McGuire Dorothy	6-14-18
McHugh Frank	5-23-1898
McKellen Ian	5-25-39
McKenna Siobhan	5-24-23
McKenna Virginia	6-7-31
McLaglen Victor	12-11-1886
McNally Stephen	7-29-13
McNeil Claudia	8-13-17
McQueen Butterfly	1-7-11
McQueen Steve	3-24-30
McShane Ian	9-29-42
Meade Julia	12-17-28
Medina Patricia	7-19-19
Meek Donald	7-14-1880
Meeker Ralph	11-21-20
Melato Mariangela	1938
Mell Marisa	2-25-39
Melton Sid	5-23-20
Menjou Adolphe	2-18-1890
Merchant Vivien	7-22-29
Mercouri Melina	10-18-25

Meredith Burgess	11-16-08
Merkel Una	12-10-03
Merrill Dina	12-9-25
Merrill Gary	8-2-14
Michaels Beverly	1927
Middleton Robert	5-13-11
Mifune Toshiro	4-1-20
Miles Sarah	12-31-43
Miles Sylvia	9-9-32
Miles Vera	8-23-30
Milland Ray	1-3-05
Miller Colleen	11-10-32
Miller Jason	4-22-39
Miller Jonathan	7-21-34
Miller Penelope Ann	1-13-64
Mills Hayley	4-18-46
Mills John	2-22-08
Mimieux Yvette	1-8-39
Mineo Sal	1-10-39
Minkus Barbara	8-15-43
Miou-Miou	2-22-50
Miranda Isa	7-5-09
Mitchell Cameron	11-4-18
Mitchell Millard	1900
Mitchell Thomas	7-11-1892
Mitchum Christopher	10-16-43
Mitchum James	5-8-41
Mitchum Robert	8-6-17
Modine Matthew	3-22-59
Moffat Donald	12-26-30
Monroe Marilyn	6-1-26
Montand Yves	10-13-21
Montez Maria	6-6-18
Montgomery Robert	5-21-04
Moody Ron	1-8-24
Moore Cleo	10-31-28
Moore Demi	11-11-62
Moore Dudley	4-19-35
Moore Kieron	10-5-24
Moore Norma	2-20-35
Moore Roger	10-14-27
Moore Terry	1-7-29
Morales Esai	10-2-62
More Kenneth	9-20-14
Moreau Jeanne	1-23-28
Moreno Rita	12-11-31

Morgan Frank	6-1-1890
Morgan Michelle	2-29-20
Morgan Ralph	7-6-1888
Moriarty Cathy	11-29-60
Morita Pat	6-28-30
Morley Karen	12-12-05
Morley Robert	5-26-08
Morris Anita	3-14-43
Morris Chester	2-16-01
Morrow Jeff	1-13-13
Morrow Jo	11-1-39
Mowbray Alan	8-18-1896
Muir Gavin	9-8-09
Muir Jean	2-13-11
Muni Paul	9-22-1895
Munro Caroline	1951
Munson Ona	6-16-06
Murphy Mary	1-26-31
Murphy Rosemary	1-13-27
Murray Barbara	9-27-29
Muse Clarence	10-7-1889
Nagel Anne	9-30-12
Naish J Carrol	1-21-00
Napier Alan	1-7-03
Neagle Anna	10-20-04
Neal Patricia	1-20-26
Neal Tom	1-28-14
Neeson Liam	6-7-52
Neff Hildegarde	12-28-25
Nelligan Kate	3-16-51
Nelson Barry	4-16-20
Nelson Judd	11-28-59
Nero Franco	11-23-41
Nesbitt Cathleen	11-24-1888
Newman Paul	1-26-25
Newton Robert	6-1-05
Nicholson Jack	4-22-37
Niven David	3-1-09
Nixon Marion	10-20-04
Nolan Lloyd	8-11-02
Nolte Nick	2-8-41
North Sheree	1-17-33
Novak Kim	2-13-33
Nuyen France	7-31-39
O'Brien Edmond	9-10-15
O'Brien Pat	11-11-1899

O'Brien Virginia	4-8-21
O'Brien-Moore Erin	5-2-08
O'Connell Arthur	3-29-08
O'Donnell Cathy	7-6-25
O'Donnell Chris	6-26-70
O'Driscoll Martha	3-4-22
O'Hanlon George	11-23-17
O'Hara Maureen	8-17-20
O'Herlihy Dan	5-1-19
O'Keefe Dennis	3-29-08
O'Keefe Michael	4-24-55
O'Neal Patrick	9-26-27
O'Neal Ron	9-1-37
O'Neal Ryan	4-20-41
O'Neal Tatum	11-5-63
O'Neil Barbara	7-10-09
O'Neil Tricia	3-11-45
O'Shea Michael	3-17-06
O'Shea Milo	6-2-26
O'Sullivan Maureen	5-17-11
O'Toole Annette	4-1-53
O'Toole Peter	8-2-32
Oakie Jack	11-12-03
Oates Warren	7-5-28
Ober Philip	3-23-02
Oberon Merle	2-19-11
Ohmart Carol	6-3-28
Oland Warner	10-3-1880
Oldman Gary	3-21-58
Olin Lena	3-22-55
Oliver Edna May	11-9-1883
Oliver Susan	2-13-36
Olivier Laurence	5-22-07
Olson Nancy	7-14-28
Opatashu David	1-30-18
Ormond Julia	1965
Ouspenskaya Maria	7-29-1867
Owen Reginald	8-5-1887
Owens Patricia	1-17-27
Pacino Al	4-25-40
Page Anita	8-4-10
Page Gale	7-23-13
Page Geraldine	11-22-24
Paget Debra	8-19-33
Paige Robert	12-21-10
Palance Holly	8-5-50

Palance Jack	2-18-20		Philipe Gerard	12-4-22
Pallette Eugene	7-8-1889		Phillips Lou Diamond	2-17-62
Palmer Gregg	1-25-27		Phoenix River	8-23-70
Palmer Lilli	5-24-14		Piazza Ben	7-30-34
Paluzzi Luciana	6-11-39		Pidgeon Walter	9-23-1897
Papas Irene	9-3-26		Pine Phillip	7-16-25
Parker Cecil	9-3-1897		Pisier Marie-France	5-10-44
Parker Cecilia	4-26-05		Pitt Brad	12-18-65
Parker Eleanor	6-26-22		Pitt Ingrid	11-21-45
Parker Jean	8-11-12		Platt Louise	8-3-14
Parker Sarah Jessica	3-25-65		Pleasence Donald	10-5-19
Parks Hildy	3-12-24		Plimpton Martha	11-16-70
Parks Larry	12-13-14		Plowright Joan	10-28-29
Parrish Helen	3-12-22		Plummer Amanda	3-23-57
Parrish Leslie	3-18-35		Plummer Christopher	12-13-27
Parsons Estelle	11-20-27		Podesta Rossana	6-20-34
Patric Jason	6-17-66		Poitier Sidney	2-20-24
Patrick Gail	6-20-11		Pollard Michael J	5-30-39
Patrick Lee	11-22-06		Powell William	7-29-1892
Patrick Nigel	5-2-13		Power Tyrone	5-15-14
Patterson Neva	2-10-22		Powers Mala	12-29-21
Paulsen Albert	12-13-27		Prentiss Paula	3-4-39
Pavan Marisa	6-19-32		Presle Micheline	8-22-22
Paxinou Katina	12-17-00		Preston Kelly	10-13-62
Paxton Bill	5-17-55		Preston Robert	6-8-18
Paymer David	8-30-54		Price Dennis	6-23-15
Payne John	5-23-12		Price Vincent	5-27-11
Payton Barbara	11-16-27		Prince William	1-26-13
Pearson Beatrice	7-27-20		Prouty Jed	4-6-1879
Peck Gregory	4-5-16		Pryce Jonathan	6-1-47
Pena Elizabeth	9-23-59		Pryor Nicholas	1-28-35
Pendleton Nat	8-8-1895		Pryor Roger	8-27-01
Penn Sean	8-17-60		Pullman Bill	12-17-53
Perez Rosie	9-6-64		Purdom Edmund	12-19-26
Perkins Anthony	4-14-32		Quaid Dennis	4-9-54
Perkins Elizabeth	11-18-60		Quaid Randy	10-1-50
Perkins Millie	5-12-38		Quarry Robert	11-3-24
Perrine Valerie	9-3-43		Quayle Anna	10-6-36
Pesci Joe	2-9-43		Quayle Anthony	9-7-13
Peters Brock	7-2-27		Quillan Eddie	3-31-07
Peters Jean	10-15-26		Quine Richard	11-12-20
Peters Susan	7-3-21		Quinlan Kathleen	11-19-54
Petit Pascale	2-27-38		Quinn Aidan	3-8-59
Pettet Joanna	11-16-44		Quinn Anthony	4-21-16
Petty Lori	1965		Raft George	9-26-1895
Pfeiffer Michelle	4-29-57		Ragland Rags	8-23-06

Rainer Luise	1-12-09
Raines Ella	8-6-21
Rainey Ford	8-8-08
Rains Claude	11-10-1889
Rampling Charlotte	2-5-46
Randell Ron	10-8-18
Randolph Jane	10-30-19
Rasulala Thalmus	11-15-39
Rathbone Basil	6-13-1892
Ratoff Gregory	4-20-1897
Ray Aldo	9-25-26
Raymond Gene	8-13-08
Raymond Paula	11-23-23
Rea Stephen	10-31-43
Reagan Ronald	2-6-11
Redford Robert	8-18-37
Redgrave Corin	7-16-39
Redgrave Lynn	3-8-43
Redgrave Michael	3-20-08
Redgrave Vanessa	1-30-37
Reed Oliver	2-13-38
Reeve Christopher	9-25-52
Reeves Keanu	9-2-64
Reid Beryl	6-17-20
Reid Elliott	1-16-20
Reid Frances	12-9-18
Reid Kate	11-4-30
Reinhold Judge	5-21-56
Remick Lee	12-14-35
Rennie Michael	8-29-09
Revere Anne	6-25-03
Revier Dorothy	4-18-04
Revill Clive	4-18-30
Rey Fernando	9-20-15
Reynolds Burt	2-11-36
Reynolds Joyce	10-7-24
Rhue Madlyn	10-3-34
Rialson Candy	1950
Rice Florence	2-14-07
Rice Joan	2-3-30
Richards Ann	12-20-18
Richards Jeff	11-1-22
Richardson Joely	1-9-65
Richardson Lee	9-11-26
Richardson Miranda	3-3-58
Richardson Natasha	5-11-63

Rickman Alan	2-21-46
Ridgely John	9-6-09
Riegert Peter	4-11-47
Ringwald Molly	2-18-68
Ritter Thelma	2-14-05
Riva Emmanuelle	2-24-27
Robards Jason Jr	7-26-22
Robbins Gale	5-7-24
Robbins Tim	10-16-58
Roberti Lyda	5-20-06
Roberts Beverly	5-19-14
Roberts Eric	4-18-56
Roberts Julia	10-25-67
Roberts Rachel	9-20-27
Roberts Tony	10-22-39
Robertson Willard	1-1-1886
Robin Dany	4-14-27
Robinson Edward G	12-12-1893
Robinson Jay	4-14-30
Roc Patricia	6-7-18
Rochefort Jean	4-29-30
Rodrigues Percy	6-13-24
Rogers Mimi	1-27-56
Rogers Will Jr	10-12-12
Roland Gilbert	12-11-05
Roman Ruth	12-23-24
Romero Cesar	2-15-07
Rooney Mickey	9-23-20
Rossellini Isabella	6-18-52
Rossi Drago Eleonora	9-23-25
Rourke Mickey	9-16-53
Rowe Misty	1950
Rowlands Gena	6-19-36
Royle Selena	11-6-04
Ruehl Mercedes	2-28-48
Ruggles Charles	2-8-1892
Rule Janice	8-15-31
Rush Barbara	1-4-27
Russell Gail	9-21-24
Russell Jane	6-21-21
Russell Kurt	3-17-51
Russell Rosalind	6-4-08
Russell Theresa	3-20-57
Russo Rene	1955
Rutherford Ann	11-2-17
Rutherford Margaret	5-11-1892

Ryan Meg	11-19-61
Ryan Robert	11-11-09
Ryan Sheila	6-8-21
Ryder Alfred	1-5-19
Ryder Winona	10-29-71
Sabu (Dastagir)	1-27-24
Saint Eva Marie	7-4-24
Sakall S Z 'Cuddles'	2-2-1883
Salmi Albert	3-11-28
Sanda Dominique	3-11-48
Sanders George	7-3-06
Sands Diana	8-22-34
Sands Julian	1-15-58
SanGiacomo Laura	11-14-61
SanJuan Olga	3-16-27
Sarandon Chris	7-24-42
Sarandon Susan	10-4-46
Sarrazin Michael	5-22-40
Savage Ann	2-19-21
Sawyer Joe	1907
Scacchi Greta	2-18-60
Scala Gia	3-3-34
Scheider Roy	11-10-35
Schell Maria	1-15-26
Schell Maximilian	12-8-30
Schildkraut Joseph	3-22-1895
Schneider Maria	3-27-52
Schneider Romy	9-23-38
Schwarzenegger Arnold	7-30-47
Schygulla Hanna	12-25-43
Sciorra Annabella	3-24-64
Scofield Paul	1-21-22
Scott Campbell	7-19-62
Scott George C	10-18-27
Scott Gordon	8-3-27
Scott Janette	12-14-38
Scott Lizabeth	9-29-22
Scott Martha	9-22-14
Scott Pippa	11-10-35
Scott Zachary	2-24-14
Sears Heather	9-28-35
Sebastian Dorothy	4-26-03
Seberg Jean	11-13-38
Sedgwick Kyra	8-19-65
Segal George	2-13-34
Sellars Elizabeth	5-6-23

Sernas Jacques	7-30-25
Servais Jean	9-24-10
Severance Joan	12-23-58
Seymour Dan	2-22-15
Seyrig Delphine	4-10-32
Shannon Peggy	1-10-07
Sharif Omar	4-10-32
Shaughnessy Mickey	1920
Shaw Robert	8-9-27
Shaw Stan	7-14-52
Shawlee Joan	3-5-29
Shearer Norma	8-10-00
Sheedy Ally	6-12-62
Sheen Charlie	9-3-65
Sheen Martin	8-3-40
Shelley Barbara	1933
Sheridan Ann	2-21-15
Shields Brooke	5-31-65
Shigeta James	1933
Shimkus Joanna	10-10-43
Shire Talia	4-25-46
Shirley Anne	4-17-18
Showalter Max	6-2-17
Shue Elisabeth	10-6-63
Sidney Sylvia	8-8-10
Siemaszko Casey	3-17-61
Signoret Simone	3-25-21
Silvera Frank	7-24-14
Sim Alastair	10-9-00
Simmons Jean	1-31-29
Simms Hilda	4-15-20
Simon Simone	4-23-11
Sinclair Hugh	5-19-03
Sinden Donald	10-9-23
Singleton Penny	9-15-08
Sinise Gary	3-17-55
Skye Ione	9-4-71
Slater Christian	8-18-69
Slezak Walter	5-3-02
Smith Alexis	6-8-21
Smith C Aubrey	7-21-1863
Smith Charles Martin	10-30-53
Smith Kent	3-19-07
Smith Kurtwood	7-3-42
Smith Maggie	12-28-34
Smith Rex	9-19-56

****

Snipes Wesley	7-31-62
Snodgress Carrie	10-27-46
Sokoloff Vladimir	12-26-1889
Sommer Elke	11-5-41
Sothern Ann	1-22-09
Spaak Catherine	4-4-45
Spacek Sissy	12-25-49
Spader James	2-7-60
St Jacques Raymond	3-1-32
St John Howard	10-9-05
St John Jill	8-19-40
Stallone Sylvester	7-6-46
Stamp Terence	7-22-39
Stander Lionel	1-11-08
Stanley Kim	2-11-25
Stanton Harry Dean	7-14-26
Stanwyck Barbara	7-16-07
Stapleton Maureen	6-21-25
Steel Anthony	5-21-20
Steele Barbara	12-29-37
Steenburgen Mary	2-8-53
Steiger Rod	4-14-25
Sten Anna	12-3-07
Sterling Jan	4-3-23
Sterling Tisha	12-10-44
Stern Daniel	8-28-57
Stevens K T	7-20-19
Stevens Kaye	7-21-33
Stevens Mark	12-13-15
Stevens Onslow	3-29-06
Stevens Stella	10-1-36
Stevenson Venetia	3-10-38
Stewart Alexandria	6-10-39
Stewart Catherine Mary	4-22-59
Stewart Elaine	5-31-29
Stewart Freddie	3-25-25
Stewart James	5-20-08
Stewart Paul	3-13-08
Stockwell Guy	11-16-34
Stoltz Eric	1961
Stone George E	5-23-03
Stone Lewis	11-15-1879
Stone Sharon	3-10-58
Stowe Madeline	8-18-58
Straight Beatrice	8-2-18
Strasberg Susan	5-22-38

****

****

Strauss Robert	11-8-13
Streep Meryl	6-22-49
Strode Woody	7-25-14
Strudwick Shepperd	9-22-07
Stuart Gloria	7-14-10
Sullavan Margaret	5-16-09
Sullivan Barry	8-29-12
Sullivan Francis L	1-6-03
Sutherland Donald	7-17-34
Sutherland Kiefer	12-21-66
Sutton John	10-22-08
Suzman Janet	2-9-39
Swayze Patrick	8-18-52
Sweeney D B	1961
Tamiroff Akim	10-29-1889
Tate Sharon	1-24-43
Taylor Don	12-13-20
Taylor Elizabeth	2-27-32
Taylor Kent	5-11-07
Taylor Robert	8-5-11
Taylor-Young Leigh	1-25-44
Thatcher Torin	1-15-05
Thaxter Phyllis	11-20-21
Thompson Carlos	6-7-16
Thompson Emma	4-15-59
Thompson Fred Dalton	8-19-42
Thompson Lea	5-31-61
Thompson Marshall	11-27-25
Thulin Ingrid	1-27-29
Thurman Uma	4-29-70
Ticotin Rachel	11-1-58
Tierney Gene	11-20-20
Tierney Lawrence	3-15-19
Tiffin Pamela	10-13-42
Tilly Jennifer	9-16-58
Tilly Meg	2-14-60
Tobin Genevieve	11-29-01
Todd Ann	1-24-09
Todd Richard	6-11-19
Todd Thelma	7-29-05
Toler Sidney	4-28-1874
Tomei Marisa	12-4-64
Tomlinson David	5-7-17
Tompkins Angel	12-20-42
Tone Franchot	2-27-05
Toomey Regis	8-13-02

****

****

Topol Chaim	9-9-35
Toren Marta	5-21-26
Torn Rip	2-6-31
Totter Audrey	12-20-18
Tracy Lee	4-14-1898
Tracy Spencer	4-5-00
Tracy William	12-1-17
Travers Bill	1-3-22
Travis June	8-7-14
Travis Nancy	9-21-61
Travis Richard	4-17-13
Travolta John	2-18-54
Treacher Arthur	7-23-1894
Tree Dorothy	5-21-09
Trevor Claire	3-8-09
Trintignant Jean-Louis	12-11-30
Tryon Tom	1-14-26
Tucker Forrest	2-12-19
Tucker Lorenzo	6-27-07
Tufts Sonny	7-16-11
Tully Tom	8-21-02
Turner Kathleen	6-19-54
Turner Lana	2-8-20
Turturro John	2-28-57
Tushingham Rita	3-14-42
Twelvetrees Helen	12-25-07
Ullmann Liv	12-16-39
Ure Mary	2-18-33
Ustinov Peter	4-16-21
Vaccaro Brenda	11-18-39
Valli Alida	5-3-21
Vallone Raf	2-17-16
VanDevere Trish	3-9-43
VanDoren Mamie	2-6-33
VanDreelan John	5-5-22
VanEyck Peter	7-16-13
VanFleet Jo	12-30-19
VanPallandt Nina	7-15-32
VanPeebles Mario	1-15-57
VanVooren Monique	3-23-33
Varsi Diane	2-23-38
Veidt Conrad	1-22-1893
Velez Lupe	7-18-08
Venable Evelyn	10-18-13
Ventura Lino	7-14-19
Vernon John	2-24-32

****

Vickers Martha	5-28-25
Vinson Helen	9-17-07
Vitale Milly	7-16-38
Vitti Monica	11-3-33
Vlady Marina	3-10-38
Voight Jon	12-29-38
vonFurstenberg Betsy	8-16-31
vonSydow Max	4-10-29
Walburn Raymond	9-9-1887
Walken Christopher	3-31-43
Walker Robert	10-13-18
Wallace Jean	10-12-23
Wallach Eli	12-7-15
Wallis Shani	4-16-33
Wanamaker Sam	6-14-19
Ward Fred	12-30-42
Ward Simon	10-19-41
Warner David	7-29-41
Washington Denzel	12-28-54
Washington Fredi	12-23-03
Wayne David	1-30-14
Wayne John	5-26-07
Wayne Patrick	7-15-39
Weaver Sigourney	10-8-49
Webb Clifton	11-19-1891
Welch Raquel	9-5-40
Weld Tuesday	8-27-43
Weller Peter	6-24-47
Werner Oskar	11-13-22
West Mae	8-17-1892
Westman Nydia	2-19-02
Weston Jack	8-21-24
Whalen Michael	6-30-02
Whalley-Kilmer Joanne	8-25-64
Whelan Arleen	9-16-16
Whitaker Forest	7-15-61
White Carol	4-1-42
Whitelaw Billie	6-6-32
Whitman Stuart	2-1-26
Whitmore James	10-1-21
Whorf Richard	6-4-06
Widmark Richard	12-26-14
Wiest Diane	3-28-48
Wilcoxon Henry	9-8-05
Wilde Cornel	10-13-15
Wilder Gene	6-11-33

****

Wilding Michael	7-23-12
William Warren	12-2-1894
Williams Billy Dee	4-6-37
Williams JoBeth	12-6-48
Williams John	4-15-03
Williams Treat	12-1-51
Williamson Nicol	9-14-38
Willis Bruce	3-19-55
Wills Chill	7-18-03
Wilson Dooley	4-3-1894
Windsor Marie	12-11-22
Winger Debra	5-16-55
Winter Alex	7-17-65
Winters Roland	11-22-04
Winters Shelley	8-18-22
Wiseman Joseph	5-15-18
Withers Googie	3-12-17
Wood Natalie	7-20-38
Woodard Alfre	11-8-53
Woodbury Joan	12-17-15
Woods Donald	12-2-04
Woods James	4-18-47
Woodward Joanne	2-27-30
Woodward Morgan	9-16-25
Woolley Monty	8-17-1888
Wray Fay	9-15-07
Wright Cobina	8-14-21
Wright Teresa	10-27-18
Wyatt Jane	8-12-12
Wyman Jane	1-4-14
Wymore Patrice	12-17-26
Wynn Keenan	7-27-16
Wynter Dana	6-8-32
York Michael	3-27-42
York Susannah	1-9-42
Young Burt	4-30-40
Young Gig	11-4-13
Young Loretta	1-6-13
Young Robert	2-22-07
Young Roland	11-11-1887
Young Sean	11-20-59
Yulin Harris	11-5-37
Yung Victor Sen	10-18-15
Zadora Pia	5-4-56
Zetterling Mai	5-24-25
Zucco George	1-11-1886

FILM JUVENILES

Baby LeRoy (Winebrenner)	5-12-32
Baby Peggy (Montgomery)	10-26-18
Baby Sandy (Henville)	1-14-38
Bartholomew Freddie	3-28-24
Beckett Scotty	10-4-29
Boyd Jimmy	1-9-40
Brown Kenneth 'Buddy'	1-20-32
Carlson June	4-16-24
Coghlan Junior	3-15-16
Culkin Macaulay	8-26-80
Cummings Quinn	8-13-67
DeWilde Brandon	4-9-42
Driscoll Bobby	5-3-37
Ernest George	11-20-21
Garner Peggy Ann	2-8-31
Gillis Ann	2-12-27
Haley Jackie Earle	7-14-61
Hodges Eddie	3-5-47
Howell C Thomas	12-7-66
Hunt Jimmy	12-4-39
Ivo Tommy	4-18-36
Jarman Claude Jr	9-27-34
Jenkins Jackie 'Butch'	8-19-37
Jones Marcia Mae	8-1-24
Kelly Tommy	4-6-25
Kent Marjorie	6-3-39
Kilburn Terry	11-25-26
Lauren Tammy	11-16-69
Lenhart Bill 'Butch'	12-14-30
Lester Mark	7-11-58
Mauch Billy & Bobby	7-6-22
Miller Cheryl	2-4-43
Moore Dickie	9-12-25
O'Brien Clay	5-6-61
O'Brien Margaret	1-15-37
O'Rourke Heather	12-27-75
Patten Luana	7-6-38
Perreau Gigi	2-6-41
Sheffield Johnny	4-11-31
Simms Larry	10-1-34
Temple Shirley	4-23-28
Thomas Henry	9-8-69
Weidler Virginia	3-21-27
Wild Jack	9-30-52
Withers Jane	4-12-26

OUR GANG/LITTLE RASCALS

Beard Matthew 'Stymie'	1-1-25
Bond Tommy 'Butch'	9-16-27
Chaney Norman 'Chubby'	1-18-18
Cobb Joe	11-7-17
Condon Jackie	3-25-18
Daniels Mickey	10-11-14
Darling Jean	8-23-22
DeBorba Dorothy 'Echo'	3-28-25
Hood Darla	11-4-31
Hoskins Allen 'Farina'	8-9-20
Hutchins Bobby 'Wheezer'	3-29-25
Jackson Mary Ann	1-14-23
Kaye Darwood 'Waldo'	9-8-29
Kornman Mary	12-27-17
Laughlin William 'Froggy'	7-5-32
Lee Eugene 'Porky'	10-25-33
McFarland George 'Spanky'	10-2-28
Spear Harry	12-16-21
Switzer Carl 'Alfalfa'	8-8-27
Thomas William 'Buckwheat'	3-12-31

BOWERY BOYS

Bartlett Bennie	8-16-27
Benedict Billy	4-16-17
Clements Stanley	7-16-26
Dell Gabriel	10-4-19
Gorcey Leo	6-3-15
Hall Huntz	8-15-19
Halop Billy	5-11-20
Jordan Bobby	4-1-23
Punsly Bernard	7-11-22

* * * * * * * * * * * * * * * *

SERIALS

Aldridge Kay	7-9-17
Alyn Kirk	10-8-10
Crabbe Buster	2-7-07
Gifford Frances	12-7-20
Hadley Reed	1-8-11
Holdren Judd	10-16-15
Lowery Robert	1914
Middleton Charles	10-3-1879
Powell Lee	1909
Purcell Dick	8-6-08
Richmond Kane	12-23-06
Rogers Jean	3-25-16
Stirling Linda	10-11-23

FILM WESTERNS

Acord Art	1890
Alexander Dick	1903
Allen Bob	3-28-06
Allen Rex	12-31-22
Anderson 'Broncho Billy'	3-21-1882
Ankrum Morris	8-27-1896
Anthony Tony	10-16-37
Ates Roscoe	1-20-1892
Autry Gene	9-29-07
Baker Bob	11-8-14
Ballew Smith	1-21-02
Bannon Jim	1911
Barcroft Roy	9-7-02
Bardette Trevor	11-19-02
Barry Don 'Red'	1-11-12
Bell Rex	10-16-05
Blue Monte	1-11-1890
Booth Adrian	7-26-24
Boyd William	6-5-1898
Bradford Lane	1923
Brady Pat	12-31-14
Bridge Alan	2-26-1891
Brown Johnny Mack	9-1-04
Burnette Smiley	3-18-11
Buttram Pat	6-19-16
Calhoun Rory	8-8-18
Cameron Rod	12-7-12
Carey Harry	1-16-1878
Carson Sunset	11-12-22
Chandler Lane	6-4-1899
Chesebro George	7-29-1888
Cobb Edmund	6-23-1892
Cody Bill	1-5-1891
Cody Iron Eyes	4-3-15
Corrigan Ray 'Crash'	2-14-02
Curtis Dick	5-11-02
Custer Bob	10-18-1898
Davis Gail	10-5-25
Dean Eddie	7-9-07
Devine Andy	10-7-05
Duncan Kenne	2-17-02
Edwards Penny	8-24-19
Elliott Wild Bill	10-16-03
Ellison James	5-4-10
Evans Dale	10-31-12

Fletcher Tex	3-8-10
Foran Dick	6-18-10
Fowley Douglas	5-30-11
Geary Bud	1899
Gibson Hoot	8-6-1892
Hackett Karl	1893
Hale Monte	6-8-21
Hart William S	12-6-1870
Harvey Harry	1901
Hatton Raymond	7-7-1887
Hayden Russell	6-12-12
Hayes George 'Gabby'	5-7-1885
Healey Myron	6-8-22
Hill Terence	3-29-41
Holt Jack	5-31-1888
Holt Jennifer	11-10-20
Holt Tim	2-5-18
Houston George	1898
Hoxie Jack	1-24-1855
Ingram Jack	1903
January Lois	10-5-13
Jolley I Stanford	1900
Johnson Ben	6-13-18
Johnson Chubby	1903
Jones Buck	12-12-1888
Jones Gordon	4-5-11
Keene Tom	12-20-1898
King Charles	2-21-1895
King John 'Dusty'	7-11-09
Knight Fuzzy	5-9-01
Kohler Fred	4-20-1889
Kortman Bob	12-24-1887
Lane Allan 'Rocky'	9-22-04
Larson Christine	1918
LaRue Lash	6-14-17
Lease Rex	2-11-01
Lee Mary	10-24-24
Lewis George J	12-10-03
Livingston Robert	12-9-08
London Tom	8-24-1883
Luden Jack	2-6-02
MacDonald Francis	8-22-1891
MacDonald Kenneth	1902
Maloney Leo	1888
Martin Chris-Pin	11-19-1893
Martin Richard	12-12-17

Mason LeRoy	1903
Maynard Ken	7-21-1895
Maynard Kermit	9-20-02
McCoy Tim	4-10-1891
McCrea Joel	11-5-05
Merton John	1901
Mix Tom	1-6-1880
Montgomery George	8-29-16
Moore Dennis	1914
Morris Wayne	2-17-14
Murphy Audie	6-20-24
Newill James	8-12-11
O'Brien Dave 'Tex'	5-31-12
O'Brien George	4-19-00
Osborne Bud	7-20-1888
Perrin Jack	7-26-1896
Pickens Slim	6-29-19
Randall Jack	5-12-06
Reed Marshall	5-28-17
Ritter Tex	1-12-07
Roberts Lynn	11-22-19
Rogers Roy	11-5-12
Russell Reb	5-31-05
Scott Fred	2-14-02
Scott Randolph	1-23-03
St John Al 'Fuzzy'	9-10-1893
Starrett Charles	3-28-03
Steele Bob	1-23-06
Stewart Peggy	6-5-23
Storey June	1920
Strange Glenn	8-16-1899
Taliaferro Hal	11-13-1895
Taylor Dub 'Cannonball'	1909
Teal Ray	1-12-02
Terhune Max	2-12-1891
Thomson Fred	2-26-1890
Thundercloud Chief	4-12-1899
Tyler Tom	8-9-03
VanCleef Lee	1-9-25
Wakely Jimmy	2-16-14
Waller Eddy	1889
Wilkerson Guy	1898
Williams Guinn 'Big Boy'	4-26-1899
Wilson Whip	6-16-19
Woods Harry	1889
Yowlachie Chief	8-15-1891

STAGE ACTORS

Aaron Caroline	8-7-54
Aaron Jack	5-1-33
Abel Walter	6-6-1898
Abraham F Murray	10-24-39
Abuba Ernest	8-25-47
Adamson David	5-30-40
Adamson Ellen	7-13-56
Adler Bruce	11-27-44
Adler Stella	2-10-02
Adrian Max	11-1-03
Aidem Betsy	10-28-57
Albert Wil	8-22-30
Albrecht Johanna	7-30-40
Alda Robert	2-26-14
Aldredge Tom	2-28-28
Alexander James	6-15-41
Alexander Jane	10-28-39
Alice Mary	12-3-41
Allen Joan	8-20-56
Allen Seth	7-13-41
Allen Sheila	10-22-32
Almquist Gregg	12-1-48
Amendolia Don	2-1-45
Anderman Maureen	10-26-46
Anders Glen	9-1-1890
Anderson Arthur	8-29-22
Anderson Douglas	6-26-48
Anderson Judith	2-10-1898
Andros Douglas	11-27-31
Anglim Philip	2-11-53
Aranas Raul	10-1-47
Arbeit Herman	4-19-25
Arliss Dimitra	10-23-32
Arlt Lewis	12-5-49
Arnold Madison	2-7-35
Arnold Victor	7-1-36
Arthur Helen-Jean	11-2-33
Ashcroft Peggy	12-22-07
Ashley Mary Ellen	6-11-38
Atherton William	7-30-47
Atkinson Peggy	10-1-43
August Ron	12-25-42
Austin Elizabeth	5-23-52
Avari N Erick	4-13-52
Ayr Michael	9-8-53

Backer Brian	12-5-56
Backus Richard	3-28-45
Baclanova Olga	8-19-1899
Baer Marian	8-18-26
Baff Regina	3-31-49
Bailey Dennis	4-12-53
Bailey Janet	9-8-52
Baker Mark	10-2-46
Baker Raymond	7-9-48
Ballantyne Paul	7-8-09
Bamman Gerry	9-18-41
Banes Lisa	7-9-55
Bankhead Tallulah	1-31-03
Banks Leslie	6-9-1890
Bankston Arnold	6-2-55
Bansavage Lisa	3-22-53
Baranski Christine	5-2-52
Barbour Thomas	7-25-21
Barker Clive	6-29-31
Barker Margaret	10-10-08
Barner Stockman	7-26-21
Baron Evalyn	4-21-48
Barone John	3-14-54
Barrat Robert	7-10-1891
Barre Gabriel	8-26-57
Barrett Brent	2-28-57
Barrett Leslie	10-30-19
Barrs Norman	11-6-17
Barry Raymond J	3-14-39
Bartenieff George	1-24-33
Bartlett Lisabeth	2-28-56
Bartlett Robin	4-22-51
Barton Daniel	1-23-49
Barton James	11-1-1890
Basescu Elinor	3-5-27
Battista Lloyd	5-14-37
Bauersmith Paula	7-26-09
Baum Susan J	7-12-50
Bavan Yolande	6-1-42
Baxter Keith	4-29-35
Beachner Louis	6-9-23
Bean Reathel	8-24-42
Bedford-Lloyd John	1-2-56
Beecher Janet	10-21-1884
Bennett Richard	5-21-1873
Bentley John	1-31-40

Berezin Tanya	3-25-41
Berghof Herbert	9-13-09
Bergner Elisabeth	8-22-00
Berman Donald F	1-23-54
Berridge Elizabeth	5-2-62
Berry Eric	1-9-13
Bessette Mimi	1-15-56
Best Edna	3-3-00
Bevans Philippa	2-10-16
Beverley Trazana	8-9-45
Billington Lee	7-15-32
Birney Reed	9-11-54
Bishop Joe	3-4-31
Bivens Diane E	6-19-48
Blackburn Robert	1-21-25
Blackman Ian	9-2-59
Blackmer Sidney	7-13-1896
Blaisdell Nesbitt	12-6-28
Blakely Gene	6-8-22
Blount Helon	1-15-29
Blum Mark	5-14-50
Blumenfeld Robert	2-26-43
Bobbie Walter	11-18-45
Boland Mary	1-28-1880
Bolin Shannon	1-1-17
Bond Sudie	7-13-28
Bonynge Leta	5-11-17
Bonds R J	11-30-46
Bordo Edwin	3-3-31
Bosco Philip	9-26-30
Bouley Frank	5-6-28
Boutsikaris Dennis	12-21-52
Bova Joseph	5-25-24
Bovasso Julie	8-1-30
Boyden Peter	7-19-45
Boyle Robert	3-28-50
Brady Alice	11-2-1892
Brannum Tom	6-17-41
Braun Roger	9-4-41
Breed Helen Lloyd	1-27-11
Brennan Mike	2-4-48
Brennan Tom	4-16-26
Brent Romney	1-26-02
Brian Michael	11-14-58
Briggs Richard	5-28-19
Brill Fran	9-30-46

Brochu James	8-16-46
Brogger Ivar	1-10-47
Bromka Elaine	1-6-50
Brookes Jacqueline	7-24-30
Brooks Alan	7-11-50
Brooks Jeff	4-7-50
Brown Kermit	2-3-37
Brown Pamela	7-8-18
Bruno Jean	12-7-26
Brutsman Laura	7-31-61
Brydon W B	9-20-33
Bubriski Peter	8-20-53
Buell Bill	9-21-52
Buffaloe Katharine	11-7-53
Buka Donald	12-18-21
Buloff Joseph	12-6-07
Burk Terence	8-11-47
Burke Robert	7-25-48
Burnell Peter	8-29-50
Burr Robert	3-5-22
Burrell Fred	9-18-36
Burrell Pamela	8-4-45
Burrows Vinie	11-15-28
Burstyn Mike	7-1-45
Burton Kate	9-10-57
Bussert Meg	10-21-49
Byers Ralph	1-10-50
Byron John	1-5-20
Cahill James	5-31-40
Cain William B	5-27-31
Caldwell Zoe	9-14-33
Cameron Hope	2-21-20
Camp Joanne	4-4-51
Carden William	2-2-47
Carlin Thomas A	12-10-28
Carlo Johann	5-21-57
Carlson Leslie	2-24-33
Carricart Robertson	12-28-47
Carruthers James	5-26-31
Carver Mary	5-3-24
Cass Peggy	5-21-26
Castang Veronica	4-22-38
Castanos Luz	7-15-35
Cates Madlyn	3-8-25
Catlin Faith	9-19-49
Cellario Maria	6-19-48

Cerveris Michael	11-6-60
Chaikin Shami	4-21-31
Chalfant Kathleen	1-14-45
Challenger Rudy	10-2-28
Champagne Michael	4-10-47
Chandler Jeffrey Alan	9-9-45
Chapin Miles	12-6-54
Chapman Roger	1-1-47
Charles Paul	7-29-47
Charney Deborah	8-1-51
Chase Ilka	4-8-05
Chatterton Ruth	12-24-1893
Chianese Dominic	2-24-32
Chibas Marissa	6-13-61
Chobanian Haig	10-26-37
Christian Robert	12-27-39
Christians Mady	1-19-00
Claire Ludi	4-15-27
Clark Bryan E	4-5-29
Clark Josh	8-16-55
Clark Phillip	8-12-41
Clarke Caitlin	5-3-52
Clay Louise	3-3-38
Coates Carolyn	4-29-30
Coco James	3-21-29
Coe John	10-19-25
Coffin Frederick	1-16-43
Colby Barbara	7-2-40
Coleman Nancy	12-30-14
Coles Zaida	9-10-33
Colitti Rik	2-1-34
Collier Constance	1-22-1878
Collinge Patricia	9-20-1894
Collins Bill	3-27-35
Collins Paul	7-25-37
Collins Peter	8-7-23
Conklin Peggy	11-2-10
Connell David	11-24-35
Connell Gordon	3-19-23
Connell Jane	10-27-25
Connolly John P	9-1-50
Connolly Walter	4-8-1887
Conolly Patricia	8-29-33
Conroy Jarlath	9-30-44
Conry Kathleen	11-15-47
Conwell Patricia	8-17-51

Coonan Sheila	6-28-22
Cooney Dennis	9-19-38
Cooper Gladys	12-18-1888
Copeland Joan	6-1-22
Corbett Leonora	6-28-08
Corfman Caris	5-18-55
Cornell Katherine	2-16-1898
Cortez Katherine	9-28-50
Costa Joseph	6-8-46
Costallos Suzanne	4-3-53
Costigan Ken	4-1-34
Countryman Michael	9-15-55
Courtneidge Cicely	4-1-1893
Courtney Alexander	3-21-40
Cowl Jane	12-14-1884
Craven Robin	9-20-10
Creswell Saylor	11-18-39
Cristofer Michael	1-22-45
Cromwell David	2-16-46
Cronin Jane	4-4-36
Cronyn Hume	7-18-11
Crook Peter	3-17-58
Crothers Joel	1-28-41
Crouse Lindsay	5-12-48
Croxton Darryl	4-5-46
Cuervo Alma	8-13-51
Cunningham Sarah	9-8-18
Curry Christopher	10-22-48
Curtis Keene	2-15-25
Cwikowski Bill	8-4-45
Dabdoub Jack	2-5-25
Dalton Lezlie	8-12-52
Dana Barbara	12-28-40
Dana Leora	4-1-23
Daneel Sylvia	6-20-30
Danette Leila	8-23-09
Danson Randy	4-30-50
Dantuono Michael	7-30-42
daSilva Howard	5-4-09
David Jean	5-4-31
Davidson Jack	7-17-36
Davidson Richard M	5-10-40
Deal Frank	10-7-58
DeAlmeida Joaquin	3-15-57
Dean Laura	5-27-63
DeAnda Peter	3-10-40

****

DeAngelis Rosemary	4-26-33
DeFrank Robert	11-29-45
DeGanon Matt	7-10-62
delaGiroday Francois	3-18-52
DelMedico Michael	10-3-33
Demas Carole	5-26-40
Dempsey Jerome	3-1-29
Dengel Jake	6-19-33
Dennis Sandy	4-27-37
Desai Shelly	12-3-35
Devlin Jay	5-8-29
Devlin John	1-26-37
DeVries Jon	3-26-47
Digges Dudley	6-9-1880
Dillon Mia	7-9-55
Dinehart Alan	10-3-1889
Dixon MacIntyre	12-22-31
Don Carl	12-15-16
DonHowe Gwyda	10-20-34
Donnelly Donal	7-6-31
Dorin Phoebe	6-26-40
Dorn Dolores	3-3-35
Douglas Lucien	8-5-49
Dowling Eddie	12-11-1894
Downing David	7-21-43
Drake Christopher	7-19-29
Draper Ruth	12-2-1884
Drischell Ralph	11-26-27
Driver John	1-16-47
Drummond Alice	5-21-29
Dudley Craig	1-22-45
Duell William	8-30-23
Dufour Val	2-5-28
Dukakis Olympia	6-20-31
Duke Robert	6-22-17
DuVal Herbert	5-4-41
Dwyer Frank	2-1-45
Ebert Joyce	6-23-33
Eckhouse James	2-14-55
eda-Young Barbara	1-30-45
Ede George	12-22-31
Edenfield Dennis	7-23-46
Edwards Burt	1-11-28
Egan Michael	8-24-26
Eldridge Florence	9-5-01
Elic Josep	3-21-21

****

****

Ellin David	1-10-25
Elliott Alice	8-22-50
Ellis William	12-5-29
Elston Robert	5-29-34
Emmet Robert	10-3-52
Emmett Robert	9-28-21
Engelhardt Wallace	4-30-23
Enserro Michael	10-5-18
Epstein Alvin	5-14-25
Epstein Pierre	7-27-30
Eskenas Linda	9-11-50
Evans Dillon	1-2-21
Evans Maurice	6-3-01
Evans Peter	5-27-50
Everett Tom	10-21-48
Everhart Rex	6-13-20
Evers Brian	2-14-42
Faber Ron	2-16-33
Fairservis Elf	5-19-57
Falkenhain Patricia	12-3-26
Fancy Richard	8-2-43
Farr Kimberly	10-16-48
Farrar Martha	4-22-28
Felder Clarence	9-2-38
Field Crystal	12-10-42
Fielding Anne	1-30-43
Fitzpatrick Jim	11-26-50
Flanagan Pauline	6-29-25
Flanagan Walter	10-4-28
Fleischman Mark	11-25-35
Fletcher Bramwell	2-20-04
Fletcher Jack	4-21-21
Florek Dave	5-19-35
Fontaine Luther	4-14-47
Fontanne Lynn	12-6-1887
Forbes Francine	4-25-60
Ford Clebert	1-29-32
Ford Frances	11-10-39
Ford Ruth	7-7-15
Ford Spence	2-25-54
Ford Suzanne	9-22-49
Ford Sydney	2-28-38
Foster Frances	6-11-24
Foster Gloria	11-15-36
Fowler Clement	12-27-24
Fox Colin	11-20-38

****

Franco Ramon	9-12-63
Frank Judy	11-26-36
Franz Elizabeth	6-18-41
Franz Joy	6-13-45
Fraser Alison	7-8-55
Frelich Phyllis	2-29-44
French Bruce	7-4-45
French Valerie	3-11-32
Friedman Peter	4-24-49
Frisch Richard	5-9-33
Frost Lauren	2-7-45
Furs Eddie L	7-23-57
Gable June	6-5-45
Gaines Boyd	5-11-53
Gale David	10-2-36
Gallagher Peter	8-19-55
Gallogly John	8-23-52
Galloway Jane	2-27-50
Gantry Donald	6-11-36
Garber Victor	3-16-49
Garfield David	2-6-41
Garfield Julie	1-10-46
Garland Geoff	6-10-32
Garrick Beulah	6-12-21
Gassell Sylvia	7-1-23
Gatto Peter	1-24-46
Gavon Igors	11-14-37
Gelke Becky	2-17-53
Genest Edmond	10-27-43
Gentles Avril	4-2-29
George Gladys	9-13-04
Geraci Frank	9-8-39
Gerdes George	2-23-48
Gerroll Daniel	10-16-51
Gielgud John	4-14-04
Giletto John Basil	9-27-50
Gilpin Jack	5-31-51
Gingold Hermione	12-9-1897
Gionson Mel	2-23-54
Girardeau Frank	10-19-42
Glanville Maxwell	2-11-18
Gleason James	9-30-52
Gleason Joanna	6-2-50
Gleason Paul	5-4-41
Glover John	8-7-44
Glushak Joanna	5-27-58

Gnat Michael	12-13-55
Goetz Peter Michael	12-10-41
Gold Russell	10-23-17
Golden Annie	10-19-51
Goldsmith Merwin	8-7-37
Goldstein Leslie	1-22-40
Gonzalez Ernesto	4-8-40
Goodman Robyn	8-24-47
Gordon Carl	1-20-32
Gordon Ruth	10-30-1896
Gossett Robert	3-3-54
Gould Ellen	12-30-50
Gould Gordon	5-4-30
Goutman Christopher	12-19-52
Grainger Gawn	10-12-40
Grant David Marshall	6-21-55
Gray Sam	7-18-23
Greene James	12-1-26
Greene Richard	1-8-46
Griffith Kristin	9-7-53
Grimes Tammy	1-30-34
Grollman Elaine	10-22-28
Gross Gene	2-17-20
Guida Maria	5-1-53
Gunton Bob	11-15-45
Gwillim Jack	12-15-15
Hadary Jonathan	10-11-48
Hagen Uta	6-12-19
Hall George	11-19-16
Hamilton Lawrence	9-14-54
Hampden Walter	6-30-1879
Hanan Stephen	1-7-47
Hardie Russell	5-20-06
Hardwicke Cedric	2-19-1893
Harper Charles Thomas	3-29-49
Harrington Delphi	8-26-42
Harris Barbara	7-25-35
Harris Baxter	11-18-40
Harris Julie	12-2-25
Harron Donald	9-19-24
Hart Paul E	7-20-39
Hawkins Trish	10-30-45
Haydon Julie	6-10-10
Hayes Helen	10-10-00
Hayle Douglas	1-11-42
Hays Rex	6-17-46

****

Hearn George	6-18-34
Heath Gordon	9-20-18
Heflin Marta	3-29-45
Herbert Diana	12-25-28
Herlie Eileen	3-8-20
Heyman Barton	1-24-37
Hicks Lois Diane	9-3-40
Higgins James	6-1-32
Higgins Michael	1-20-26
Hilbrandt James	8-13-34
Hines Patrick	3-17-30
Hodapp Ann	5-6-46
Hogan Jonathan	6-13-51
Holbrook Ruby	8-28-30
Holmes George	6-3-35
Hornish Rudy	1-26-38
Horton Russell	11-11-41
Houts Rod	12-15-06
Hovis Joan	4-3-32
Hoxie Richmond	7-21-46
Hudson Charles	3-29-31
Hughes Barnard	7-16-15
Hughes Tresa	9-17-29
Hull Josephine	1-3-1886
Hurst Lillian	8-13-49
Hurt Mary Beth	9-26-48
Hurt Tom	2-25-45
Hyman Earle	10-11-26
Impert Margaret	6-4-46
Ivanek Zjelko	8-15-57
Ivey Dana	8-12-41
James Jessica	10-31-33
James Stephen	2-2-52
Jamrog Joseph	12-21-32
Jay Mary	12-23-39
Jenney Lucinda	4-23-54
Jennings Ken	10-10-47
Jochim Keith	1-26-42
Johnson Page	8-25-28
Johnston Audre	7-22-39
Jones Gordon G	11-1-41
Jones Jeffrey	9-28-47
Jones Jen	3-23-27
Joy Robert	8-17-51
Judd Robert	8-3-27
Jude Patrick	2-25-51

****

Kan Lilah	9-4-31
Kane John	8-29-20
Karr Patti	7-10-32
Kaufman Michael	7-28-50
Kelly K C	11-12-52
Kennedy Laurie	2-14-48
Kenyon Laura	11-23-48
Kepros Nicholas	11-8-32
Kerner Norberto	7-19-29
Keyes Daniel	3-6-14
Killmer Nancy	12-16-36
Kingsley Peter	8-14-45
Kiser Terry	8-1-39
Kliban Ken	7-26-42
Klunis Tom	4-29-30
Knudson Kurt	9-7-36
Koloc Bonnie	2-6-46
Kosleck Martin	3-24-14
Kotler Jill	10-3-52
Kudan John	9-13-55
Kurek Annette	2-6-50
Lally James	10-2-56
Lance Rory	4-10-54
Landau Vivien	1-31-40
Landfield Timothy	8-22-50
Landon Sofia	1-24-49
Lane Nathan	2-3-56
Lang Stephen	7-11-52
Lange Ann	6-24-53
Lantzy Tom	5-27-51
Larsen Liz	1-16-59
Laub Sandra	12-15-56
Laudicino Dino	12-22-39
Lawrence Delphi	3-23-32
Leary David	8-8-39
Lederer Suzanne	9-9-48
Lee Irving Allen	11-21-48
Lee Jerry	1-23-46
Lee Kaiulani	2-28-50
Lee-Aranas Mary	9-23-59
Leffert Joel	12-8-51
LeGallienne Eva	1-11-1899
LeMassena William	5-23-16
LeNoire Rosetta	8-8-11
Leone Marianne	1-2-52
LeRoy Ken	8-17-27

****

Lessane Leroy	8-5-42
Leversee Loretta	3-26-28
Lewis Gilbert	4-6-41
Lewis Jenifer	1-25-57
Lewis Marcia	8-18-38
Lewis Timothy	6-28-47
Lide Miller	8-10-35
Lipman David	5-12-38
Lippin Renee	7-26-46
Lipson Clifford	2-10-47
Lipson Paul	12-23-13
Listman Ryan	12-30-39
Locante Sam	9-12-18
Lombard Michael	8-8-34
London Chet	4-8-31
London Howard	10-19-27
Lonergan Lenore	6-2-28
Long Jodi	1-7-54
Lopez Michael	10-10-56
Lopez Priscilla	2-26-48
Lord Barbara	11-21-37
Love Phyllis	12-21-29
Lovelace Cindie	8-31-58
Lowery Marcella	4-27-45
Lubar Cynthia	4-16-54
Lucas J Frank	3-15-20
Luce Claire	10-15-03
Lum Alvin	5-28-31
Lunt Alfred	8-19-1892
Lute Denise	8-2-54
Lyndeck Edmund	10-4-25
MacGrath Leueen	7-3-14
MacIntosh Joan E	11-25-45
Macy W H	3-13-50
Madden Donald	11-5-33
Madden Sharon	7-8-47
Mahaffey Valerie	6-16-53
Mahone Juanita M	9-12-52
Maillard Carol Lynn	3-4-51
Mais Michele	7-30-54
Malina Judith	6-4-26
Malet Arthur	9-24-27
Mantell Bernard	11-21-53
Maraden Frank	8-9-44
Margulies David	2-19-37
Marks Jack R	2-28-35

Marr Richard	5-12-28
Marshall Larry	4-3-44
Marshall Norman Thomas	4-28-39
Martin Lucy	2-8-42
Martin W T	1-17-47
Matz Jerry	11-15-35
May Beverly	8-11-27
May Winston	2-3-37
Mayer Jerry	5-12-41
McCann Christopher	9-29-52
McClarnon Kevin	8-25-52
McCrane Paul	1-19-61
McDermott Keith	9-28-53
McDonald Tanny	2-13-39
McFarland Robert	5-7-31
McGrath Katherine	12-11-44
McGregor-Stewart Kate	10-4-44
McGuire Mitchell	12-26-36
McHenry Don	2-25-08
McInerney Bernie	12-4-36
McIntyre Marilyn	5-23-49
McKay Scott	5-28-15
Meacham Paul	8-5-39
Meredith Lee	10-22-47
Merson Susan	4-25-50
Meryl Cynthia	9-25-50
Michalski John	6-7-48
Milgrim Lynn	3-17-44
Miller Betty	3-27-25
Miller Gregory	10-2-54
Moldow Deborah	12-18-48
Monson Lex	3-11-26
Monteith John	11-1-48
Monti Mary Elaine	9-18-48
Moor Bill	7-13-31
Moore Charlotte	7-7-39
Moore Maureen	8-12-51
Moore Peter	1-27-56
Morath Kathy	3-23-55
Morden Roger	3-21-39
Morfogen George	3-30-33
Morris Nat	3-13-51
Morrisey Bob	8-15-46
Murray Brian	10-9-39
Nakahara Ron	7-20-47
Nastasi Frank	1-7-23

Natwick Mildred	6-19-08
Negro Mary-Joan	11-9-48
Nelson Mark	9-26-55
Nesbit Cathleen	11-24-1889
Neuman Joan	10-4-26
Newman Ellen	9-5-50
Newman William	6-15-34
Newton John	11-2-25
Nichols Robert	7-20-24
Niles Richard	5-19-46
Nixon Cynthia	4-9-66
Noonan Tom	4-12-51
Noto Lore	6-9-23
Nugent Elliott	9-20-1899
O'Brien Sylvia	5-4-24
O'Connor Kevin	5-7-38
O'Karma Alexandra	9-28-48
O'Neill Gene	4-7-51
O'Rourke Kevin	1-25-56
Oliver Rochelle	4-15-37
Owens Elizabeth	2-26-38
Pagano Giulia	7-8-48
Palmieri Joseph	8-1-39
Palminteri Chazz	5-15-51
Parady Ron	3-12-40
Parker Paula	8-14-50
Parker Rochelle	2-26-40
Parry William	10-7-47
Passeltiner Bernie	11-21-31
Patterson James	6-29-32
Patton Will	6-14-54
Pearlman Stephen	2-26-35
Pearthree Pippa	9-23-56
Pen Polly	3-11-54
Pendleton Austin	3-27-40
Pendleton Wyman	4-18-16
Pentecost George	7-15-39
Perez Lazaro	12-17-45
Perri Paul	11-6-53
Pessano Jan	8-10-44
Phillips Garrison	10-8-29
Phillips Peter	12-7-49
Pierce Harvey	6-24-17
Pinero John	1-31-45
Polito Jon	12-29-50
Ponazecki Joe	1-7-34

Poole Roy	3-31-24
Price Lonny	3-9-59
Primont Marian	10-2-13
Rachelle Bernie	10-7-39
Rackleff Owen S	7-16-34
Ramos Richard Russell	8-23-41
Ramsay Remak	2-2-37
Ramsel Gena	2-19-59
Rebhorn James	9-1-48
Redfield Adam	11-4-59
Reed Gavin	6-3-35
Rees Roger	5-5-44
Reinhardsen David	1-13-49
Rey Antonia	10-12-27
Richardson Ralph	12-19-02
Richie Chuck	4-2-47
Riley Larry	6-21-52
Robbins Rex	3-30-35
Roberts Marilyn	10-30-39
Roberts Ralph	8-17-22
Robson Flora	3-28-02
Rockafellow Marilyn	1-22-39
Rodgers Enid	4-29-24
Rogan Peter	5-11-39
Rogers Paul	3-22-17
Rolfing Tom	9-6-49
Rose Cristine	1-31-51
Rose George	2-19-20
Ross Alan	12-1-20
Ross Jamie	5-4-39
Rothman John	6-3-49
Rounds David	10-9-30
Rowe Hansford	5-12-24
Rowe Stephen	6-3-48
Rucker Bo	8-17-48
Ruisinger Thomas	5-13-30
Russell Cathy	8-6-55
Ryland Jack	7-2-35
Sabin David	4-24-37
Sachs Ann	1-23-48
Salisbury Fran	2-9-45
Sanchez Jaime	12-19-38
Saputo Peter J	2-2-39
Saunders Nicholas	6-2-14
Sbarge Raphael	2-12-64
Scardino Don	2-17-48

****

Schenkkan Robert	3-19-53
Schimmel John	10-12-48
Schnabel Stefan	2-2-12
Schneider Jana	10-24-51
Schweid Carole	10-5-46
Scott Seret	9-1-49
Seamon Edward	4-15-37
Seaton Joanna	3-15-49
Seff Richard	9-23-27
Segal Kathrin King	12-8-47
Selby James	8-29-48
Seldes Marian	8-23-28
Serra Raymond	8-13-37
Serrecchia Michael	3-26-51
Setrakian Ed	10-1-28
Severs William	1-8-32
Shaller Anna	4-8-40
Shallo Karen	9-28-46
Shelley Carole	8-16-39
Shepard John	12-9-52
Sherman Hiram	2-11-08
Sherwood Madeleine	11-13-26
Sherwood Toba	9-28-34
Shimizu Keenan	10-22-56
Shimono Sab	7-31-43
Short Sylvia	10-22-27
Shropshire Noble	3-2-46
Shultz Philip	7-24-53
Siegel Harvey	2-28-45
Siegler Ben	4-9-58
Silliman Maureen	12-3-49
Silver Joe	9-28-22
Skinner Cornelia Otis	5-30-01
Sleeper Martha	6-24-07
Smith Lois	11-3-30
Snow Norman	3-29-50
Sommer Josef	6-26-34
Spaisman Zipora	1-2-20
Sparer Kathryn C	1-5-56
Spindell Ahvi	6-26-54
Spivak Alice	8-11-35
St John Betta	11-26-29
Stanley Gordon	12-20-51
Stattel Robert	11-20-37
Steinberg Roy	3-24-51
Stenborg Helen	1-24-25

****

****

Sterner Steve	5-5-51
Stevens Fisher	11-27-63
Stevensen Scott	5-4-51
Stickney Dorothy	6-21-00
Stinton Colin	3-10-47
Stoneburner Sam	2-24-34
Strimpell Stephen	1-17-37
Stroman Guy	9-11-51
Stuthman Fred	6-27-19
Sullivan Brad	11-18-31
Sullivan Kim	7-21-52
Surovy Nicolas	6-30-44
Sutton Henry	8-24-26
Talman Ann	9-13-57
Tandy Jessica	6-7-09
Tarlow Florence	1-19-29
Tate Dennis	8-31-38
Taylor George	9-18-30
Taylor Holland	1-14-43
Taylor Laurette	4-1-1884
Teitel Carol	8-1-29
Thacker Russ	6-23-46
Thompson Evan	9-3-31
Thompson Jeffrey V	3-21-52
Tippit Wayne	12-19-32
Tolaydo Michael	7-23-46
Torres Andy	8-10-45
Torres Liz	9-27-47
Tsoutsouvas Sam	8-20-48
Tucci Maria	6-19-41
Twomey Anne	6-7-51
Urla Joe	12-25-58
Umeki Miyoshi	4-3-29
Utley Byron	11-4-54
Vale Michael	6-28-22
Valentine James	2-18-33
VanHunter William	2-1-47
VanNorden Peter	12-16-50
Vannuys Ed	12-28-30
Varon Susan	5-5-52
Vennema John C	8-24-48
Ventriss Jennie	8-7-35
Vinovich Steve	1-22-45
Vipond Neil	12-24-29
Voigts Richard	11-25-34
vonScherler Sasha	12-12-39

****

34

****

****

Vye Murvyn	7-15-13	**RADIO ACTORS**	
Waldren Peter	9-7-33	Adams Mason	2-26-19
Waldrop Mark	7-30-54	Allenby Peggy	1901
Walker June	6-14-04	Allison Jone	1923
Wallace Lee	7-15-30	Allman Elvia	1905
Wallace Marie	5-19-39	Ameche Don	5-31-08
Warden Yvonne	1-16-28	Ameche Jim	1915
Warfield Marlene	6-19-41	Backus Jim	2-25-13
Warren Joseph	6-5-16	Barney Jay	3-14-16
Watkins James	6-6-33	Barrett Tony	5-24-16
Watt Billie Lou	6-20-24	Barrier Edgar	3-4-07
Weaver Fritz	1-19-26	Beemer Brace	1903
Weber Fredricka	12-22-40	Begley Ed	3-25-01
Webster Margaret	3-15-05	Benaderet Bea	4-4-06
Weddell Mimi	2-15-15	Berg Gertrude	10-3-1899
Weeks James Ray	3-21-42	Blaine Martin	1914
Weiner Arn	7-19-31	Booth Shirley	8-20-1898
Weiss Joel	9-21-53	Bouchey Bill	1895
Weldon Charles	6-1-40	Bradley Curley	1911
Westenberg Robert	10-26-53	Briggs Donald	1-28-11
White Charles	8-29-20	Brown John	1904
White Jane	10-30-22	Bryan Arthur Q	1899
Whitton Margaret	11-30-50	Bunce Alan	6-28-03
Williams Ellis	6-28-51	Butterfield Herb	1896
Willoughby Ronald	6-3-37	Campbell Patsy	1919
Wilson K C	8-10-45	Collyer Bud	6-18-08
Wilson Mary Louise	11-12-36	Conreid Hans	4-15-15
Wilson Trey	1-21-48	Conte John	9-15-15
Wolfe Joel	9-19-36	Cotsworth Staats	2-17-08
Wolpe Lenny	3-25-51	Curtin Joseph	1913
Wong B D	10-24-62	Damon Les	1909
Woods Richard	5-9-21	Darnay Toni	8-11-22
Woronov Mary	12-8-46	Darvas Lili	4-10-02
Worth Irene	6-23-16	DeCamp Rosemary	11-14-10
Wright Mary Catherine	3-19-48	deCorsia Ted	1904
Xifo Ray	9-3-42	Dehner John	11-23-15
Yancey Kim	9-25-59	DeKoven Roger	10-22-07
Yoshida Peter	5-28-45	Doyle Len	1893
Yurka Blanche	6-18-1887	Duff Howard	11-24-17
Zacharias Emily	7-27-53	Erskine Marilyn	4-24-24
Zachary Alaina	10-6-46	Felton Verna	7-20-1890
Zala Nancy	7-10-36	Fitzmaurice Michael	4-28-08
Zang Edward	8-19-34	Flynn Bernardine 'Sade'	1-2-04
Zeller Mark	4-20-32	Frees Paul	6-22-20
Zien Chip	3-20-47	Frost Alice	8-1-09
Zorich Louis	2-12-24	Garde Betty	9-19-05

******************************* ***********************************

****

Gardner Ed	6-29-05
Gilbert Jody	3-18-16
Goff Norris 'Abner'	5-30-06
Graser Earle W	1909
Greaza Walter	1-1-1897
Gregg Virginia	3-6-16
Haines Larry	8-3-17
Halop Florence	1-23-23
Harris Stacy	1918
Hayworth Vinton	1906
Hersholt Jean	7-12-1886
Higby Mary Jane	1916
Hurt Marlin	1906
Irving Charles	1913
Jameson House	12-17-02
Janney Leon	4-1-17
Jostyn Jay	1902
Julian Joseph	1911
Keane Teri	10-24-22
Kelk Jackie	8-6-23
Kilpack Bennett	1883
Kinsella Walter	8-16-00
Kruschen Jack	3-20-22
Larkin John	4-11-12
Lauck Chester 'Lum'	2-9-02
Lewis Abby	1-14-10
Lewis Cathy	1918
Lewis Elliott	1902
Lewis Forrest	1900
Lovejoy Frank	3-28-14
Luddy Barbara	1908
Lynch Ken	1910
Mann Gloria	1928
Mather Jack	1908
McCambridge Mercedes	3-17-18
McCormick Myron	2-8-07
McGrath Paul	4-11-04
McIntire John	6-27-07
Meighan James	1904
Miner Jan	10-15-17
Mitchell Shirley	11-4-19
Mohr Gerald	5-11-14
Morgan Claudia	6-12-12
Morrison Bret	1912
Moss Arnold	1-28-10
Nelson Frank	1911

****

****

Nolan Jeannette	12-30-11
Ortega Santos	1900
Pawley Edward	3-16-01
Petrie George	11-16-15
Phillips Barney	10-20-13
Pious Minerva	3-5-03
Randolph Amanda	1902
Randolph Lillian	1915
Redfield William	1-26-27
Reed Alan	8-20-07
Robinson Bartlett	12-9-12
Ross Earle	3-29-1888
Ruick Melville	7-8-1898
Sands Dorothy	3-5-00
Seymour Anne	9-11-09
Sloane Everett	10-1-09
Smart J Scott	1903
Sorel Guy	8-12-14
Soule Olan	2-28-09
Stafford Hanley	9-22-1898
Stone Ezra	12-2-17
Studebaker Hugh	1901
Swenson Karl	7-23-08
Tedrow Irene	8-3-10
Thomas Ann	7-8-15
Thompson Bill	7-8-13
Tozere Frederick	7-19-01
Tremayne Les	4-16-13
Trout Dink	6-18-1898
Tuttle Lurene	8-29-06
VanHarvey Art 'Vic'	8-23-1883
VanRooten Luis	11-29-06
Vigran Herb	1910
Waldo Janet	1930
Walter Wilmer	2-9-1884
Waterman Willard	1914
Weber Karl	3-17-16
Weeks Barbara	1907
Wever Ned	1899
Wheel Patricia	12-9-25
Whiting Barbara	5-19-31
Williams Florence	1912
Wilson Marie	12-30-16
Wright Ben	1915
Yarborough Barton	1900
Young Carleton G	5-26-07

****

TV ACTORS

Aames Willie	7-15-60
Acker Sharon	4-2-35
Ackerman Bettye	2-28-28
Ackroyd David	5-30-40
Acovone Jay	8-30-55
Actman Jane	4-6-49
Adams Don	4-19-26
Adams Jeb	4-10-61
Adams Marla	8-28-38
Addams Dawn	9-21-30
Addison-Altman Nancy	3-21-50
Addy Wesley	8-4-13
Aidman Charles	1-31-25
Akins Claude	5-25-18
Alann Lloyd	8-15-52
Albee Denny	3-19-49
Albert Edward	2-20-51
Albertson Jack	6-16-07
Albright Lola	7-20-24
Alda Alan	1-28-36
Alden Norman	9-13-24
Aletter Frank	1-14-26
Alex Marilyn	10-30-30
Alexander Ben	5-26-11
Alexander Denise	11-11-39
Alexander Jason	9-23-59
Alexander Terry	3-23-47
Alfonso Kristian	9-5-54
Allan Jed	3-1-38
Allen Sian Barbara	7-12-46
Alley Kirstie	1-12-55
Ames Rachel	11-2-29
Amos John	12-27-39
Amsterdam Morey	12-14-14
Ana-Alicia (Ortiz)	12-12-56
Anders Merry	5-22-33
Anderson Barbara	11-27-45
Anderson Daryl	7-1-51
Anderson Gillian	8-9-68
Anderson Harry	10-14-52
Anderson Herbert	3-30-17
Anderson John	10-20-22
Anderson Loni	8-5-45
Anderson Melody	12-3-55
Anderson Michael Jr	8-6-43

Anderson Richard	8-8-26
Anderson Richard Dean	1-23-50
Andes Keith	7-12-20
Andrews Tige	3-19-23
Andrews Tod	11-10-14
Ansara Michael	4-15-22
Anspach Susan	11-23-39
Antonio Lou	1-23-34
Archer Beverly	7-19-48
Arden Eve	4-30-12
Argenziano Carmen	10-27-43
Arkin Adam	8-19-56
Armstrong Bess	12-11-53
Arnaz Lucie	7-17-51
Arnold Tichina	6-28-69
Arrants Rod	9-5-44
Arthur Beatrice	5-13-26
Ashford Matthew	1-29-60
Ashton John	2-22-48
Asner Ed	11-15-29
Assante Armand	10-4-49
Astin John	3-30-30
Atkins Christopher	2-21-61
Atterbury Malcolm	2-20-07
Atwater Edith	4-22-11
Auberjonois Rene	6-1-40
Aubrey Skye	12-20-45
Aubuchon Jacques	10-30-24
Austin Teri	4-17-59
Autry Alan	7-31-52
Avery Phyllis	11-14-24
Azzara Candy	5-18-47
Babcock Barbara	2-27-37
Bach Catherine	3-1-54
Badler Jane	12-31-53
Baer Max Jr	12-4-37
Baggetta Vincent	12-7-47
Bailey-Smith Hillary	5-25-57
Bain Barbara	9-13-32
Bain Conrad	2-4-23
Baio Scott	9-22-61
Baker Blanche	12-20-56
Baker Kathy	6-8-50
Baker Mark-Linn	6-17-54
Baker Scott Thompson	9-15-61
Bakula Scott	10-9-54

Bal Jeanne	5-3-28
Balaban Bob	8-16-45
Ballantine Carl	9-27-22
Banks Jonathan	1-31-47
Banner John	1-28-10
Bannon Jack	6-14-40
Baragrey John	4-15-18
Barbeau Adrienne	6-11-45
Barnes Joanna	11-15-34
Barnes Priscilla	12-7-55
Baron Sandy	5-5-37
Barr Douglas	5-1-49
Barr Hayley	4-27-71
Barr Julia	2-8-49
Barrett Majel	2-23-32
Barrie Barbara	5-23-31
Barrow Bernard	12-30-27
Barry Gene	6-14-19
Barth Eddie	9-29-31
Bartlett Bonnie	6-20-29
Bauer Charita	12-20-23
Bauer Jaime Lyn	3-9-49
Baur Elizabeth	12-11-47
Bavier Frances	1-14-05
Baxter-Birney Meredith	6-21-47
Bayer Gary	6-25-44
Beacham Stephanie	8-23-49
Beaird Betty	3-11-39
Beasley Allyce	7-6-54
Beaumont Hugh	2-16-09
Beavers Louise	3-8-02
Beck John	1-28-43
Beck Michael	2-4-49
Beck Noelle	12-14-68
Bedford Brian	2-16-35
Beery Noah Jr	8-10-13
Begley Ed Jr	9-16-49
Belafonte Shari	9-22-54
Belford Christine	1-14-49
BelGeddes Barbara	10-31-22
Bell Lauralee	12-22-68
Bellaver Harry	2-12-05
Beller Kathleen	2-10-55
Bellwood Pamela	6-26-51
Beltran Robert	11-19-53
Benedict Dirk	3-1-44

Benedict Paul	9-17-38
Benet Brenda	8-14-45
Bennett Meg	10-4-48
Benoit Patricia	2-21-27
Benson Lucille	7-17-22
Benton Barbi	1-28-50
Beradino John	5-1-17
Bergen Candice	5-9-46
Bergman Peter	6-11-43
Berlinger Warren	8-31-37
Bernard Crystal	9-30-64
Bernard Ed	7-4-39
Bernardi Herschel	10-30-23
Bernau Christopher	6-2-40
Bernsen Corbin	9-7-54
Berry Ken	11-3-33
Bertinelli Valerie	4-23-60
Bessell Ted	3-20-35
Best James	7-26-26
Bethune Zina	2-17-45
Betz Carl	3-9-20
Billingsley Barbara	12-22-22
Bindiger Emily	5-10-55
Binns Edward	9-12-16
Birney David	4-23-39
Bishop William	7-16-17
Bisoglio Val	5-7-26
Bissett Josie	10-5-70
Bixby Bill	1-22-34
Blacque Taurean	5-10-46
Blake Robert	9-18-33
Bleeth Yasmine	6-14-72
Blocker Dirk	7-31-57
Bochner Lloyd	7-29-24
Boen Earl	8-8-41
Bogazianos Vasili	2-1-49
Bohay Heidi	12-15-59
Bond Steve	4-22-53
Bonerz Peter	8-6-38
Bonner Frank	2-28-42
Booke Sorrell	1-4-26
Boone Randy	1-17-42
Boone Richard	6-18-17
Boothe Powers	6-1-49
Bornlenghi Matt	5-25-67
Bosley Tom	10-1-27

Bosson Barbara	11-1-39
Bottoms Joseph	4-22-54
Bottoms Sam	10-17-55
Bottoms Timothy	8-30-51
Boxleitner Bruce	5-12-50
Boyle Lara Flynn	3-24-70
Boynton Peter	11-4-55
Braeden Eric	4-3-43
Brainard Michael	11-23-65
Brand Neville	8-13-21
Brandon Michael	4-20-45
Brandon Peter	7-11-26
Brands X	7-24-27
Braugher Andre	1962
Braverman Bart	2-1-46
Bray Robert	10-23-17
Breeding Larry	9-28-46
Bremseth Lloyd	7-27-48
Brettschneider Mark	9-2-69
Brickell Beth	11-13-41
Brimley Wilford	9-27-34
Brittany Morgan	12-5-51
Broderick Beth	2-24-59
Broderick James	3-7-27
Brolin James	7-18-40
Brooks Avery	10-2-48
Brooks Joel	12-17-49
Brooks Martin	11-30-25
Brosnan Pierce	5-16-52
Brown Clancy	1-5-59
Brown Georg Stanford	6-24-43
Brown Johnny	6-11-37
Brown Lisa	8-2-54
Brown Peter	10-5-35
Bruce David	1-6-14
Bruns Philip	5-2-31
Bryant Lee	8-31-45
Bryce Edward	9-24-21
Bryggman Larry	12-21-38
Buktenica Ray	8-6-43
Bulifant Joyce	12-16-37
Bundy Brooke	8-8-47
Burch Shelly	3-19-60
Burghoff Gary	5-24-34
Burke Chris	8-26-65
Burke Delta	7-30-56

Burke Maggie	5-2-36
Burke Paul	7-21-26
Burns Catherine	9-25-45
Burns Jere	10-15-54
Burns Michael	12-30-47
Burr Raymond	5-21-17
Burton LeVar	2-16-57
Burton Warren	10-23-44
Busfield Timothy	6-12-57
Butkus Dick	12-9-42
Butler Dean	5-20-56
Byrde Edye	1-19-29
Byrne Martha	12-23-69
Byrnes Edd	7-30-33
Cadorette Mary	3-31-57
Caffrey Steve	9-27-61
Caine Howard	1-2-28
Calabro Thomas	2-3-59
Call Anthony	8-31-40
Callan Michael	11-22-35
Calvin Henry	5-25-18
Cameron Joanna	9-20-50
Camp Hamilton	10-30-34
Campanella Joseph	11-21-27
Campbell Alan	4-22-57
Campbell Nicholas	3-24-52
Campbell William	10-30-26
Canary David	8-25-38
Cannon J D	4-24-32
Cannon Katherine	9-6-53
Canova Diana	6-2-53
Carey Macdonald	3-15-13
Carey Philip	7-15-25
Carey Ron	12-11-35
Carlson Linda	5-12-45
Carmel Roger C	9-27-32
Carmen Julie	4-4-54
Carney Mary	1-26-50
Carradine David	10-8-36
Carson Crystal	6-24-67
Carter Dixie	5-25-39
Carter Lynda	7-24-51
Caruso David	1-17-56
Casnoff Philip	8-3-53
Cason Barbara	11-15-33
Cass Christopher	9-30-58

Cassidy Joanna	8-2-44
Catlett Mary Jo	9-2-38
Cazenove Christopher	12-17-45
Chamberlain Richard	3-31-35
Chapman Lonny	10-1-20
Charleson Leslie	2-22-45
Chiklis Michael	8-30-63
Childress Alvin	1907
Chris Marilyn	5-19-39
Christian Robert	12-27-39
Christie Audrey	6-27-11
Christopher Thom	10-5-40
Christopher William	10-20-32
Churchill Sarah	10-7-14
Cioffi Charles	10-31-35
Clanton Ralph	9-11-14
Clark Candy	6-20-47
Clark Fred	3-9-14
Clark Susan	3-8-44
Clarke Brian Patrick	8-1-52
Clarke Gary	8-16-36
Clary Robert	3-1-26
Clooney George	5-6-61
Clute Sidney	4-21-16
Coffield Peter	7-17-45
Colasanto Nicholas	1-19-24
Cole Carol	10-17-44
Cole Dennis	7-19-43
Cole Gary	9-20-57
Cole Michael	7-3-45
Cole Olivia	11-26-42
Coleman Dabney	1-3-32
Coleman Jack	2-21-58
Colin Margaret	1957
Collins Gary	4-30-38
Collins Jessica	4-1-71
Collins Joan	5-23-33
Collins Kate	5-6-59
Collins Ray	12-10-1889
Collins Stephen	10-1-47
Colomby Scott	9-19-52
Combs David	6-10-49
Compton Forrest	9-15-25
Compton John	6-21-23
Conaway Jeff	10-5-50
Conn Didi	7-13-51

Connelly Christopher	9-8-41
Connolly Norma	8-20-30
Connors Mike	8-15-25
Conrad Michael	10-16-25
Conrad Robert	3-1-35
Conrad William	9-27-20
Constantine Michael	5-22-27
Converse Frank	5-22-38
Conway Gary	2-4-36
Conway Shirl	6-13-16
Cook Nathan	4-9-50
Cooper Jeanne	10-25-28
Cooper Roy	1-22-30
Copley Teri	5-10-61
Corbett Glenn	8-17-29
Corbett Gretchen	8-13-47
Corbin Barry	10-16-40
Corby Ellen	6-13-14
Cord Alex	8-3-31
Corley Pat	6-1-30
Cornthwaite Robert	4-18-17
Corsaut Aneta	11-3-33
Cossart Valerie	6-27-07
Coster Nicolas	12-30-34
Cote Suzy	9-17-68
Council Richard	10-1-47
Courtney Jacqueline	9-24-46
Cover Franklin	11-20-28
Cox Courteney	6-15-64
Cox Richard	5-6-48
Cox Ronny	8-23-38
Cox Wally	12-6-24
Craig Yvonne	5-16-38
Crane Bob	7-13-28
Crane Dagne	3-8-34
Crane Matt	5-4-67
Crenna Richard	11-30-26
Cristal Linda	2-24-35
Crosby Cathy Lee	12-2-48
Crosby Denise	1957
Crosby Gary	6-27-33
Crosby Mary Frances	9-14-59
Crowley Kathleen	12-26-31
Crowley Pat	9-17-29
Cryer Jon	4-16-65
Cullum John	3-2-30

****

Culp Robert	8-16-30
Cypher Jon	1-13-32
D'Andrea Tom	5-15-09
D'Arbanville Patti	1951
Dabney Augusta	10-23-20
Dailey Irene	9-12-20
Daily Bill	8-30-28
Dalton Abby	8-15-35
Daly James	10-23-18
Daly Timothy	3-1-56
Daly Tyne	2-21-46
Damian Michael	4-26-62
Damon Cathryn	9-11-30
Damon Stuart	2-5-37
Daniels William	3-31-27
Dano Linda	5-12-43
Dano Royal	11-16-22
Danova Cesare	3-1-26
Danson Ted	12-29-47
Danza Tony	4-21-51
Darden Severn	11-9-29
Darling Joan	4-15-35
Darren James	6-8-36
Davalos Dick	11-5-35
David Thayer	3-4-27
Davila Diane	11-5-47
Davis Ann B	5-5-26
Davis Clifton	10-4-45
Davis Jim	8-26-16
Davis Phyllis	7-17-40
Davis Terry	7-23-51
Davis-Voss Sammi	6-21-64
Dawber Pam	10-18-51
Dawson Curt	12-5-41
Deacon Richard	5-14-22
DeCarlo Yvonne	9-1-24
DeFore Don	8-25-17
DeFreitas Scott	9-9-69
Delany Dana	3-13-57
DeLuise Peter	11-6-66
Demarest William	2-27-1892
Dennehy Brian	7-9-38
Denning Richard	3-27-14
Dennison Rachel	8-31-59
Denniston Leslie	5-19-50
Denver Bob	1-9-35

****

****

Derwin Mark	10-28-60
DeSantis Joe	6-15-09
Desiderio Robert	9-9-51
Devane William	9-5-37
DeVito Danny	11-17-44
DeWitt Joyce	4-23-49
Dey Susan	12-10-52
DeYoung Cliff	2-12-45
Dhiegh Khigh	1910
Diamond Selma	8-5-20
Dickinson Angie	9-30-31
Dicopoulos Frank	1-3-57
Dierkop Charles	9-11-36
Dion Colleen	12-26-64
Dishy Bob	1933
Dixon Donna	7-20-57
Dixon Ivan	4-6-31
Dobson Kevin	3-18-44
Dodson Jack	5-16-31
Doherty Shannen	4-12-71
Dolan Ellen	10-16-55
Dolenz Ami	1-8-69
Donahue Elinor	4-19-37
Donaldson Norma	1939
Donat Peter	1-20-38
Donnell Jeff	7-10-21
Donohue Amanda	6-29-62
Doohan James	3-3-20
Dooley Paul	2-22-28
Dorn Michael	12-9-52
Douglas Diana	1-22-23
Douglas Donna	9-26-39
Douglass Robyn	6-21-53
Doyle David	12-1-25
Drake Larry	2-21-50
Draper Polly	6-15-56
Dubbins Don	6-28-29
DuBois Ja'net	8-5-38
Duchovny David	1960
Duffy Julia	6-27-51
Duffy Patrick	3-17-49
Dugan Dennis	9-5-46
Duggan Andrew	12-28-23
Duke Patty	12-14-46
Dukes David	6-6-45
Duncan Sandy	2-20-46

****

```
* * * * * * * * * * * * * * * * * * * * * * * * * * * * * * *
```

Dunn Michael	10-20-34
Durning Charles	2-28-23
Durrell Michael	10-6-43
Dusenberry Ann	9-13-52
Dussault Nancy	6-30-36
Dutton Charles S	1-30-51
Dysart Richard	3-30-29
Dzundza George	7-19-45
Earley Candice	8-18-50
Easton Michael	2-16-66
Ebsen Buddy	4-2-08
Edelman Herb	11-5-30
Eden Barbara	8-23-34
Edmonds Louis	9-24-23
Edwards Anthony	1-19-62
Edwards Vince	7-7-28
Egan Eddie	1-3-30
Eikenberry Jill	1-21-47
Eisley Anthony	1-19-25
Elcar Dana	10-10-27
Elizondo Hector	12-22-36
Ellingsen Maria	1-22-64
Elliot Jane	1-17-47
Elliott David James	9-21-60
Elliott Patricia	7-21-42
Ely Ron	6-21-38
Engel Georgia	7-28-48
Englund Morgan	8-25-65
Englund Robert	6-6-47
Enriquez Rene	11-25-33
Eplin Tom	10-25-60
Ericson John	9-25-26
Estrada Erik	3-16-49
Evans Linda	11-18-42
Evans Michael	7-27-22
Evans Mike	11-3-49
Everett Chad	6-11-36
Evers Jason	1-2-27
Evigan Greg	10-14-53
Fabares Shelley	1-19-42
Fahey Jeff	1956
Fairchild Morgan	2-3-50
Falk Peter	9-16-27
Farentino James	2-24-38
Fargas Antonio	8-14-43
Farina Dennis	2-29-44

```
* * * * * * * * * * * * * * * * * * * * * * * * * * * * * * *
```

Farr Jamie	7-1-34
Farrell Mike	2-6-39
Farrell Sharon	12-24-46
Faso Laurie	4-11-46
Fawcett Farrah	2-2-47
Feinstein Alan	9-8-41
Feldon Barbara	3-12-41
Feldshuh Tovah	12-27-48
Fell Norman	3-24-24
Fenn Sherilyn	2-1-65
Ferrell Conchata	3-28-43
Ferrer Miguel	2-7-55
Fiedler John	2-3-25
Fisher Gail	8-18-35
Fitzsimmons Tom	10-28-47
Flanagan Fionnula	12-10-41
Flanders Ed	12-29-34
Flanery Sean Patrick	10-11-65
Flannery Susan	7-31-43
Flood Ann	11-12-32
Fluegel Darlanne	1956
Flynn Joe	11-8-25
Fogel Jerry	1-17-36
Ford Constance	7-1-29
Ford Faith	9-14-64
Ford Paul	11-2-01
Ford Steven	5-19-56
Forrest Steve	9-29-25
Forster Robert	7-13-42
Forsythe Henderson	9-11-17
Forsythe John	1-29-18
Foster Meg	5-10-48
Foster Phil	3-29-14
Fox Michael	2-27-21
Fox Michael J	6-9-61
Foxworth Robert	11-1-41
Frabotta Don	12-23-41
Frakes Jonathan	8-19-52
Franciosa Tony	10-25-28
Francis Anne	9-16-30
Francis Genie	5-26-62
Franciscus James	1-31-34
Franklin Bonnie	1-6-44
Franklin Don	12-15-60
Frann Mary	2-27-43
Franz Dennis	10-28-44

****

Frawley William	2-26-1893
Freed Bert	11-3-19
Freeman Al Jr	3-21-34
Freeman Kathleen	2-17-19
French Victor	12-4-34
Frewer Matt	1-4-58
Frid Jonathan	12-2-24
Fudge Alan	2-27-44
Fulton Eileen	9-13-33
Furst Stephen	5-8-55
Furth George	12-14-32
Gabet Sharon	1-13-52
Gabor Eva	2-11-21
Gail Max	4-5-43
Gallagher Helen	7-19-26
Gallagher Megan	2-6-60
Galloway Don	7-27-37
Garber Terri	12-28-60
Garland Beverly	10-17-26
Garrett Joy	3-2-45
Garth Jennie	1972
Gates Larry	9-24-15
Gateson Marjorie	1-17-1891
Gautier Dick	10-30-31
Geary Anthony	5-29-47
Geer Ellen	8-29-41
Geer Will	3-9-02
George Anthony	1-29-25
George Christopher	2-25-29
George Lynda Day	12-11-44
Georgiade Nick	2-5-33
Gerard Gil	1-23-43
Getty Estelle	7-25-23
Getz John	1947
Gian Joseph	7-13-61
Gibb Cynthia	12-14-63
Gibbs Marla	6-14-46
Gibbs Timothy	4-17-66
Gilbert Melissa	5-8-64
Ging Jack	11-30-31
Ginty Robert	11-14-48
Givens Robin	11-27-64
Glaser Paul Michael	3-25-43
Glass Ron	7-10-45
Gless Sharon	5-31-43
Goddard Mark	7-24-36

****

****

Gold Missy	7-14-70
Golonka Arlene	1-23-36
Goodeve Grant	7-6-52
Goodman John	6-20-52
Gordon Barry	12-21-48
Gordon Bruce	6-20-19
Gordon Gale	2-2-06
Gordon Phil	5-5-22
Gorman Cliff	10-13-36
Gosfield Maurice	1-28-13
Gossett Louis Jr	5-27-36
Gould Harold	12-10-23
Grammer Kelsey	2-21-45
Grandy Fred	6-29-48
Grant Faye	7-16-58
Grant Jennifer	2-26-66
Grassle Karen	2-25-44
Graves Ernest	5-5-19
Graves Peter	3-18-26
Graves Teresa	1-10-49
Gray Erin	1-7-52
Gray Linda	9-12-40
Greason Staci	5-23-64
Green Brian	3-9-62
Greer Dabbs	4-2-17
Gregory James	12-23-11
Grieco Richard	3-23-64
Griffith Andy	6-1-26
Groh David	5-21-39
Gross Michael	6-21-47
Grubbs Gary	11-14-49
Guido Michael	1-13-50
Guilbert Ann Morgan	10-16-28
Guillaume Robert	11-30-28
Gulager Clu	11-16-28
Guy Jasmine	3-10-64
Gwynne Fred	7-10-26
Hack Shelley	7-6-52
Hagen Jean	8-3-24
Haggerty Dan	11-19-41
Hagman Larry	9-21-31
Haid Charles	6-2-43
Haig Sid	7-14-39
Haigh Kenneth	3-25-30
Hairston Jester	7-9-01
Hale Alan Jr	3-8-18

****

****

Hale Barbara	4-18-22
Hall Deidre	10-31-48
Hall Grayson	1927
Halsey Brett	6-20-33
Hamel Veronica	11-20-43
Hamilton Carrie	12-5-63
Hamlin Harry	10-30-51
Hammer Ben	12-8-25
Hampton James	7-9-36
Hanley Bridget	2-3-41
Hansen Peter	12-5-21
Harewood Dorian	8-6-50
Hargitay Mariska	1-23-64
Harmon Mark	9-2-51
Harper Jessica	10-10-49
Harper Ron	1-12-36
Harper Valerie	8-22-40
Harrelson Woody	7-23-61
Harrington Pat Jr	8-13-29
Harris Jonathan	11-6-14
Harris Mel	7-12-56
Harrison Gregory	5-31-50
Harrison Jenilee	6-21-59
Harrison Noel	1-29-36
Harrold Kathryn	8-2-50
Hartley Mariette	6-21-40
Hartman Lisa	6-1-56
Harty Patricia	11-5-41
Haskell Peter	10-15-34
Hasselhoff David	7-17-52
Hastings Bob	4-18-25
Hastings Don	4-1-34
Hatch Richard	5-21-47
Hauser Wings	12-12-47
Hayes Bill	6-5-25
Hayes Margaret	12-5-24
Hayes Susan Seaforth	7-11-43
Haynes Lloyd	10-19-34
Hays Robert	7-24-47
Headley Shari	7-15-63
Hearst Rick	1-4-65
Hedaya Dan	7-24-40
Hedison David	5-20-29
Heffley Wayne	7-15-27
Hegyes Robert	5-7-51
Helmond Katherine	7-5-33

****

Hemsley Sherman	2-1-38
Henderson Florence	2-14-34
Henderson Marcia	7-22-29
Henner Marilu	4-6-52
Henning Linda Kaye	9-16-44
Henry Emmaline	11-1-31
Hensley Pamela	10-3-50
Herring Lynn	9-22-58
Heslov Grant	5-15-63
Hesseman Howard	2-27-40
Hewett Christopher	4-5-22
Hewitt Alan	1-21-15
Hewitt Virginia	1925
Hexum Jon-Erik	11-5-57
Heydt Louis Jean	4-17-05
Hickman Darryl	7-28-31
Hickman Dwayne	5-18-34
Hicks Catherine	8-6-51
Hicks Hilly	5-4-50
Higgins Joel	9-28-44
Hill Arthur	8-1-22
Hill Steven	2-24-22
Hillerman John	12-20-32
Hindle Art	7-21-48
Hirsch Judd	3-15-35
Holbrook Hal	2-17-25
Holden Rebecca	6-12-53
Holland Kristina	2-25-44
Holliday Kene	6-25-49
Holliday Polly	7-2-37
Holliman Earl	9-11-28
Holly Ellen	1-16-31
Holly Lauren	10-28-66
Hooks Kevin	9-19-58
Hooks Robert	4-18-37
Hopkins Bo	2-2-42
Hopkins Kaitlin	2-1-64
Hopper William	1-26-15
Horsford Anna Maria	3-6-45
Horsley Lee	5-15-55
Horton Peter	8-20-53
Horton Robert	7-29-24
Houser Jerry	7-14-52
Hovis Larry	2-20-36
Howard Clint	4-20-59
Howard Ken	3-28-44

****

Howard Rance	11-17-28	Johnson Don	12-15-49
Howard Ron	3-1-54	Johnson Georgann	8-15-26
Howard Susan	1-28-42	Johnson Joanna	12-31-61
Howland Beth	5-28-47	Johnson Laura	8-1-58
Hoyt John	10-5-04	Johnson Russell	11-9-24
Hubley Season	5-14-51	Jones Carolyn	4-28-29
Huddleston David	9-17-30	Jones Christopher	8-18-41
Hudgins Wayne	6-19-50	Jones Henry	8-1-12
Hudson Ernie	12-17-45	Jones Sam J	8-12-54
Hugh-Kelly Daniel	8-10-49	Jordan Richard	7-19-38
Hughes Finola	10-29-60	Joyce Elaine	12-19-45
Hughes Kathleen	11-14-28	Jump Gordon	4-1-27
Hugo Larry	12-22-17	Kaczmarek Jane	12-21-55
Hunley Leann	2-25-55	Kalember Patricia	12-30-54
Hunt Helen	6-15-63	Kallman Dick	7-7-33
Hunter Ronald	6-14-43	Kampmann Steven	5-31-40
Hurst Rick	1-1-46	Kanakaredes Melina	4-23-68
Hutchison Fiona	5-17-60	Kanaly Steve	3-14-46
Hutton Jim	5-31-36	Kane Carol	6-18-52
Hyland Diana	1-25-36	Kaplan Gabe	3-31-45
Ironside Michael	2-12-50	Kaplan Marvin	1-24-27
Irvine Paula	6-22-68	Karlen John	5-28-33
Ito Robert	7-2-31	Karns Roscoe	9-7-1893
Jackee (Harry)	8-14-57	Kasdorf Lenore	7-27-48
Jackson Andrew	9-11-62	Katt William	2-16-50
Jackson Kate	10-29-48	Kavner Julie	9-7-51
Jacobs Lawrence-Hilton	9-4-53	Keach Stacy	6-2-41
Jacquet Jeffrey	10-15-66	Kean Betty	12-15-17
Jaeckel Richard	10-10-26	Kean Jane	4-10-24
Jaffe Sam	3-8-1891	Kearns Joseph	1907
James Clifton	5-29-21	Keating Larry	1896
James John	4-18-56	Keep Stephen	8-24-47
Jameson Joyce	9-26-32	Keim Betty Lou	9-27-38
Janis Conrad	2-11-28	Keith Brian	11-14-21
Janssen David	3-27-30	Keleghan Peter	9-16-59
Jarrett Renne	1-28-46	Kelley DeForest	1-20-20
Jarvis Graham	8-25-30	Kellin Mike	4-26-22
Jason Rick	5-21-26	Kelly Paula	10-21-42
Jefferson Herb Jr	9-28-46	Kelsey Linda	7-28-46
Jeffreys Anne	1-26-23	Kelton Pert	10-14-07
Jeffries Lang	6-7-31	Kennedy George	2-18-25
Jensen Maren	9-23-56	Kennedy Jayne	10-27-51
Jensen Sanford	8-11-53	Kennedy Mimi	9-25-49
Jeter Michael	8-26-52	Kercheval Ken	7-15-35
Jillian Ann	1-29-51	Kerns Joanna	2-12-53
Johnson Anne-Marie	7-18-60	Kerwin Brian	10-25-49

Ketchum Dave	1928	Langdon Sue Ane	3-8-36
Kilpatrick Lincoln	2-12-36	Lange Ted	1-5-47
Kimbrough Charles	5-23-36	Lanning Jerry	5-17-43
King Perry	4-30-48	Lansbury Angela	10-16-25
King Wright	1-11-27	Lansing John	10-16-49
Kirby Bruno	4-28-49	Lansing Joi	4-6-28
Kirk Phyllis	9-18-26	Lansing Robert	6-5-29
Klemperer Werner	3-22-19	LaPlaca Allison	12-16-59
Klous Pat	10-19-55	Larroquette John	11-25-47
Klugman Jack	4-27-22	Larson Jack	2-8-33
Knight Jack	2-26-39	Larson Jill	10-7-47
Knight Michael E	5-7-59	LaSalle Eriq	1962
Knight Ted	12-7-23	Lasser Louise	4-11-37
Knotts Don	7-21-24	Laughlin Lori	7-28-65
Knox Terence	12-16-51	Lauria Dan	4-12-47
Kobe Gail	3-19-29	Lauter Ed	10-30-40
Koenig Walter	9-14-36	Lavin Linda	10-15-37
Koock Guich	7-22-44	Lawrence Elizabeth	9-6-22
Kopell Bernie	6-21-33	Lawrence Sharon	6-29-61
Korf Mia	11-1-65	Leachman Cloris	4-30-26
Korot Alla	11-1-70	Learned Michael	4-9-39
Kotto Yaphet	11-15-37	LeBlanc Christian	8-25-58
Kove Martin	3-6-47	Lee Anna	1-2-13
Kozak Harley Jane	1-28-57	Lee Michele	6-24-42
Kraft Jill	9-29-30	Lee Ruta	5-30-36
Kramer Stepfanie	8-6-56	Leguizamo John	7-22-65
Kuhlman Ron	3-6-48	Leighton Laura	7-24-68
Kulky Henry	8-11-11	Leisure David	11-16-50
Kulp Nancy	8-28-21	Lembeck Harvey	4-15-23
Kurth Wallace	7-31-58	Lembeck Michael	6-25-48
Kurtz Swoosie	9-6-44	Lemmon Chris	6-22-54
Kusatsu Clyde	9-13-48	Lenard Mark	10-15-27
Ladd Cheryl	7-2-51	Lenihan Deirdre	5-19-46
Laire Judson	8-3-02	Lenz Kay	3-4-53
Lamas Lorenzo	1-20-58	Lenz Rick	11-21-39
Lambert Robert	7-28-60	Leo Melissa	9-14-60
Lampert Zohra	5-13-36	Leslie Bethel	8-3-29
Landau Martin	6-30-25	Lester Tom	9-23-38
Lander David L	6-22-47	Lewis Al	4-30-23
Landers Audrey	7-18-59	Lewis David	10-19-15
Landers Harry	4-3-21	Lewis Geoffrey	7-31-35
Landers Judy	10-7-61	Lien Jennifer	8-24-74
Landesburg Steve	11-3-45	Light Judith	2-9-49
Lando Joe	12-9-59	Lime Yvonne	4-7-38
Lane Nancy	6-16-51	Linden Hal	3-20-31
Laneuville Eric	7-14-52	Lindley Audra	9-24-18

Lindsey George	12-17-35
Linke Paul	1948
Linn-Baker Mark	6-17-53
Linville Larry	9-29-39
Lipton Peggy	8-30-47
Litel John	12-30-1894
Lloyd Christopher	10-22-38
Lloyd Norman	11-8-14
LoBianco Tony	10-19-36
Lockhart Anne	9-6-53
Lockhart June	6-25-25
Locklear Heather	9-25-61
Lockwood Gary	2-21-37
Logan Robert	5-29-41
Long Nia	10-30-70
Long Richard	12-17-27
Long Shelley	8-23-49
Lopez Perry	7-22-31
Lord Jack	12-30-28
Lord Marjorie	7-26-18
Loring Gloria	12-10-46
Loring Lisa	2-16-58
Loring Lynn	7-13-44
Lorne Marion	8-12-1888
Louis-Dreyfuss Julia	1-13-61
Louise Tina	2-11-34
Lu Lisa	1932
Lucci Susan	12-23-46
Luckinbill Lawrence	11-21-34
Luisi James	11-11-28
Lumley Joanna	5-1-46
LuPone Robert	7-29-46
Lupton John	8-22-26
Lupus Peter	6-17-37
Lyman Dorothy	4-18-47
Lynch Richard	4-26-36
Lynde Janice	3-28-47
Lyons Gene	1923
MacArthur James	12-8-37
Macchio Ralph	11-4-61
MacCorkindale Simon	2-12-52
MacDonald Susan	9-4-53
MacLachlan Kyle	2-22-59
MacLeod Gavin	2-28-30
MacNee Patrick	2-6-22
MacNicol Peter	4-10-54

MacRae Elizabeth	2-22-39
MacRae Meredith	5-30-45
MacRae Sheila	9-24-24
Macy Bill	5-18-22
Madden Dave	12-12-34
Magee Jack	5-12-50
Maharis George	9-1-28
Mahoney John	6-20-40
Maitland Beth	5-12-59
Majors Lee	4-23-40
Mandan Robert	2-2-32
Mandel Howie	11-29-55
Manetti Larry	7-23-38
Manoff Dinah	1-25-58
Mantooth Randolph	9-19-45
Maples Marla	10-27-63
Marchand Nancy	6-19-28
Marcovicci Andrea	11-18-48
Margolin Stuart	1-31-37
Marinaro Ed	3-31-50
Markham Monte	6-21-35
Marlowe Hugh	1-30-11
Mars Kenneth	4-4-35
Marshall E G	6-18-10
Marshall Ken	1953
Marshall Mort	8-17-18
Marshall Penny	10-15-42
Martin Jared	12-21-43
Martin Kiel	7-26-45
Martin Pamela Sue	1-5-53
Martin Ross	3-22-20
Martinez A	9-27-49
Martinez Tony	1-27-20
Masur Richard	11-20-48
Matheson Tim	12-31-47
Mathews Carmen	5-8-18
Mattson Robin	6-1-56
Mayer Ken	1919
Mayo Whitman	11-15-30
Mayron Melanie	10-20-52
McBain Diane	5-18-41
McCalla Irish	12-25-29
McCallum David	9-19-33
McCay Peggy	11-3-31
McClanahan Rue	2-21-34
McClory Sean	3-8-24

McCloskey Leigh	6-21-55
McCook John	6-20-45
McCord Kent	9-26-42
McCormack Patty	8-21-45
McCracken Jeff	9-12-52
McCullough Kimberly	3-5-78
McEachin James	5-20-30
McFadden Gates	3-2-49
McGavin Darren	5-7-22
McGill Everett	10-21-45
McGillin Howard	11-5-53
McGiver John	11-5-13
McGoohan Patrick	3-19-28
McGuire Biff	10-25-26
McIntire Tim	1944
McKay Gardner	6-10-32
McKean Michael	10-17-47
McKinsey Beverlee	8-9-40
McLaughlin Emily	12-1-28
McMahon Horace	5-17-07
McMillan Kenneth	7-2-34
McMurray Sam	4-15-52
McNear Howard	1905
McQuade Arlene	5-29-36
McRaney Gerald	8-19-48
McVey Patrick	3-17-10
McWilliams Caroline	4-4-45
Meacham Anne	7-21-25
Meadows Audrey	2-8-19
Meadows Jayne	9-27-21
Meaney Colm	5-30-53
Mekka Eddie	6-14-52
Melville Sam	8-20-40
Menzies Heather	12-3-49
Metcalf Laurie	6-16-55
Michaels Tommy J	2-8-81
Middendorf Tracey	1-26-71
Miller Barry	2-6-58
Miller Mark	11-20-25
Mills Alley	5-9-51
Mills Donna	12-11-43
Mills Judson	5-10-69
Mills Juliet	11-21-41
Milner Martin	12-28-27
Miner Rachel	7-29-80
Mintz Eli	3-1-04

Mitchell Ann	10-23-36
Mitchell Don	3-17-43
Mitchell James	2-29-20
Mitchell Scoey	3-12-30
Molinaro Al	6-24-19
Moll Richard	1-13-43
Moncrieff Karen	12-20-63
Montalban Ricardo	11-25-20
Montgomery Belinda J	7-23-50
Montgomery Elizabeth	4-15-33
Mooney William	5-2-36
Moore Jonathan	3-24-23
Moore Mary Tyler	12-29-37
Moore Tim	12-9-1887
Moorehead Agnes	12-6-06
Morgan Harry	4-10-15
Moriarty Michael	4-5-41
Morris Greg	9-27-34
Morrow Rob	9-21-62
Morrow Vic	2-14-32
Morse Barry	6-10-18
Morse David	10-11-53
Morton Joe	10-18-47
Moses William R	11-17-59
Moss Ronn	3-4-52
Mostel Josh	12-21-46
Mr T	5-21-52
Muldaur Diana	8-19-38
Mulgrew Kate	4-29-55
Mulhare Edward	4-8-23
Mullaney Jack	9-18-32
Mullavey Greg	9-10-39
Mulligan Richard	11-13-32
Murney Chris	7-20-43
Murphy Michael	5-5-38
Murray Don	7-31-29
Murray Mary Gordon	11-13-53
Musante Tony	6-30-36
Mustin Burt	2-8-1884
Nabors Jim	6-12-32
Nader George	10-19-21
Nader Michael	2-19-45
Naughton James	12-6-45
Neill Noel	11-25-20
Nelson Craig T	4-4-46
Nelson David	10-24-36

Nelson Ed	12-21-28
Nelson Harriet	7-18-14
Nelson Lori	8-15-33
Nelson Ozzie	3-20-06
Nelson Rick	5-8-40
Nelson Tracy	10-25-63
Nettleton Lois	8-16-29
Neuchateau Corinne	7-20-52
Newland John	11-23-17
Newman Barry	11-7-38
Newman Christine Tudor	6-22-51
Newmar Julie	8-16-35
Nicholas Denise	7-12-44
Nichols Barbara	12-30-29
Nichols David Bruce	1-16-46
Nichols Nichelle	12-28-33
Nielsen Leslie	2-11-26
Nielsen Tom	1-30-55
Nigh Jane	2-25-25
Nimoy Leonard	3-26-31
Noble James	3-5-22
Noble Trisha	2-3-44
Nolan Kathleen	9-27-33
Norris Christopher	10-7-53
Nouri Michael	12-9-45
O'Brien Joan	2-14-36
O'Connor Carroll	8-2-24
O'Connor Glynnis	11-19-56
O'Heaney Caitlin	8-16-53
O'Loughlin Gerald S	12-23-21
O'Mara Kate	8-10-39
O'Neill Dick	8-29-28
O'Neill Ed	4-12-46
O'Neill Jennifer	2-20-49
Oakes Randi	8-19-52
Oakland Simon	8-28-18
Ogilvy Ian	9-30-43
Olin Ken	7-30-54
Olmos Edward James	2-24-47
Olson James	10-8-30
Ontkean Michael	1-24-46
Orbach Jerry	10-20-35
Osterwald Bibi	2-3-20
Overall Park	3-15-57
Oxenberg Catherine	9-22-61
Page Harrison	8-27-41

Page LaWanda	10-19-20
Palillo Ron	4-2-54
Palmer Betsy	11-1-26
Paris Jerry	7-25-25
Parker Ellen	9-30-49
Parker Jameson	11-18-47
Parker Lara	10-27-42
Parkins Barbara	5-22-42
Parks Michael	4-4-38
Pastorelli Robert	6-21-55
Patrick Dennis	3-14-18
Patterson Hank	10-9-1888
Patterson Kelly	2-22-64
Patterson Lee	3-31-29
Patterson Lorna	7-1-56
Patterson Melody	4-16-47
Paul Alexandra	7-29-63
Pavia Ria	10-8-67
Pays Amanda	6-6-59
Pearce Alice	10-16-13
Peck J Eddie	10-10-58
Peluso Lisa	7-29-64
Penny Joe	6-24-56
Peppard George	10-1-28
Perlman Rhea	3-31-48
Perlman Ron	4-13-50
Perry John Bennett	1-4-41
Perry Luke	10-11-66
Perry Roger	5-7-33
Persoff Nehemiah	8-14-20
Pescow Donna	3-24-54
Peterson Lenka	10-16-25
Pettiford Valarie	7-8-60
Petty Ross	8-29-46
Peyser Penny	2-9-51
Pflug Jo Ann	5-2-47
Phillips Ethan	2-8-50
Phillips Grace	5-3-64
Phillips Jeff	7-3-68
Phillips Mackenzie	11-10-59
Phillips Wendy	1-2-52
Picardo Robert	10-27-53
Picerni Paul	12-1-22
Pickett Cindy	4-18-47
Pickles Christina	2-17-38
Pinchot Bronson	5-20-59

****

Pine Robert	7-10-41
Pinkins Tonya	5-30-62
Place Mary Kay	9-23-47
Plank Melinda	2-27-42
Platt Edward C	2-4-16
Pleshette John	7-27-42
Pleshette Suzanne	1-31-37
Ponce Poncie	4-10-33
Porter Don	9-24-12
Porter Nyree Dawn	1940
Porter Rick	1-21-51
Posey Parker	11-8-68
Post Markie	11-4-50
Poston Tom	10-17-27
Potter Carol	5-21-48
Potts Annie	10-28-52
Potts Cliff	1-5-45
Pounder C C H	12-25-52
Powers Stefanie	11-2-42
Presley Priscilla	5-24-45
Pressman Lawrence	7-10-39
Price Lindsay	12-6-76
Priest Pat	1936
Priestley Jason	8-28-69
Primus Barry	2-16-38
Prince Clayton	2-17-65
Princi Elaine	12-14--
Principal Victoria	1-3-45
Prine Andrew	2-14-36
Prinz Rosemary	1-1-31
Prosky Robert	12-13-30
Provine Dorothy	1-20-37
Purcell Lee	6-15-47
Purl Linda	9-2-55
Pyle Denver	5-11-20
Quinn Bill	5-6-12
Rachins Alan	10-10-47
Rae Charlotte	4-22-26
Rafferty Frances	6-26-22
Raffin Deborah	3-13-53
Raines Cristina	2-28-53
Rambo Dack & Dirk	11-13-41
Randall Sue	1935
Randall Tony	2-26-20
Randolph Bill	10-11-53
Randolph John	6-1-15

****

****

Randolph Joyce	10-21-25
Rappaport David	11-23-52
Rasche David	8-7-44
Rashad Phylicia	6-19-48
Rattray Heather	4-26-65
Ratzenberger John	4-6-47
Reagan Maureen	1-4-41
Reason Rex & Rhodes	11-20-28
Redeker Quinn	5-2-36
Reed Donna	1-27-21
Reed Pamela	4-2-49
Reed Robert	10-19-32
Reed Tracy	8-21-41
Reeves George	4-6-14
Regalbuto Joe	8-24-49
Reid Daphne Maxwell	7-13-48
Reid Tim	12-19-44
Reilly Hugh	1920
Reilly John	11-11-40
Reilly Luke	4-3-49
Reiner Rob	3-6-45
Reinhardt Sandra	3-23-67
Reinholt George	8-22-40
Repp Stafford	4-26-18
Rey Alejandro	2-8-30
Reynolds James	8-10-46
Reynolds Marjorie	8-12-21
Reynolds William	12-9-31
Rhoades Barbara	3-23-46
Rhodes Hari	4-10-32
Rhys-Davis John	5-5-44
Rice Rosemary	1928
Rice-Taylor Allyson	11-26-63
Richards Michael	7-24-49
Richardson Patricia	2-23-51
Richardson Susan	3-11-52
Richman Peter Mark	4-16-27
Rigg Diana	7-20-38
Riley Jack	12-30-37
Ritter John	9-17-48
Roberts Doris	11-4-29
Roberts Roy	3-19-00
Roberts Tanya	10-15-55
Robertson Cliff	9-9-25
Robinson Chris	11-5-38
Robinson Holly	9-18-64

****

****

Robinson Roger	5-2-41
Rocco Alex	2-29-36
Roche Eugene	9-22-28
Rockwell Robert	10-5-21
Rodd Marcia	7-8-40
Roerick William	12-17-12
Rogers Gil	2-4-34
Rogers Suzanne	7-9-47
Rogers Tristan	6-3-46
Rogers Wayne	4-7-33
Roker Roxie	8-28-29
Rolle Esther	11-8-22
Rollins Howard Jr	10-17-50
Ronnie Julie	3-21-63
Rorke Hayden	10-23-10
Rose Jamie	11-26-59
Rose Jane	2-7-12
Rose-Marie (Mazetta)	8-15-23
Rosenberg Alan	10-4-51
Ross Katharine	1-29-43
Ross Marion	10-25-28
Rossovich Rick	8-28-57
Roundtree Richard	9-7-42
Rowland Jada	2-23-43
Rubinstein John	12-8-46
Ruick Barbara	12-23-30
Runyeon Frank	8-24-53
Russ Tim	1956
Ruttan Susan	9-16-49
Ryan Irene	10-17-03
Ryan Michael M	3-19-29
Ryan Mitchell	1-11-28
Ryan Roz	7-7-51
Sabatino Michael	6-25-55
Sagal Katey	1955
Saget Bob	5-17-56
Saint-James Susan	8-14-46
Saldana Theresa	8-20-54
Salt Jennifer	9-4-44
Samms Emma	8-28-60
Sand Paul	3-5-35
Sanders Jay O	4-16-53
Sanders Richard	8-23-40
Sanderson William	1-10-48
Sandy Gary	12-25-45
Sanford Isabel	8-29-27

****

****

Santiago Saundra	4-13-57
Santos Joe	6-9-34
Sargent Dick	4-19-33
Saunders Lori	10-4-41
Savage John	8-25-49
Savalas Telly	1-21-23
Savant Douglas	6-21-64
Saxon John	8-5-35
Scalia Jack	11-10-50
Schaal Richard	5-5-30
Schaal Wendy	7-2-54
Schafer Natalie	11-5-02
Schallert William	7-6-22
Schell Ronnie	12-23-31
Schmidtke Ned	6-19-42
Schneider John	4-8-54
Schnetzer Stephen	6-11-48
Schroder Rick	4-3-70
Schuck John	2-4-40
Schultz Dwight	11-24-47
Scoggins Tracy	11-13-59
Scolari Peter	9-12-54
Scott Debralee	4-2-53
Scott Melody Thomas	4-18-56
Scotti Vito	1-26-18
Selby David	2-5-41
Sellecca Connie	5-25-55
Selleck Tom	1-29-45
Seymour Jane	2-15-51
Shackelford Ted	6-23-46
Sharkey Ray	11-14-52
Shatner William	3-22-31
Shaud Grant	10-17-61
Shaver Helen	2-24-51
Shaw Reta	9-13-12
Shea John	4-14-49
Sheehan Douglas	4-27-49
Shelton Sloane	3-17-34
Shepherd Cybill	2-18-50
Shera Mark	7-10-49
Sheridan Jamey	7-12-51
Sheridan Nicollette	11-21-63
Shimerman Armin	11-5-49
Shipp John Wesley	1-22-55
Show Grant	2-27-62
Shriner Kin	12-6-53

****

Shue Andrew	2-20-67
Shull Richard B	2-24-29
Siebert Charles	3-9-38
Sikes Cynthia	1-3-51
Sikking James B	3-5-34
Silva Henry	1928
Silver Ron	7-2-46
Silverman Jonathan	8-5-66
Silvers Cathy	5-27-61
Sinclair Madge	4-28-38
Singer Lori	5-6-62
Sirtis Marina	3-29-59
Skerritt Tom	8-25-33
Slate Jeremy	2-17-26
Slater Helen	12-14-63
Slattery Richard X	6-26-25
Slezak Erika	8-5-46
Sloan Tina	2-1-43
Smart Jean	9-13-51
Smith Cotter	5-29-49
Smith Jaclyn	10-26-47
Smith Lane	4-29-36
Smith Roger	12-18-32
Smith Shelley	10-25-52
Smith Will	9-25-68
Smith William	5-24-32
Smithers Jan	7-3-49
Smithers William	7-10-27
Smitrovich Bill	5-16-47
Smits Jimmy	7-9-55
Smythe Marcus	3-26-50
Snyder Arlen Dean	3-3-33
Solomon Bruce	1944
Somers Brett	7-11-27
Somers Suzanne	10-16-46
Sommars Julie	4-15-42
Soo Jack	10-28-15
Sorkin Arleen	10-14-56
Sorvino Paul	4-13-39
Soul David	8-28-40
Spain Fay	1933
Spano Joe	7-7-46
Spelling Tori	5-16-75
Spielberg David	3-6-39
St John Kristoff	7-15-66
Stack Robert	1-13-19

Stahl Richard	1-4-32
Stamos John	8-19-63
Stapleton Jean	1-19-23
Stauffer Jack	12-3-45
Stephens James	5-18-51
Sterling Robert	11-13-17
Sternhagen Frances	1-13-30
Stevens Andrew	6-10-55
Stevens Craig	7-8-18
Stevens Inger	10-18-34
Stevens Warren	11-2-19
Stevenson MacLean	11-14-29
Stevenson Parker	6-4-52
Stewart Byron	5-1-56
Stewart Patrick	7-13-40
Stiers David Ogden	10-31-42
Stockwell Dean	3-5-36
Stoddard Haila	11-14-13
Stone Cynthia	2-26-26
Stone Milburn	7-5-04
Storm Gale	4-5-22
Stovall Count	1-15-46
Strasser Robin	5-7-45
Strassman Marcia	4-28-48
Strauss Peter	2-20-47
Strickland Gail	5-18-46
Stringfield Sherry	6-24-65
Stroud Don	9-1-37
Struthers Sally	7-28-48
Stuart Mary	7-4-26
Stuart Patrick	6-16-66
Sullivan Susan	11-18-44
Sullivan Tom	3-27-47
Susman Todd	1-17-47
Sutton Frank	10-23-23
Svenson Bo	2-13-41
Swan William	2-6-28
Sward Anne	12-9-49
Sweet Dolph	7-18-20
Swenson Inga	12-29-32
Swit Loretta	11-4-37
Szarabajka Keith	12-2-52
Tabori Kristoffer	8-4-52
Takei George	4-20-39
Talbot Lyle	2-8-02
Talbot Nita	8-8-30

****

Talbott Gloria	2-7-31
Talman William	2-4-15
Tambor Jeffrey	7-8-44
Tarantina Brian	3-27-59
Tatum Bill	5-6-47
Tayback Vic	1-6-29
Taylor Buck	5-13-38
Taylor Meshach	4-11-47
Taylor Regina	1959
Taylor Rod	1-11-29
Templeton Christopher	2-26-52
Tennant Victoria	9-30-50
Tewes Lauren	10-28-53
Theus BJ	10-19-47
Thicke Alan	3-1-47
Thinnes Roy	4-6-38
Thomas Betty	7-27-48
Thomas Frankie	4-9-21
Thomas Heather	9-8-57
Thomas Jay	7-12-48
Thomas Marlo	11-21-37
Thomas Philip Michael	5-26-49
Thomas Richard	6-13-51
Thomas-Scott Melody	4-18-56
Thompson Sada	9-27-29
Thomson Gordon	3-2-51
Thor Jerome	1-5-15
Thorne-Smith Courtney	11-8-67
Thorson Linda	6-18-47
Thrower Joey	4-30-68
Tighe Kevin	8-13-44
Tilton Charlene	12-1-59
Tirelli Jaime	3-4-45
Todd Russell	3-14-58
Tolkan James	6-20-31
Tolsky Susan	4-6-43
Tom Heather	11-4-75
Tomei Concetta	12-30-45
Towers Constance	5-20-33
Travanti Daniel J	3-7-40
Tucker Michael	2-6-44
Tunie Tamara	3-14-59
Turco Paige	5-17-65
Turner Janine	12-6-62
Tweed Shannon	3-10-57
Tyler Judy	1932

****

Tylo Hunter	7-3-62
Tyson Cicely	12-19-33
Underwood Blair	8-25-64
Urich Robert	12-19-46
Valentine Karen	5-25-47
VanArk Joan	6-16-43
Vance Vivian	7-26-03
VanderVlis Diana	6-9-35
VanDyke Barry	7-31-51
VanPatten Dick	12-9-28
VanPatten Joyce	3-9-34
VanPatten Timothy	6-10-59
VanPatten Vincent	10-17-57
VanValkenburgh Deborah	8-29-52
Vassey Liz	8-9-72
Vaughn Robert	11-22-32
Vel-Johnson Reginald	8-16-52
verDorn Jerry	11-23-49
Verdugo Elena	4-20-26
Vereen Ben	10-10-46
Vigoda Abe	2-24-21
Villechaize Herve	4-23-43
Vincent Jan-Michael	7-15-44
Viscardi John	8-18-61
Visitor Nana	7-26-58
Vivyan John	5-31-16
Vogel Lesley	4-11-58
Waggoner Lyle	4-13-35
Wagner Helen	9-13-18
Wagner Jack P	10-3-59
Wagner Lindsay	6-22-49
Wagner Robert	2-10-30
Wahl Ken	2-14-53
Wainwright James	3-5-38
Waite Ralph	6-22-28
Walden Robert	9-25-43
Walker Jimmie	6-25-49
Walker Nancy	5-10-21
Wallace Marcia	11-1-42
Walley Deborah	8-12-43
Walsh M Emmet	3-22-35
Walston Ray	11-2-14
Walter Jessica	1-31-40
Ward Burt	7-6-45
Ward Rachel	9-12-57
Ward Sela	7-11-56

****

* *

Ward Stuart	11-19-62
Warden Jack	9-18-20
Warfield Marsha	3-5-55
Warren Jennifer	8-12-41
Warren Lesley Ann	8-16-46
Warren Michael	3-5-46
Warrick Ruth	6-29-16
Waterston Sam	11-15-40
Watkins Carlene	6-4-52
Watson Douglass	2-24-21
Watson Mills	7-10-40
Waxman Al	3-2-35
Weaver Dennis	6-4-25
Webb Jack	4-2-20
Webb Richard	9-9-15
Webber Robert	10-14-24
Wedgeworth Ann	1-21-35
Weitz Bruce	5-27-43
Wells Dawn	10-18-38
Wendt George	10-17-48
Wesley Kassie	3-21-61
West Adam	9-19-29
Weston Ellen	4-19-39
Wettig Patricia	12-4-51
Weatherly Shawn	1960
Wheatley Alan	4-19-07
White Betty	1-17-22
White Jesse	1-3-18
Whitfield Dondre	5-27-69
Whitfield Lynn	2-15-54
Whitney Grace Lee	4-1-30
Wickes Mary	6-13-16
Widdoes James	11-15-53
Widdoes Kathleen	3-21-39
Wilcox Frank	3-13-07
Wilcox Larry	8-8-47
Wilcox Ralph	1-30-51
Wilkof Lee	6-25-57
Willey Walt	1-26-51
Williams Ann	5-18-35
Williams Cara	6-29-25
Williams Cindy	8-22-47
Williams Clarence III	8-21-39
Williams Darnell	3-3-55
Williams Dick Anthony	8-9-38
Williams Grant	8-18-30

* *

Williams Guy	1-14-24
Williams Hal	12-14-38
Williams Spencer	7-14-1893
Williams Van	2-27-34
Wilson Demond	10-13-46
Wilson Elizabeth	4-4-25
Wilson Sheree J	12-12-58
Wilson Theodore	12-10-43
Windom William	9-28-23
Winfield Paul	5-22-41
Winkler Henry	10-30-45
Winningham Mare	5-16-59
Winter Edward	6-3-37
Winters Gloria	11-28-33
Wintersole William	7-30-31
Wood Peggy	2-9-1892
Woods Robert S	3-13-50
Woodward Edward	6-1-30
Wopat Tom	9-9-51
Wright Max	8-2-43
Wright Robin	4-8-66
Wyler Gretchen	2-16-32
Wynant H M	2-12-27
Yarnell Bruce	12-28-35
York Dick	9-4-28
Young Stephen	5-19-39
Zaslow Michael	11-1-42
Zeman Jacklyn	3-6-53
Zerbe Anthony	5-20-36
Zimbalist Efrem Jr	11-30-23
Zimbalist Stephanie	10-8-56
Zimmer Kim	2-2-55
Zmed Adrian	3-14-54
Zuniga Daphne	10-28-63

* * * * * * * * * * * * * * * *

PUBLIC TV ACTORS

Andrews Anthony	1-12-48
Andrews Harry	10-10-11
Annis Francesca	5-14-44
Atkins Eileen	6-16-34
Baddeley Angela	7-4-04
Bailey Robin	10-5-19
Baker Tom	1-20-36
Bean Sean	4-17-58
Beeny Christopher	7-7-41
Booth Connie	1941

* *

****

Bowles Peter	10-16-36
Brett Jeremy	11-3-33
Burke David	5-25-34
Carmichael Ian	6-18-20
Charles Maria	9-22-29
Collins Pauline	9-3-40
Cropper Anna	5-13-38
Curry Julian	12-8-37
Dance Charles	10-10-46
Dobie Alan	6-2-32
Dotrice Karen	11-9-55
Down Lesley-Anne	3-17-54
Drake Fabia	1-20-04
Ellis Robin	1944
Follows Megan	3-14-68
Fry Stephen	8-24-57
Gambon Michael	10-19-40
Gordon Hannah	4-9-41
Hampshire Susan	5-12-38
Hardwicke Edward	8-7-32
Hartnell William	1-8-08
Havers Nigel	11-6-49
Hawthorne Nigel	4-5-29
Hickson Joan	8-5-06
Hodge Patricia	9-29-46
Huntley Raymond	4-23-04
Jackson Gordon	12-19-23
Jacobi Derek	10-22-38
James Geraldine	7-6-50
Jeffrey Peter	4-18-29
Jones Gemma	12-4-42
Jones Simon	7-27-50
Keith Penelope	4-2-40
Kempson Rachel	5-28-10
Leach Rosemary	12-18-35
Malik Art	11-13-52
Marsden Roy	6-25-41
Marsh Jean	7-1-34
McAnally Ray	3-30-26
McKern Leo	3-16-20
Michell Keith	12-1-26
Mirren Helen	7-26-45
Mohyeddin Zia	6-20-33
Moore Stephen	12-11-37
Neill Sam	9-14-47
Pagett Nicola	6-15-45

****

****

Parfitt Judy	11-7-35
Pertwee Jon	7-7-19
Petherbridge Edward	8-3-36
Pigott-Smith Tim	5-13-46
Porter Eric	4-8-28
Powell Robert	6-1-44
Quinn Patricia	1944
Rodgers Anton	1-10-33
Scales Prunella	6-22-32
Stephens Robert	7-14-31
Stevenson Juliet	10-30-56
Suchet David	5-2-46
Thaw John	1-3-42
Thorpe-Bates Peggy	8-11-14
Townsend Jill	1-25-45
Treacher Bill	6-4-36
Troughton Patrick	3-25-20
Tutin Dorothy	4-8-30
Williams Simon	6-16-46

****

TV WESTERNS

Adams Nick	7-10-31
Arness James	5-26-23
Blake Amanda	2-20-29
Blocker Dan	12-10-27
Breck Peter	3-13-30
Bromfield John	6-11-22
Carrillo Leo	8-6-1880
Connors Chuck	4-10-21
Crawford Johnny	3-26-46
Curtis Ken	7-12-16
Drury James	4-18-34
Duel Peter	1940
Elliott Sam	8-9-44
Fleming Eric	1925
Forbes Scott	1921
Fuller Robert	7-29-34
Garrison Sean	10-19-37
Grant Kirby	11-24-11
Greene Lorne	2-12-15
Hardin Ty	1-1-30
Hart John	1921
Hutchins Will	5-5-32
Jones Dick	2-25-27
Kelly Jack	9-16-27
Kennedy Douglas	9-14-15

****

Landon Michael	10-31-36
Larsen Keith	6-17-25
Madison Guy	1-19-22
Mahoney Jack	2-7-19
Maunder Wayne	12-19-42
McClure Doug	5-11-35
McGrath Frank	2-2-03
Miller Denny (Scott)	4-25-34
Moore Clayton	9-14-14
Murphy Ben	3-6-41
O'Brian Hugh	4-19-25
Parker Fess	8-16-25
Parker Willard	2-5-12
Preston Wayde	9-10-30
Renaldo Duncan	4-23-04
Roberts Pernell	5-18-28
Robertson Dale	7-14-23
Russell John	1-8-21
Silverheels Jay	5-26-19
Simmons Richard	8-19-18
Smith John	3-6-31
Walker Clint	5-30-27
Williams Bill	5-15-16
Wilson Terry	9-3-23

****

TV JUVENILES

Aaker Lee	9-24-43
Allen Chad	6-5-74
Anderson Melissa Sue	9-26-62
Applegate Christina	11-25-71
Astin Sean	2-25-71
Baio Jimmy	3-15-62
Bank Frank	4-12-42
Bateman Jason	1-14-69
Bateman Justine	2-19-66
Beckham Brice	2-11-76
Bialik Mayim	12-12-75
Bledsoe Tempestt	8-1-73
Bonaduce Danny	8-13-59
Bonet Lisa	11-16-67
Brandon Clark	12-30-58
Bridges Todd	5-27-66
Brisebois Danielle	6-28-69
Brissette Tiffany	12-26-74
Buntrock Bobby	8-4-52
Cameron Candace	4-6-76

Cameron Kirk	10-12-70
Cartwright Angela	9-9-52
Chapin Lauren	5-23-45
Cohn Mindy	5-20-66
Cohoon Patti	1-27-59
Coleman Gary	2-8-68
Considine Tim	12-10-41
Copage Mark	6-21-62
Corcoran Donna	9-29-42
Corcoran Kevin	6-10-45
Corcoran Noreen	10-20-43
Cotler Kami	6-17-65
Crabbe Cullen	9-4-44
Cruz Brandon	5-28-62
Diamond Bobby	8-23-43
Dow Tony	4-13-45
Drier Moosie	8-6-64
Eisenmann Ike	7-21-62
Faustino David	3-3-74
Feldman Corey	7-16-71
Fields Kim	5-12-69
Frank Gary	10-9-50
Frye Soleil Moon	8-6-76
Garrett Leif	11-8-61
Gerritsen Lisa	12-21-57
Gertz Jami	10-28-65
Gilbert Sara	1-29-75
Gold Tracey	5-16-69
Grady Don	6-8-44
Gray Billy	1-13-38
Gregory Benji	5-26-78
Haje Khrystyne	12-21-66
Hamer Rusty	2-15-47
Hardin Melora	6-29-67
Harper David W	10-4-61
Harris Neil Patrick	6-15-73
Hart Melissa Jean	4-18-76
Hendler Lauri	4-22-65
Hill Dana	5-6-64
Hinton Darby	8-19-57
Houlihan Keri	7-3-75
Huston Martin	2-8-41
Jackson Sherry	2-15-42
Jacoby Scott	11-26-55
James Sheila	2-9-41
Jones Anissa	12-13-58

TV Juveniles Kay-Pol

Kay Dianne	3-29-55
Keith Richard	12-1-50
Kerwin Lance	11-6-60
Kiff Kaleena	10-23-74
Knight Christopher	11-7-57
Kristen Marta	2-26-45
Laborteaux Matthew	12-8-66
Lawrence Joey	4-20-76
Lawrence Matthew	2-11-80
Lewis Emmanuel	3-9-71
Link Michael	6-12-62
Linker Amy	10-19-66
Livingston Barry	12-17-53
Livingston Stanley	11-24-50
Lookinland Mike	12-19-60
Martin Lori	4-18-47
Mathers Jerry	6-2-48
Mathews Larry	8-15-55
McCormick Maureen	8-5-56
McDonough Mary Elizabeth	5-4-61
McKeon Doug	6-10-66
McKeon Nancy	4-4-66
McKeon Phillip	11-11-64
McNichol Jimmy	7-2-61
McNichol Kristy	9-11-62
Milano Alyssa	12-19-72
Miller Jeremy	10-21-76
Moran Erin	10-18-61
Morgan Robin	1-29-42
Most Donny	8-8-53
Mumy Billy	2-1-54
Nolan Tommy	1-15-48
North Jay	8-3-52
Norton-Taylor Judy	1-29-58
Nucci Danny	9-15-68
Olsen Mary Kate & Ashley	6-13-88
Olsen Susan	8-14-61
Osmond Ken	6-7-43
Patrick Butch	6-2-53
Peluce Meeno	2-26-69
Pera Radames	9-14-60
Petersen Paul	9-23-44
Pintauro Danny	1-6-76
Plato Dana	11-7-64
Plumb Eve	4-29-57
Polley Sarah	1-8-79

TV Juveniles Pon-Mickey Mouse Club

Ponce Danny	9-4-72
Price Marc	2-23-68
Provost Jon	3-12-50
Pulliam Keshia Knight	4-9-79
Raven-Symone (Pearman)	12-10-85
Rettig Tommy	12-10-41
Rich Adam	10-12-68
Richards Kim	9-19-64
Rippy Rodney Allen	7-29-68
Rudie Evelyn	3-28-47
Savage Fred	7-9-76
Scott Eric	10-20-58
Shore Roberta	4-7-43
Smith Allison	12-9-69
Stone Rob	9-22-62
Valentine Scott	6-3-58
Vogel Mitch	1-17-56
Walmsley Jon	2-6-56
Ward Jonathan	2-26-70
Warner Malcolm-Jamal	8-18-70
Washbrook John	10-16-44
Watson Debbie	1-17-49
Wheaton Wil	7-29-72
Whelan Jill	9-29-66
Whelchel Lisa	5-29-63
Whitaker Johnny	12-13-59
White Jaleel	11-27-76
Williams Anson	9-25-49
Williams Barry	9-30-54
Winkelman Michael	1946
Yothers Tina	5-5-73
Zal Roxana	11-8-69
MICKEY MOUSE CLUB	
Baird Sharon	8-16-43
Burgess Bobby	5-19-41
Burr Lonnie	5-31-43
Cole Tommy	12-20-41
Dodd Jimmie	3-28-10
Funicello Annette	10-22-42
Gillespie Darlene	4-8-41
Holdridge Cheryl	6-20-44
Kirk Tommy	12-10-41
O'Brien Cubby	7-14-46
Pendleton Karen	7-1-46
Tracey Doreen	4-13-43
Williams Roy	7-30-07

COMEDIANS

Abbott Bud	10-2-1895
Ace Goodman	1-15-1899
Ace Jane	10-12-05
Adams Joey	1-16-11
Ajaye Franklin	5-13-49
Allen Byron	4-22-61
Allen Dayton	9-24-19
Allen Fred	5-31-1894
Allen Gracie	7-26-06
Allen Marty	3-23-22
Allen Tim	6-13-53
Altman Jeff	8-13-51
Anderson Eddie 'Rochester'	9-18-05
Anderson Louie	3-23-53
Arbuckle Roscoe 'Fatty'	3-24-1887
Arnaz Desi	3-2-17
Arnold Tom	3-6-59
Arquette Cliff	12-28-05
Aykroyd Dan	7-1-52
Ball Lucille	8-6-11
Ballard Kaye	11-20-26
Barbutti Pete	5-4-34
Barth Belle	4-27-11
Bean Orson	7-22-28
Belushi John	1-24-49
Belzer Richard	8-4-44
Benny Jack	2-14-1894
Berle Milton	7-12-08
Berman Shelley	2-3-24
Bernhard Sandra	6-6-55
Bishop Joey	2-3-18
Blue Ben	9-12-01
Bodett Tom	2-23-55
Boosler Elayne	8-18-52
Brenner David	2-4-45
Brice Fanny	10-29-1891
Brooks Albert	7-22-47
Brooks Foster	5-11-12
Brown Joe E	7-28-1892
Brown Julie	8-31-58
Bruce Lenny	10-13-25
Bunny John	9-21-1863
Burnett Carol	4-26-33
Burns Bob	8-2-1893
Burns George	1-20-1896

Burns Jack	11-15-33
Butler Brett	1958
Buttons Red	2-5-19
Buzzi Ruth	7-24-36
Caesar Sid	9-8-22
Callas Charlie	12-20-24
Cambridge Godfrey	2-26-33
Candy John	10-31-50
Canova Judy	11-20-16
Cantinflas	8-12-11
Cantor Eddie	1-31-1892
Carlin George	5-12-37
Carne Judy	4-27-39
Carney Art	11-4-18
Carrey Jim	1-17-62
Carroll Pat	5-5-27
Carson Jack	10-27-10
Carson Jeannie	5-23-28
Carter Jack	6-24-23
Carvey Dana	6-2-55
Chaplin Charlie	4-16-1889
Chapman Graham	1-8-41
Chase Charley	10-20-1893
Chase Chevy	10-8-43
Cheech (Marin)	7-13-46
Cho Margaret	12-5-68
Chong Tommy	5-24-38
Clark Bobby	6-16-1888
Clay Andrew 'Dice'	1958
Cleese John	10-27-39
Close Del	3-9-34
Clyde Andy	3-25-1892
Coca Imogene	11-18-08
Cohen Myron	7-1-02
Colonna Jerry	9-17-04
Coltrane Robbie	3-30-50
Conklin Chester	1-11-1888
Conway Tim	12-15-33
Cook Joe	1890
Cook Peter	11-17-37
Corey Prof Irwin	1-29-12
Correll Charles 'Andy'	2-2-1890
Cosby Bill	7-12-37
Costello Lou	3-6-08
Crosby Norm	9-15-27
Crystal Billy	3-14-47

Comedians Cur-Got

Curtin Jane	9-6-47
Daley Cass	7-17-15
Dana Bill	10-5-24
Dangerfield Rodney	11-22-21
Davis Joan	6-29-07
DeGeneres Ellen	1-1-58
Delmar Kenny	1910
DeLuise Dom	8-1-33
DeWolfe Billy	3-6-07
Diller Phyllis	7-17-17
Donald Peter	1918
Drescher Fran	12---57
Duke Robin	3-13-54
Dunn Nora	4-29-52
Durante Jimmy	2-10-1893
Ebersole Christine	2-21-53
Einstein Bob	11-20-40
Elder Ann	9-21-42
Elliott Bob	3-26-23
Elliott Chris	5-31-60
Faye Joey	7-12-10
Fazenda Louise	6-17-1895
Feldman Marty	7-8-33
Fernandel	5-8-03
Fields Totie	5-7-31
Fields W C	4-9-1879
Flaherty Joe	6-21-40
Flagg Fannie	9-21-42
Fleischer Charles	8-27-50
Fontaine Frank	4-19-20
Foxx Redd	12-9-22
Freberg Stan	8-7-26
Gallagher (Leo)	7-24-47
Gardner Brother Dave	6-11-26
Gayle Jackie	3-1-28
Ghostley Alice	8-14-26
Gibson Henry	9-21-35
Gilliam Stu	7-27-43
Gilliam Terry	11-22-40
Gleason Jackie	2-26-16
Gobel George	5-20-20
Goldthwait Bob	5-26-62
Goodman Dody	10-28-22
Gorshin Frank	4-5-34
Gosden Freeman 'Amos'	5-5-1899
Gottfried Gilbert	2-28-55

Comedians Gou-Kor

Goulding Ray	3-20-22
Graham Ronny	8-26-19
Greene Shecky	4-8-25
Gregory Dick	10-12-32
Grier David Alan	6-30-55
Gross Mary	3-25-53
Guest Christopher	2-5-48
Hackett Buddy	8-11-24
Hall Anthony Michael	4-14-68
Hall Brad	3-21-58
Hardy Oliver	1-18-1892
Harris Phil	6-24-06
Harris Robin	8-30-53
Hartman Phil	9-24-48
Henry Buck	12-9-30
Henry Pat	8-28-23
Hill Benny	1-21-25
Hines Mimi	7-17-33
Hodge Stephanie	12-24-56
Hoffa Portland	1910
Hooks Jan	4-23-57
Idle Eric	3-29-43
Ingels Marty	3-9-36
Jackson Victoria	8-2-59
James Sidney	5-8-13
Jewell Geri	9-13-56
Johnson Arte	1-20-34
Johnson Chic	3-5-1891
Jones Terry	2-1-42
Jordan Jim 'Fibber'	11-16-1896
Jordan Marian 'Molly'	4-15-1898
Jordan Will	7-27-30
Katz Mickey	6-15-09
Kaufman Andy	1-17-49
Kaye Danny	1-18-13
Kazurinsky Tim	3-3-50
Keaton Buster	10-4-1896
Kelly Patsy	1-12-10
Kennedy Edgar	4-26-1890
Keymah Crystal T'Keyah	10-13-62
King Alan	12-26-27
Kinison Sam	12-8-53
Kirby George	6-8-23
Kirchenbauer Bill	2-19-53
Klein Robert	2-8-42
Korman Harvey	2-15-27

Kovacs Ernie	1-23-19
Kroeger Gary	4-13-57
Lahr Bert	8-13-1895
Lamb Gil	6-14-06
Laurel Stan	6-16-1890
Lawrence Eddie	3-2-21
Lawrence Martin	4-16-65
Leary Dennis	8-18-57
Leonard Jack E	4-24-11
Lester Jerry	2-16-10
Levenson Sam	12-28-11
Levy Eugene	12-17-46
Lewis Jerry	3-16-26
Lewis Joe E	1-12-02
Lewis Richard	6-29-47
Little Rich	11-26-38
Livingstone Mary	6-22-09
Lloyd Harold	4-20-1893
Lovitz Jon	7-21-57
Lynde Paul	6-13-26
Mabley Moms	3-19-1894
Mann Hank	1888
Manna Charlie	10-6-25
Markham Pigmeat	4-18-04
Martin Andrea	1-15-47
Martin Dick	1-30-22
Martin Steve	4-14-45
Marx Chico	3-22-1891
Marx Groucho	10-2-1890
Marx Harpo	11-23-1893
Marx Zeppo	2-25-01
Mason Jackie	6-9-31
May Elaine	4-21-32
Mayehoff Eddie	7-7-11
McCormick Pat	7-17-34
McCullough Paul	1883
Meader Vaughn	3-20-36
Meara Anne	9-20-29
Miller Dennis	11-3-53
Milligan Spike	4-16-18
Moran Polly	6-28-1883
Moranis Rick	4-18-53
Moreland Mantan	9-3-01
Morgan Henry	3-31-15
Morris Garrett	2-1-37
Morris Howard	9-4-19

Mull Martin	8-18-43
Murphy Eddie	4-3-61
Murray Bill	9-21-50
Murray Charlie	6-22-1872
Myers Mike	5-25-63
Nealon Kevin	11-18-53
Newhart Bob	9-5-29
Newman Laraine	3-2-52
Noonan Tommy	4-29-22
Normand Mabel	11-16-1894
Nye Louis	5-1-19
O'Donnell Rosie	3-21-62
O'Hara Catherine	3-4-54
Olsen Ole	11-6-1892
Palin Michael	5-5-43
Paulsen Pat	7-6-27
Pearce Al	1899
Pearl Jack	10-29-1895
Peary Harold	7-25-08
Penner Joe	11-11-04
Philips Emo	2-7-56
Piscopo Joe	6-17-51
Pollard Snub	11-9-1886
Poundstone Paula	12-29-59
Price Roger	3-6-20
Prinze Freddie	6-22-54
Pryor Richard	12-1-40
Radner Gilda	6-28-46
Ramis Harold	11-21-44
Raye Martha	8-27-16
Reilly Charles Nelson	1-13-31
Reiner Carl	3-20-22
Reiser Paul	3-30-57
Rickles Don	5-8-26
Risley Ann	9-30-49
Ritz Al	8-27-01
Ritz Harry	5-28-07
Ritz Jimmy	10-22-04
Rivers Joan	6-8-33
Rodriguez Paul	1955
Rogers Timmie	7-14-15
Rosato Tony	12-26-54
Roseanne (Arnold)	11-3-52
Ross Joe E	3-15-05
Rossi Steve	5-25-32
Rowan Dan	7-2-22

Rudner Rita	9-17-55
Russell Anna	12-27-11
Russell Mark	8-23-32
Russell Nipsey	10-13-24
Sahl Mort	5-11-27
Sarducci Father Guido	1-1-43
Savo Jimmy	1896
Schreiber Avery	4-9-35
Seinfeld Jerry	4-29-54
Sellers Peter	9-8-25
Semon Larry	7-6-1889
Shandling Garry	11-29-49
Shawn Dick	12-1-29
Shearer Harry	12-23-43
Shepherd Jean	7-26-29
Sherman Allan	11-30-24
Sherman Ransom	10-15-1898
Short Martin	3-26-50
Shriner Herb	5-29-18
Shriner Wil	12-6-53
Shuster Frank	9-5-16
Sinbad	11-10-56
Skelton Red	7-18-13
Smirnoff Yakov	1-24-51
Smothers Dick	11-20-39
Smothers Tom	2-2-37
Stang Arnold	9-28-25
Steinberg David	8-9-42
Sterling Ford	11-3-1883
Stiller Jerry	6-8-28
Storch Larry	1-8-23
Summerville Slim	7-10-1892
Sweeney Terry	3-23-60
Tati Jacques	10-9-08
Taylor Renee	3-19-35
Taylor Rip	1-13-30
Tenuta Judy	11-7-51
Terry-Thomas	7-14-11
Thomas Danny	1-16-14
Thomas Dave	5-20-48
Tomlin Lily	9-1-37
Travalena Fred	10-6-42
Turpin Ben	9-17-1874
Ullman Tracey	12-30-59
Vague Vera	9-2-05
VanDyke Dick	12-13-25

VanDyke Jerry	7-27-31
Varney Jim	6-15-46
Vernon Bobby	3-9-1897
Warren Rusty	3-20-30
Wayans Damon	1960
Wayans Keenen Ivory	6-8-58
Wayne Johnny	5-28-18
Weaver Doodles	5-11-14
Wheeler Bert	4-7-1895
Willard Fred	9-18-39
Williams Kenneth	2-22-26
Williams Pearl	9-10-14
Williams Robin	7-21-52
Wilson Flip	12-8-33
Winters Jonathan	11-11-25
Wisdom Norman	2-4-20
Woolsey Robert	8-14-1889
Worley Jo Anne	9-6-37
Wright Steven	12-6-55
Wynn Ed	11-9-1886
Young Alan	11-19-19
Youngman Henny	1-12-06

THREE STOOGES

Fine Larry	10-5-02
Howard Curly	10-22-03
Howard Moe	6-19-1897
Howard Shemp	3-17-1895
Besser Joe	8-12-07
DeRita Joe	7-12-09

****

DANCERS & CHOREOGRAPHERS

Adam Noelle	12-24-33
Adams Diana	3-29-26
Adams Neile	7-10-34
Ailey Alvin	1-5-31
Alexander Rod	1-23-20
Allen Debbie	1-16-50
Alonso Alicia	12-21-21
Alton Robert	1-28-02
Alum Manuel	1-23-43
Andersen Ib	12-14-54
Armour Tommy	9-27-36
Aroldingen Karin von	7-9-41
Arpino Gerald	1-14-28
Ashley Merrill	12-2-50
Ashton Frederick	9-17-06

Baker Josephine	6-3-06
Balanchine George	1-9-04
Bales William	6-27-10
Baryshnikov Mikhail	1-27-48
Bauman Art	12-22-39
Beatty Patricia	5-15-36
Bennett Michael	4-8-43
Bergman Sandahl	11-14-51
Beriosova Svetlana	9-24-32
Bessmertnova Natalya	7-19-41
Bettis Valerie	12-20-19
Bishop Kelly	2-28-44
Blair David	7-27-32
Blair Pamela	12-5-49
Brock Karena	9-21-42
Brown Kelly	9-24-28
Brown Trisha	11-25-36
Browne Leslie	6-29-57
Bruhn Erik	10-3-28
Bujones Fernando	3-9-55
Butler John	9-29-20
Castle Irene	4-7-1893
Castle Nick	3-21-10
Castle Vernon	5-2-1887
Catterson Pat	2-20-46
Charlip Remy	1-10-29
Chase Barrie	10-20-34
Chase Lucia	3-24-07
Cilento Wayne	8-25-49
Clarke Martha	6-3-44
Cole Jack	4-27-14
Cole Kay	1-13-48
Collins Janet	2-2-17
Cunningham James	4-1-38
Cunningham Merce	4-16-19
Currier Ruth	1-4-26
d'Amboise Charlotte	1964
d'Amboise Christopher	2-4-60
d'Amboise Jacques	7-28-34
Daniele Graciela	12-8-39
Danilova Alexandra	1-20-04
Dean Laura	12-3-45
DeLoatch Gary	8-24-52
DeMille Agnes	9-18-05
Dolin Anton	7-27-04
Dowell Anthony	2-16-43

Draper Paul	10-25-09
Dudley Jane	4-3-12
Dunas William	5-1-47
Duncan Isadora	5-27-1878
Duncan Jeff	2-4-30
Dunham Katherine	6-22-10
Eglevsky Andre	12-21-17
Elg Taina	3-9-31
Enters Angna	4-28-07
Erdman Jean	2-20-17
Faison George	1947
Falco Louis	8-2-42
Farber Viola	2-25-31
Farrell Suzanne	8-16-45
Fisher Nelle	12-10-14
Field Ron	1934
Fonteyn Margot	5-18-19
Fosse Bob	6-23-27
Fracci Carla	8-20-36
Franca Celia	6-25-21
Fuller Loie	1-22-1862
Garth Midi	1-28-20
Gennaro Peter	1924
Godunov Alexander	11-28-49
Graham Martha	5-11-1893
Gray Gilda	10-24-01
Greco Jose	12-23-18
Gregory Cynthia	7-8-46
Hale George	9-6-00
Halprin Ann	7-13-20
Hay Deborah	12-18-41
Hayden Melissa	4-25-23
Hightower Rosella	1-30-20
Hines Gregory	2-14-46
Holmes Anna Marie	4-17-43
Horton Lester	1-23-06
Jamison Judith	5-10-44
Jeanmaire Renee 'Zizi'	4-29-24
Joffrey Robert	12-24-30
Jones Bill T	2-14-52
Jones Janet	1-10-61
Kain Karen	3-28-51
Kaye Nora	1-17-20
Kent Allegra	8-11-38
Kidd Michael	8-12-19
King Kenneth	4-1-48

Kirkland Gelsey	12-29-52	Pomare Eleo	10-22-37
Kistler Darci	6-4-64	Posin Kathryn	3-23-45
Kylian Jiri	3-21-45	Primus Pearl	11-29-19
Lamhut Phyllis	11-14-33	Prowse Juliet	9-25-36
Lander Toni	6-19-31	Rall Tommy	12-27-29
Lang Pearl	5-29-22	Randall Carl	2-28-1898
Last Brenda	4-17-38	Redlich Don	8-17-33
Lavery Sean	8-16-56	Reinking Ann	11-10-49
Layton Joe	5-3-31	Robbins Jerome	10-11-18
Lees Michelle	3-18-47	Ruiz Brunilda	6-1-36
Leland Sara	8-2-41	Saddler Donald	1-24-20
LeRoy Hal	1913	Saltonstall Ellen	11-2-48
Lichine David	10-25-10	Sanasardo Paul	9-15-28
Limon Jose	1-12-08	Schaufuss Peter	4-26-49
Linn Bambi	4-26-26	Seymour Lynn	3-8-39
Lopez Lourdes	1958	Shawn Ted	10-21-1891
Loring Eugene	1914	Shearer Moira	1-17-26
Louis Murray	11-4-26	Slavenska Mia	2-20-16
Love Edward	6-29-52	Sokolow Anna	2-22-13
Lubovitch Lar	1943	Solomons Gus Jr	8-27-40
Lynn Mara	7-17-29	Somes Michael	9-28-17
Maiorano Robert	8-29-46	St Denis Ruth	1-20-1877
Makarova Natalia	11-21-40	Summers Elaine	2-20-25
Markova Alicia	12-1-10	Tallchief Maria	1-24-25
Martins Peter	10-11-46	Tamiris Helen	4-24-02
Massine Leonide	8-9-1896	Taylor June	1918
McBride Patricia	8-23-42	Taylor Paul	7-29-30
McKayle Donald	7-6-30	Tennant Veronica	1-15-46
McKechnie Donna	11-16-44	Tetley Glen	2-3-26
Miller Linda Kay	9-7-53	Tharp Twyla	7-1-41
Mitchell Arthur	3-27-34	Tomasson Helgi	10-8-42
Moiseyev Igor	1-21-06	Tudor Anthony	4-4-09
Molina Jose	11-19-37	Tune Tommy	2-28-39
Monk Meredith	11-20-42	VanHamel Martine	11-16-45
Moore Jack	3-18-26	Verdy Violette	12-1-33
Morris Mark	8-29-56	Villella Edward	10-1-32
Muller Jennifer	10-16-49	Wagoner Dan	7-31-32
Nagrin Daniel	5-22-17	Ward Charles	10-24-52
Neville Phoebe	9-28-41	Waring James	11-1-22
Nikolais Alwin	11-25-12	Watts Heather	9-27-53
Nureyev Rudolf	3-17-38	Wayburn Ned	3-30-1874
Panov Valery	3-12-38	Weidman Charles	7-22-01
Passloff Aileen	10-21-31	White Onna	3-24-22
Perez Rudy	11-24-29	Wilde Patricia	7-16-28
Petit Roland	1-13-24	Williams Sammy	11-13-48
Plisetskaya Maya	11-20-25	Wong Mel	12-2-38

****

VAUDEVILLE

Baker Belle	12-25-1893	Lloyd Marie	2-12-1870
Bent Marion	12-23-1879	Loftus Cissie	10-22-1876
Block Jessie	12-16-00	Lucas Nick	8-22-1897
Brendel El	3-25-1891	Mack Charles	11-22-1887
Browne Bothwell	3-7-1877	Mahoney Will	2-5-1894
Bubbles John	2-19-02	McGiveney Owen	5-4-1884
Cahill Marie	2-7-1870	Meller Raquel	3-10-1888
Carus Emma	3-18-1879	Mills Florence	1-25-1895
Chandler Anna	1887	Moran George	10-3-1881
Cohan George M	7-4-1878	Morris Elida	11-12-1886
D'Orsay Fifi	4-16-04	Nesbit Evelyn	12-25-1884
Dale Charlie (Marks)	9-6-1881	Nicholas Fayard	10-20-14
Duncan Rosetta	11-23-1896	Nicholas Harold	3-17-21
Duncan Vivian	6-17-1899	North Bobby	2-2-1884
Durant Jack	4-12-05	Norworth Jack	1-5-1879
Duprey Fred	9-6-1884	O'Connor George	8-20-1874
Edwards Gus	8-18-1879	Oakland Will	1-15-1880
Eltinge Julian	5-14-1883	Peabody Eddie	2-19-02
Fay Frank	11-17-1897	Petrova Olga	2-19-1885
Fields Benny	6-14-1894	Picon Molly	2-28-1898
Fields Lew	1-1-1867	Price Georgie	1-5-00
Foy Eddie	3-9-1854	Puck Eva	11-27-1892
Franklin Irene	6-13-1876	Ring Blanche	4-24-1877
Friganza Trixie	11-29-1870	Robinson Bill 'Bojangles'	5-25-1878
Gallagher Ed	1873	Romain Manuel	10-1-1872
Gallagher Skeets	7-28-1891	Rooney Pat Jr	7-4-1880
Goodwin Nat C	7-25-1857	Rubin Benny	2-2-1899
Greene Gene	6-9-1877	Russell Lillian	12-4-1861
Guinan Texas	1-12-1884	Sale Chic	8-25-1885
Hall Adelaide	10-20-1895	Samuels Rae	1886
Halperin Nan	1898	Schenck Joe	1891
Hanneford Poodles	1892	Seeley Blossom	7-16-1891
Hartman Grace	1-7-07	Shean Al	5-12-1868
Hartman Paul	3-1-04	Shields Ella	9-26-1879
Healy Ted	10-1-1896	Smith Joe	2-16-1884
Hilton Daisy & Violet	2-5-08	Stone Fred	8-19-1873
Holtz Lou	4-11-1893	Suratt Valeska	6-28-1882
Irwin May	6-27-1862	Tilley Vesta	5-13-1864
Janis Elsie	3-16-1889	Tucker Sophie	1-13-1884
Jessel George	4-3-1898	Van Gus	8-12-1887
Langtry Lillie	10-13-1853	Victoria Vesta	11-26-1873
Lauder Harry	8-4-1870	Waldman Ted	2-12-1899
Laurie Joe Jr	1892	Ward Fannie	2-22-1871
Leonard Eddie	10-18-1883	Weber Joe	8-11-1867
Lloyd Alice	10-20-1873	Wills Nat	7-11-1873
		Yule Joe	4-30-1894

****

STAGE MUSICALS

Ackerman Loni	4-10-49
Allen Elizabeth	1-25-34
Allen Jonelle	6-18-44
Allen Rae	7-3-26
Allmon Clinton	6-13-41
Alvarez Anita	10-13-20
Alvarez Carmen	7-2-35
Andreas Christine	10-1-51
Andrews George Lee	10-13-42
Andrews Julie	10-1-35
Andrews Nancy	12-16-24
Aronson Jonathan	6-17-53
Arthur Carol	8-4-35
Astaire Adele	9-10-1898
Avera Tom	2-21-23
Azito Tony	7-18-48
Baray John	11-29-44
Bartlett D'jamin	5-21-48
Battle Hinton	11-29-56
Beach Gary	10-10-47
Beechman Laurie	4-4-54
Bell Joan	2-1-35
Bell Vanessa	3-20-57
Benjamin P J	9-2-51
Berger Stephen	5-16-54
Bigley Isabel	2-23-28
Blaine Vivian	11-21-21
Blyden Larry	6-23-25
Bodin Duane	12-31-32
Bolger Ray	1-10-04
Bond Sheila	3-16-28
Boockvor Steven	11-18-42
Boone Michael Kelly	3-13-57
Bozyk Reizl	5-13-14
Brennan Maureen	10-11-52
Brightman Sarah	8-14-61
Broderick Helen	8-11-1891
Brooks David	9-24-17
Brown Tally	8-1-34
Browning Susan	2-25-41
Bruce Betty	5-2-21
Bruce Carol	11-15-19
Brummel David	11-1-42
Bryant David	5-26-36
Bryne Barbara	4-1-29

Buchanan Jack	4-2-1891
Buckley Betty	7-3-47
Burns David	6-22-02
Burrell Teresa	2-8-52
Callahan Bill	8-23-26
Callman Nancy	4-12-49
Cameron Madeline	3-29-55
Cannon Maureen	12-3-26
Capers Virginia	9-25-25
Cariou Len	9-30-39
Carlisle Kitty	9-3-14
Carpenter Constance	4-19-06
Carroll Danny	5-30-40
Carroll David-James	7-30-50
Carter Nell	9-13-48
Cassidy Jack	3-5-25
Channing Carol	1-31-21
Chaplin Sydney	3-30-26
Charles Walter	4-4-45
Choder Jill	12-14-48
Cibelli Renato	9-28-15
Cissel Chuck	10-3-48
Clark Dort	10-1-17
Clayton Jan	8-26-17
Clemente Rene	7-2-50
Cohen Margery	6-24-47
Cohenour Patti	10-17-52
Colker Jerry	3-16-55
Conrad Harriett	6-11-44
Cook Barbara	10-25-27
Cook Jill	2-25-54
Cooley Dennis	5-11-48
Cooper Marilyn	12-14-36
Correia Don	8-28-51
Cotsirilos Stephanie	2-24-47
Cox Catherine	12-13-50
Crabtree Don	8-21-28
Crawford Michael	1-19-42
Crofoot Leonard John	9-20-48
Crosby Kim	7-11-60
Crowley Dick	7-27-29
Cryer David	3-8-36
Cunningham John	6-22-32
Dale Grover	7-22-36
Dale Jim	8-15-35
Danek Michael	5-5-55

David Clifford	6-30-32
Davis Michael Allen	8-23-53
Dawn Hazel	3-23-1891
Dawson Mark	3-23-20
Day Frances	12-16-08
DeMirjian Denise	7-8-52
Dennis Ronald	10-2-44
DeSal Frank	4-14-43
DeShields Andre	1-12-46
Devine Loretta	8-21-49
Dickey Annamary	10-19-49
Diener Joan	2-24-34
Dillehay Kaylyn	12-1-54
Dixon Ed	9-2-48
Dooley Ray	10-30-1896
Douglas Larry	2-17-14
Douglass Stephen	9-27-21
Drake Alfred	10-7-14
Drake Donna	5-21-53
Duncan Todd	2-12-03
Edeiken Louise	6-23-56
Edmead Wendy	7-6-56
Ellington Mercedes	2-9-49
Ellis Mary	6-15-00
Ellis Scott	4-19-57
Elmore Steve	7-12-36
Ensslen Dick	12-19-26
Erwin Barbara	6-30-37
Esposito Giancarlo	4-26-58
Ewing J Timothy	4-3-54
Fabray Nanette	10-27-20
Fairchild Charlotte	6-3-30
Fickinger Steven	4-29-60
Fields Gracie	1-9-1898
Fitch Robert	4-29-34
Flagg Tom	3-30-49
Foote Gene	10-30-36
Foy Eddie Jr	2-4-05
Frey Nathaniel	8-3-18
Garnett Chip	5-8-53
Garrett Betty	5-23-19
Garrett Kelly	3-25-48
Garripoli Mary	3-15-56
Garrison David	6-30-52
Gary Harold	5-7-10
Gaxton William	12-2-1893

Gear Luella	9-5-1897
Geffner Deborah	8-26-52
Gilbert Alan	3-4-49
Gilford Jack	7-25-13
Gillette Anita	8-16-36
Gillette Priscilla	11-27-25
Giombetti Karen	5-24-55
Glynn Carlin	2-19-40
Gorrill Maggy	2-19-52
Goulet Robert	11-26-33
Goz Harry	6-23-32
Grammis Adam	12-8-47
Gray Dolores	6-7-24
Green Martyn	4-22-1899
Green Melissa Ann	3-22-56
Green Mitzi	10-22-20
Greenberg Mitchell	9-19-50
Greene Ellen	2-22-50
Greene Marty	6-19-09
Greenwood Charlotte	6-25-1893
Grenfell Joyce	2-10-10
Grey Joel	4-11-32
Grody Svetlana McLee	9-22-29
Groenendaal Cris	2-17-48
Groener Harry	9-10-51
Groody Louise	3-26-1897
Grover Stanley	3-28-26
Hajos Mitzi	4-27-1891
Haley Jack	8-10-02
Hall Juanita	11-6-01
Hall Natalie	9-23-04
Halliday Robert	4-11-1893
Haney Carol	12-24-24
Hanley Eileen	5-15-26
Haraldson Marian	9-5-33
Harney Ben	8-29-52
Hart Teddy	9-25-1897
Harum Eivind	5-24-44
Haynes Tiger	12-13-07
Heath Luise	4-18-51
Heatherton Ray	6-1-10
Hecht Paul	8-16-41
Hemsley Winston DeWitt	5-21-47
Herrera John	9-21-55
Hitchcock Raymond	10-22-1865
Holder Geoffrey	8-1-30

****

Hoit Michael	10-18-49
Holgate Ronald	5-26-37
Holliday David	8-4-37
Holliday Jennifer	10-19-60
Holloway Stanley	10-1-1890
Hopkins Linda	12-14-25
Hoty Dee	8-16-52
Howard Willie	4-13-1886
Howes Sally Ann	7-20-30
Ingram Rex	10-20-1895
Irving George S	11-1-22
Jablons Karen	7-19-51
Jarrett Jerry	9-9-18
Jerome Timothy	12-29-43
Johnson Bill	3-22-18
Johnson Kurt	10-5-52
Jones Reed	6-30-53
Kantor Kenneth	4-6-49
Karnilova Maria	8-3-20
Kaye Judy	10-11-48
Kaye Stubby	11-11-18
Kellogg Lynn	4-2-43
Kelton Gene	10-21-38
Kermoyan Michael	11-29-25
Kerns Linda	6-2-53
Kert Larry	12-5-30
Kezer Glenn	4-2-23
King Charles	10-31-1889
King Dennis	11-2-1897
Kirk Lisa	2-25-25
Kirsch Carolyn	5-24-42
Knight June	1-22-11
Kobart Ruth	8-24-24
Kuhn Judy	5-20-58
Lang Harold	12-21-20
Lawrence Gertrude	7-4-1898
Lee Sondra	9-30-30
Lenya Lotte	10-18-00
Lightner Winnie	9-17-1899
Lillie Beatrice	5-29-1898
Logan Ella	3-6-13
Losch Tilly	11-15-02
Lucas Craig	4-30-51
Lugenbeal Carol	7-14-52
LuPone Patti	4-21-49
MacDonald Christie	2-28-1875

****

Maggart Brandon	12-12-33
Magid Karen	6-2-49
Magnuson Merilee	6-11-51
March Ellen	8-18-48
Mariano Patti	6-12-45
Marshall Everett	12-31-01
Martin Leila	8-22-32
Martin Mary	12-1-13
Martin Millicent	6-8-34
Martin Virginia	12-2-32
Masiell Joe	10-27-39
May Edna	9-2-1878
McArdle Andrea	11-5-63
McCall Nancy	1-12-48
McClain Marcia	9-30-49
McCracken Joan	12-31-22
McKee Lonette	7-22-54
McLerie Allyn Ann	12-1-26
McNaughton Stephen	10-11-49
McQueen Armelia	1-6-52
McRae Calvin	2-14-55
McSpadden Becky	12-14-49
Medford Kay	9-14-20
Meiser Edith	5-9-1898
Mercer Marian	11-26-35
Merlin Joanna	7-15-31
Merman Ethel	1-16-08
Merrill Scott	7-14-22
Merritt George	7-10-42
Merritt Theresa	9-24-22
Middleton Ray	2-8-07
Milford Penelope	6-17-23
Miller Fred	9-17-22
Miller Marilyn	9-1-1898
Miller Tod	9-15-44
Miller Wynne	9-29-30
Mills Stephanie	3-22-57
Minnelli Liza	3-12-46
Misita Michael	1-10-47
Moore Victor	2-24-1876
Morison Patricia	3-19-14
Morrow Doretta	1-27-28
Morrow Karen	12-15-36
Morse Robert	5-18-31
Mostel Zero	2-28-15
Munshin Jules	2-22-15

Murray J Harold	2-17-1891
Myers Pamela	7-15-47
Myrtil Odette	6-28-1898
Newman Phyllis	3-19-35
Nielsen Alice	6-7-1876
Niesen Gertrude	7-8-10
Niles Mary Ann	5-2-23
Nype Russell	4-26-24
O'Brien Marcia	3-17-34
O'Hara Jill	8-23-47
O'Neal Zelma	5-29-07
O'Shea Tessie	3-13-18
Page Ken	1-20-54
Palmer Peter	9-20-31
Parker Lew	10-28-07
Patinkin Mandy	11-30-52
Penzner Seymour	7-29-15
Peters Bernadette	2-28-48
Playten Alice	8-28-47
Presnell Harve	9-14-33
Pritchett Lizabeth	3-12-20
Radigan Michael	5-2-49
Raitt John	1-19-17
Ralph Sheryl Lee	12-30-56
Reams Lee Roy	8-23-42
Reardon John	4-8-30
Rhodes Erik	2-10-06
Rice Sarah	3-5-55
Rich James	4-29-55
Richards Jess	1-23-43
Richert Wanda	4-18-58
Rinehart Elaine	8-16-52
Ritchard Cyril	12-1-1897
Rivera Chita	1-23-33
Robertson Guy	1-26-1892
Roos Casper	3-21-25
Roy Renee	1-2-35
Sabellico Richard	6-29-51
Sadoff Fred	10-21-26
Saffran Christina	10-21-58
Santley Joseph	1-10-1889
Seal Elizabeth	8-28-33
Segal Vivienne	4-19-1897
Sell Janie	10-1-41
Serrano Charlie	12-4-52
Shapiro Debbie	9-29-54

Shelton Reid	10-7-24
Skaggs Marsha	8-23-49
Smith Queenie	9-8-02
Smith Sheila	4-3-33
Stadlen Lewis J	3-7-47
Steele Tommy	12-17-36
Stratton Ronald Bennett	1-11-42
Stritch Elaine	2-2-25
Sullivan Jo	8-28-27
Suzuki Pat	9-23-31
Syers Mark	10-25-52
Tabbert William	10-5-21
Tamara (Drasin)	10-13-07
Tatum Marianne	2-18-51
Templeton Fay	12-25-1866
Terris Norma	11-13-04
Terry Ethelind	8-14-00
Terry Susan	5-30-53
Testa Mary	6-4-55
Theodore Donna	7-25-45
Thome David	7-24-51
Thompson Jack	8-31-40
Thorne Raymond	11-27-34
Thurston Ted	1-9-20
Toy Christine	12-26-59
Urmston Kenneth	8-6-29
Venuta Benay	1-27-11
Verdon Gwen	1-13-25
Vestoff Virginia	12-9-40
Vosburgh David	3-14-38
Walters Kelly	5-28-50
Watson Susan	12-17-38
Welch Charles C	2-2-21
Welch Elisabeth	2-27-08
White Terri	1-24-53
Whiting Jack	6-22-01
Wilkinson Colm	6-5-44
Williams Curt	11-17-35
Winninger Charles	5-26-1884
Winston Hattie	3-3-45
Withers Iva	7-7-17
Witter William C	3-15-50
Wolfington Iggie	10-14-20
Wong Janet	8-30-51
Worth Penny	3-2-50
Wyman Nicholas	5-18-50

Yeoman JoAnn	3-19-48	Gravet Fernand	12-25-04
Young Ronald	6-11-41	Grayson Kathryn	2-9-22
Ziemba Karen	11-12-57	Haver June	6-10-26
Zimmerman Mark	4-19-52	Hope Bob	5-29-03
Zorina Vera	1-2-17	Hutton Betty	2-26-21
		Jean Gloria	4-14-26

ZIEGFELD FOLLIES

Bayes Nora	1-10-1880	Jolson Al	3-26-1886
Claire Ina	10-15-1895	Jones Allan	10-14-05
Dolly Jenny & Rosie	10-25-1892	Jones Shirley	3-31-33
Eaton Mary	1902	Keel Howard	4-13-17
Held Anna	3-18-1873	Keeler Ruby	8-25-09
Joyce Peggy Hopkins	1893	Kelly Gene	8-23-12
Lorraine Lillian	1-1-1892	Lamour Dorothy	12-10-14
Pennington Ann	12-23-1892	Lanza Mario	1-31-21
Richman Harry	8-10-1895	Lee Dixie	11-5-11
Rogers Will	11-4-1879	MacDonald Jeanette	6-18-01
Tanguay Eva	8-1-1878	MacRae Gordon	3-12-21
Tashman Lilyan	10-23-1899	Manning Irene	7-17-18
Tinney Frank	3-29-1878	Matthews Jessie	3-11-07
Williams Bert	11-12-1874	McDonald Grace	6-15-18
		Miller Ann	4-12-19

****

FILM MUSICALS

Astaire Fred	5-10-1899	Miranda Carmen	2-9-09
Berkeley Busby	11-29-1895	Moore Constance	1-18-19
Breen Bobby	11-4-27	Moore Grace	12-5-01
Caron Leslie	7-1-31	Morgan Dennis	12-10-10
Carpenter Carleton	7-10-26	Murphy George	7-4-02
Carroll Nancy	11-19-05	Nelson Gene	3-24-20
Champion Gower	6-22-20	O'Connor Donald	8-28-25
Champion Marge	9-2-19	Paige Janis	9-16-22
Charisse Cyd	3-8-21	Powell Dick	11-14-04
Chevalier Maurice	9-12-1888	Powell Eleanor	11-21-12
Crosby Bing	5-2-01	Powell Jane	4-1-29
Dailey Dan	12-14-14	Preisser June	1920
Day Doris	4-3-24	Regan Phil	5-28-06
Downs Johnny	10-10-13	Reynolds Debbie	4-1-32
Dunbar Dixie	1-18-18	Rogers Ginger	7-16-11
Durbin Deanna	12-4-21	Ross Shirley	1-7-11
Eddy Nelson	6-29-01	Ryan Peggy	8-28-24
Edwards Cliff	6-14-1895	Tamblyn Russ	12-30-35
Faye Alice	5-5-12	Terry Ruth	10-21-20
Foster Susanna	12-6-24	Van Bobby	12-6-30
Frazee Jane	7-18-18	Vera-Ellen	2-16-20
Garland Judy	6-10-22	Weaver Marjorie	3-2-13
Gaynor Mitzi	9-4-30	Williams Esther	8-8-23
Grable Betty	12-18-16	Wing Toby	7-14-13
		Wonder Tommy	3-7-14

****

COUNTRY & WESTERN

Acuff Roy	9-15-03
Allanson Susie	3-17-52
Allen Deborah	9-30-53
Allen Rex Jr	8-23-47
Allen Rosalie	6-6-24
Anderson Bill	11-1-37
Anderson John	12-13-54
Anderson Lynn	9-26-47
Anglin Jack	5-13-16
Arnold Eddy	5-15-18
Arnold Kristine	11-28-56
Ashworth Ernie	12-15-28
Atcher Bob	5-11-14
Atkins Chet	6-20-24
Axton Hoyt	3-25-38
Bailey Razzy	2-14-39
Baillie Kathie	2-20-51
Bandy Moe	2-12-44
Bare Bobby	4-7-35
Bee Molly	8-18-39
Belew Carl	4-21-31
Bellamy David	9-16-50
Bellamy Howard	2-2-46
Berry John	9-14-59
Black Clint	2-4-62
Blanchard Jack	5-8-42
Bogguss Suzy	12-30-56
Bolick Bill	10-28-17
Bolick Earl	11-16-19
Bonagura Michael	3-26-53
Bond Johnny	6-1-15
Bonnie Lou (Keith)	10-27-24
Boxcar Willie	9-1-31
Britt Elton	6-27-17
Brooks Garth	2-7-62
Brooks Kit	5-12-55
Brown Bonnie	7-31-37
Brown Jim Ed	3-1-34
Brown Marty	7-25-65
Brown Maxine	4-27-32
Brown T Graham	10-30-54
Browne Jann	3-14-54
Bruce Ed	12-29-40
Burgess Wilma	6-11-39
Bush Johnny	2-17-35

****

Butler Carl	6-2-27
Butler Pearl	9-20-27
Byrd Jerry	3-9-20
Byrd Tracy	12-18-66
Campbell Glen	4-22-35
Cargill Henson	2-5-41
Carlisle Bill	12-19-08
Carlisle Cliff	5-6-04
Carlson Paulette	10-11-53
Carpenter Mary-Chapin	2-21-58
Carson Martha	5-19-21
Carter Carlene	9-26-55
Carter Maybelle	5-10-09
Carter Wilf 'Montana Slim'	12-18-04
Carter-Cash June	6-23-29
Carver Johnny	11-24-40
Cash Johnny	2-26-32
Cash Rosanne	5-24-55
Cash Tommy	4-5-40
Chesnutt Mark	9-6-63
Clark Guy	11-6-41
Clark Roy	4-15-33
Clayton Lee	10-29-42
Clement Jack	4-5-31
Clements Zeke	9-6-11
Cline Patsy	9-8-32
Cochran Hank	8-2-35
Coe David Allan	9-6-39
Collie Mark	1-18-56
Collins Tommy	9-28-30
Colter Jessi	5-25-47
Conlee John	8-11-46
Conley Earl Thomas	10-17-41
Coolidge Rita	5-1-45
Cooper Stoney	10-16-18
Cooper Wilma Lee	2-7-21
Copas Cowboy	7-15-13
Cornelius Helen	12-6-41
Craddock Billy 'Crash'	6-16-39
Cramer Floyd	10-27-33
Crowell Rodney	8-7-50
Cryner Bobbie	9-13-61
Curless Dick	3-17-32
Cyrus Billy Ray	8-25-61
Daffan Ted	9-21-12
Dalhart Vernon	4-6-1883

****

****

Dalton Lacy J	10-13-46
Damita Jo (DuBlanc)	8-5-40
Daniels Charlie	10-28-36
Davies Gail	4-4-48
Davis Danny	4-29-25
Davis Jimmie	9-11-02
Davis Linda	11-26-62
Davis Mac	1-21-42
Davis Paul	4-21-48
Davis Skeeter	12-30-31
Dean Billy	4-2-62
Dean Jimmy	8-10-28
DeHaven Penny	5-17-48
Delmore Alton	12-25-08
Delmore Rabon	12-3-10
Denver John	12-31-43
Dexter Al	5-4-02
Dickens Little Jimmy	12-19-20
Diffie Joe	12-28-58
Dottsy (Brodt)	4-6-53
Drake Pete	10-8-32
Drusky Roy	6-22-30
Dudley Dave	5-3-28
Duncan Johnny	10-5-38
Dunn Holly	8-22-57
Dunn Ronnie	6-1-53
Edwards Stoney	12-24-37
Ely Joe	2-9-47
Emmons Buddy	1-27-37
Everette Leon	6-21-48
Fairchild Barbara	11-12-50
Fargo Donna	11-10-49
Feathers Charlie	6-12-32
Felts Narvel	11-11-38
Flores Rosie	9-10-50
Foley Red	6-17-10
Ford Tennessee Ernie	2-13-19
Forester Christy	10-10-62
Forester June	9-25-56
Forester Kathy	1-4-55
Forester Kim	12-4-60
Foster Radney	7-20-59
Fox Curly	11-9-10
Frazier Dallas	10-27-39
Fricke Janie	12-19-47
Friedman Kinky	10-31-44

****

Frizzell David	9-26-41
Frizzell Lefty	3-31-28
Fromholz Steve	6-8-45
Garland Hank	11-11-30
Garnett Gale	7-17-42
Gatlin Larry	5-2-48
Gatlin Rudy	8-20-52
Gatlin Steve	4-4-51
Gayle Crystal	1-9-51
Gentry Bobbie	7-27-44
Gibbs Terri	6-15-54
Gibson Don	4-3-28
Gill Janis	3-1-55
Gill Vince	4-12-57
Gilley Mickey	3-9-36
Gilmore Jimmie Dale	5-6-45
Glaser Chuck	2-3-36
Glaser James	12-16-37
Glaser Tompall	9-3-33
Goldsboro Bobby	1-18-41
Gosdin Vern	8-5-34
Grammer Billy	8-28-25
Gray Claude	1-26-32
Gray Mark	10-24-53
Green Lloyd	10-4-37
Greene Jack	1-7-30
Greenwood Lee	12-27-42
Griff Ray	4-22-40
Griffin Rex	8-22-12
Haggard Merle	4-6-37
Hall Tom T	5-25-36
Hamblen Stuart	10-20-08
Hamilton George IV	7-19-37
Harden Arleen	3-1-45
Hargrove Linda	2-3-50
Harrell Kelly	9-13-1899
Harris Emmylou	4-2-47
Hart Freddie	12-21-26
Harvey Alex	3-10-47
Hawkins Hawkshaw	12-22-21
Head Roy	1-9-43
Hill Faith	9-21-67
Hill Goldie	1-11-33
Hobbs Becky	1-24-50
Holly Doyle	6-30-36
Horton Johnny	4-30-25

****

Country/Western Hou-Mac
****

Houston David	12-9-38
Howard Jan	3-13-32
Hunley Con	4-9-46
Husky Ferlin	12-3-25
Jackson Alan	10-17-58
Jackson Carl	9-18-53
Jackson Stonewall	11-6-32
Jackson Wanda	10-20-37
James Sonny	5-1-29
Jennings Waylon	6-15-37
Jones George	9-12-31
Judd Naomi	1-11-46
Judd Wynonna	5-30-64
Kazee Buell	8-29-00
Keith Bill	12-20-39
Kendall Jeannie	11-30-54
Kendall Royce	9-25-34
Kershaw Sammy	2-24-58
Ketchum Hal	4-9-53
Kilgore Merle	9-8-34
King Claude	2-5-33
Kirk Eddie	3-21-19
Kristofferson Kris	6-22-36
LaCosta (Tucker)	4-6-51
Lane Cristy	1-8-40
Lane Red	2-9-39
Lang K D	11-2-61
Lawrence Tracy	1-27-68
LeDoux Chris	10-2-48
Lee Brenda	12-11-44
Lee Dickey	9-21-40
Lee Johnny	7-3-46
Lloyd Bill	12-6-55
Locklin Hank	2-15-18
Loudermilk John D	3-31-34
Louvin Charlie	7-7-27
Louvin Ira	4-21-24
Loveless Patty	1-4-57
Lovett Lyle	11-1-57
Lulu Belle (Wiseman)	12-24-13
Lunn Robert	11-28-12
Lynn Judy	4-12-36
Lynn Loretta	4-14-35
Lynne Shelby	10-22-68
MacDonald Skeets	10-1-15
Mack Warner	4-2-38

****

Country/Western Mac-Oda
****

Macon Uncle Dave	10-7-1870
Maddox Rose	12-15-26
Mainer J E	7-20-1898
Mainer Wade	4-21-07
Mandrell Barbara	12-25-48
Mandrell Irlene	1-29-57
Mandrell Louise	7-13-54
Maphis Joe	5-12-21
Maphis Rose	12-29-22
Mattea Kathy	6-21-59
McAnally Mac	7-1-59
McBride Martina	7-29-66
McCall C W	11-15-28
McClain Charly	3-26-56
McClinton O B	4-25-40
McCoy Charlie	3-28-41
McCoy Neal	7-30-63
McDaniel Mel	9-6-42
McDowell Ronnie	3-26-50
McEnery 'Red River Dave'	12-15-14
McEntire Reba	3-28-54
McGraw Tim	5-1-67
McKee Maria	8-17-64
Meyers Augie	5-31-40
Miller Jody	11-29-41
Miller Roger	1-2-36
Milsap Ronnie	1-16-44
Moffatt Hugh	11-10-48
Montana Patsy	10-30-14
Montgomery John Michael	1-20-65
Montgomery Melba	10-14-38
Morgan George	6-28-25
Morgan Lorrie	6-27-59
Morris Gary	12-7-48
Mullican Moon	3-27-09
Murphey Michael Martin	3-14-42
Murray Anne	6-20-45
Naylor Jerry	3-6-39
Nelson Tracy	12-27-47
Nelson Willie	4-30-33
Newbury Mickey	5-19-40
Newton Juice	2-18-52
Noack Eddie	4-29-30
Norma Jean (Beasler)	1-30-38
O'Connor Mark	8-5-61
O'Day Molly	7-9-23

****

Oslin K T	5-15-41
Overstreet Tommy	9-10-37
Owens Bonnie	10-1-32
Owens Buck	8-12-29
Oxford Vernon	6-8-41
Parker Andy	3-17-13
Parnell Lee Roy	12-21-56
Parton Dolly	1-19-46
Parton Stella	5-4-49
Paycheck Johnny	5-31-41
Payne Leon	6-15-17
Perkins Carl	4-9-32
Phillips Bill	1-28-36
Pierce Webb	8-8-26
Pillow Ray	7-4-37
Price Kenny	5-27-31
Price Ray	1-12-26
Pride Charley	3-18-38
Prophet Ronnie	12-26-37
Pruett Jeanne	1-30-37
Puckett Riley	5-7-1884
Rabbitt Eddie	11-27-44
Rainwater Marvin	7-2-25
Raven Eddy	8-19-44
Raye Collin	8-22-59
Raye Susan	10-18-44
Reed Jerry	3-20-37
Reeves Del	7-14-33
Reeves Jim	8-20-24
Rice Bobby G	7-11-44
Rich Charlie	12-14-32
Riley Jeannie C	10-19-45
Rivers Johnny	11-7-42
Robbins Marty	9-26-25
Robison Carson J	8-4-1890
Rodgers Jimmie	9-8-1897
Rodriguez Johnny	12-10-51
Rogers David	3-27-36
Rogers Kenny	8-21-38
Rowland Dave	1-26-42
Royal Billy Joe	4-3-42
Russell Johnny	1-23-32
Sahm Doug	11-6-41
Scotty (Wiseman)	11-8-09
Seals Troy	11-16-38
Seely Jeannie	7-16-40

Sessions Ronnie	12-7-48
Shaver Billy Joe	8-16-39
Shay Dorothy	4-11-21
Shelton Ricky Van	1-12-52
Shepard Jean	11-21-33
Sheppard T G	7-20-42
Sizemore Asher	6-6-06
Sizemore Little Jimmy	1-29-28
Skaggs Ricky	7-18-54
Smith Arthur 'Guitar Boogie'	4-1-21
Smith Cal	4-7-32
Smith Carl	3-15-27
Smith Connie	8-14-41
Smith Margo	4-9-42
Smith Sammi	8-5-43
Snow Hank	5-9-14
Sovine Red	7-17-18
Spears Billie Jo	1-14-37
Stafford Jim	1-16-44
Stampley Joe	6-6-43
Starr Kenny	9-21-53
Stegall Keith	11-1-54
Stevens Ray	1-24-39
Stewart Gary	5-28-45
Stewart Redd	5-27-21
Stewart Wynn	6-7-34
Stone Doug	6-19-56
Strait George	5-18-52
Street Mel	10-21-33
Stuart Marty	9-30-58
Stuckey Nat	12-17-37
Supernaw Doug	9-26-60
Swan Billy	5-12-42
Sylvia (Allen)	12-9-56
Talley James	11-9-44
Texas Ruby (Fox)	6-4-10
Thomas B J	8-7-42
Thompson Hank	9-3-25
Tillis Mel	8-8-32
Tillis Pam	7-24-57
Tillman Floyd	12-8-14
Tippin Aaron	7-3-58
Trask Diana	6-23-40
Travis Merle	11-29-17
Travis Randy	5-4-59
Trevino Rick	5-16-71

****

Tritt Travis	2-9-64
Tubb Ernest	2-9-14
Tubb Justin	8-20-35
Tucker Tanya	10-10-58
Twitty Conway	9-1-33
VanDyke Leroy	10-4-29
Vanwarmer Randy	3-30-55
Wagoner Porter	8-12-27
Walker Billy	1-14-29
Walker Charlie	11-2-26
Walker Clay	8-19-69
Walker Jerry Jeff	3-16-42
Wallace Jerry	12-15-33
Wariner Steve	12-25-54
Watson Doc	3-2-23
Watson Gene	10-11-43
Watson Merle	2-8-49
Weller Freddy	9-9-47
Wells Kitty	8-30-18
West Dottie	10-11-32
West Shelly	5-23-58
West Speedy	1-25-24
Wheeler Billy Edd	12-9-32
Wheeler Cheryl	7-10-51
Whitley Keith	7-1-55
Whitman Slim	1-20-24
Wilburn Doyle	7-7-30
Wilburn Teddy	11-30-31
Williams Don	5-27-39
Williams Hank	9-17-23
Williams Hank Jr	5-26-49
Williams Leona	1-7-43
Williams Lucinda	1-26-53
Willis Guy	7-15-15
Willis Kelly	10-1-68
Willis Skeeter	12-20-17
Willis Vic	5-31-22
Wood Del	2-22-20
Wooley Sheb	4-10-21
Wright Bobby	3-30-42
Wright Johnny	5-13-14
Wright Michelle	7-1-61
Wynette Tammy	5-5-42
Yearwood Tricia	9-19-64
Yoakum Dwight	10-23-56
Young Faron	2-25-32

****

ALABAMA

Cook Jeff	8-27-49
Gentry Teddy	1-22-52
Herndon Mark	5-11-55
Owen Randy	12-13-49

OAK RIDGE BOYS

Allen Duane	4-29-43
Bonsall Joe	5-18-44
Golden William Lee	1-12-39
Sterban Richard	4-24-43

STATLER BROTHERS

Balsley Philip	8-8-39
DeWitt Lew	3-8-38
Reid Don	6-5-45
Reid Harold	8-21-39

****

ZYDECO & CAJUN

Arceneaux Fernest	8-27-40
August Lynn	8-7-48
Chenier Clifton	6-25-25
Choates Harry	12-26-22
Doucet Michael	1951
Dural Stanley 'Buckwheat'	11-17-47
Kershaw Doug	1-24-36
Newman Jimmy C	8-27-27
Queen Ida	1-15-29
Richard Zachary	9-8-50
Simien Terrance	9-3-65
Sonnier Jo-El	10-2-46
Terry Al	1-14-22
Wilson Justin	4-24-14

****

BLUEGRASS

Adcock Eddie	6-21-38
Allen Lee	6-19-46
Auldridge Mike	12-30-38
Clements Vassar	4-25-28
Crowe J D	8-27-37
Dillard Doug	3-6-37
Dillard Rodney	5-18-42
Flatt Lester	6-28-14
Grisman Dave	3-23-45
Jesse (McReynolds)	7-9-29
Jim (McReynolds)	2-13-27
Krauss Alison	7-23-71
Martin Jimmy	8-10-27

****

McCoury Del	2-1-39
Monroe Bill	9-13-11
Osborne Bob	12-7-31
Osborne Sonny	10-29-37
Reno Don	2-2-27
Scruggs Earl	1-6-24
Smiley Red	5-17-25
Stanley Carter	8-27-25
Stanley Ralph	2-25-27
Story Carl	5-29-16
White Clarence	6-7-44
Wiseman Mac	5-23-25

WESTERN SWING

Boyd Bill	9-29-10
Brown Milton	9-8-03
Bruner Cliff	4-25-15
Callahan Homer/Bill	3-27-12
Callahan Walter/Joe	1-27-10
Commander Cody (Geo Frayne)	7-19-44
Cooley Spade	2-22-10
Crow Alvin	9-29-50
Duncan Tommy	1-11-11
Gimble Johnny	5-30-26
Howard Paul	7-10-08
King Pee Wee	2-18-14
McAuliffe Leon	1-3-17
Penny Hank	8-18-18
Rausch Leon	10-2-27
Steagall Red	12-22-37
Tyler T Texas	6-20-16
Western Johnny	10-28-34
Whitley Ray	12-5-01
Williams Tex	8-23-17
Wills Bob	3-6-05
Wills Johnnie Lee	9-2-12

ASLEEP AT THE WHEEL

Benson Ray	3-16-51
Levin Danny	1949
O'Connell Chris	3-21-53
Oceans Lucky	4-22-51
Ryan Pat 'Taco'	7-14-53

RIDERS IN THE SKY

Ranger Doug (Green)	3-20-46
Paul Woody	8-23-49
Too Slim (Fred LaBour)	6-3-48

SONS OF THE PIONEERS

Farr Hugh	12-6-03
Farr Karl	4-25-09
Nolan Bob	4-1-08
Perryman Lloyd	1-29-17
Spencer Tim	7-7-08

COUNTRY COMEDY

Andrews Andy	5-22-59
Bowman Don	8-26-37
Campbell Archie	11-17-14
Childre Lew	11-1-01
Clower Jerry	9-28-26
Duke of Paducah (Whitey Ford)	6-12-01
Homer (Henry Haynes)	7-27-17
Jethro (Kenneth Burns)	3-10-20
Jones Grandpa	10-20-13
Lonzo (John Sullivan)	7-7-17
Oscar (Rollin Sullivan)	1-19-19
Pearl Minnie	10-25-12
Roman Lulu	1947
Samples Junior	8-10-26
Stringbean (David Akeman)	6-17-15

FOLK

Andersen Eric	2-14-43
Baez Joan	1-9-41
Bibb Leon	1935
Bookbinder Roy	10-5-43
Brand Oscar	2-7-20
Bromberg David	9-19-45
Carawan Guy	7-28-27
Chandler Len	5-27-35
Clayton Paul	3-3-33
Cohen Leonard	9-21-34
Collins Judy	5-1-39
Colvin Shawn	1-10-56
Dane Barbara	5-12-27
Davis Meg	1-28-53
Dawson Jim	6-27-46
DeMent Iris	1-5-61
Drapkin Livia	4-18-51
Driftwood Jimmie	6-20-17
Dyer-Bennet Richard	10-6-13
Dylan Bob	5-24-41
Elliott Ramblin' Jack	8-1-31

****

Fadden Jimmie	3-9-48
Farina Mimi	4-30-45
Gibson Bob	11-16-31
Gilkyson Terry	6-17-16
Goodman Steve	7-25-48
Grey Sara	3-22-40
Griffith Nanci	7-6-52
Guthrie Arlo	7-10-47
Guthrie Woody	7-14-12
Hammond John Jr	11-13-42
Hanna Jeff	8-11-47
Hartford John	12-30-37
Havens Richie	1-21-41
Henske Judy	1942
Hester Carolyn	1-28-37
Hopkins Doc	1-26-1899
Houston Cisco	8-18-18
Ian (Tyson)	9-25-33
Ives Burl	6-14-09
Kilby-Snow John	5-28-05
Koerner John 'Spider'	8-31-38
Kweskin Jim	7-18-40
Ledbetter Huddie 'Leadbelly'	1-29-1885
Lehrer Tom	4-9-28
Lightfoot Gordon	11-17-38
Lomax Alan	1-15-15
Makeba Miriam	3-4-32
Marais (Josef)	11-17-05
McEuen John	12-19-45
McGarrigle Anna	12-4-44
McGarrigle Kate	2-6-46
McGowan Rattlesnake Annie	12-26-41
Miranda	1-9-12
Mitchell Chad	12-5-36
Mitchell Howie	2-22-32
Mitchell Joni	11-7-43
Morrissey Bill	11-25-51
Niles John Jacob	4-28-1892
Ochs Phil	12-19-40
Odetta	12-31-30
Okun Milton	12-23-23
Paxton Tom	10-31-37
Prine John	10-10-46
Redpath Jean	4-28-37
Ringer Jim	2-29-36
Rinzler Ralph	7-20-34

****

Ritchie Jean	12-8-22
Robinson Earl	7-2-10
Rush Tom	2-8-41
Sainte-Marie Buffy	2-20-41
Seeger Peggy	6-17-35
Sky Patrick	10-2-40
Sorrels Rosalie	6-24-33
Spoelstra Mark	6-30-40
Stracke Win	2-20-08
Stuart Alice	6-15-42
Sylvia (Fricker)	9-19-40
Turner Gil	5-6-33
Vanaver Bill	9-1-43
VanRonk Dave	6-30-36
Wainwright Loudon III	9-5-46
Warner Jeff	3-9-43
West Hedy	4-6-38
White Josh	2-11-08
Williams Victoria	12-23-58
Wolf Kate	1-27-42
Young Jesse Colin	11-22-41
KINGSTON TRIO	
Guard Dave	10-19-34
Reynolds Nick	7-27-33
Shane Bob	2-1-34
Stewart John	9-5-39
LIMELIGHTERS	
Gottlieb Lou	1923
Hassilev Alex	7-11-32
Yarborough Glenn	1-12-30
NEW CHRISTY MINSTRELS	
McGuire Barry	10-15-35
Settle Mike	3-20-41
Sparks Randy	7-29-33
Williams Terry Benson	6-6-47
NEW LOST CITY RAMBLERS	
Cohen John	8-2-32
Paley Tom	3-19-28
Schwarz Tracy	11-13-38
Seeger Mike	8-15-33
NEW SEEKERS	
Doyle Peter	7-28-49
Graham Eve	4-19-43
Kristian Marty	5-27-47
Layton Paul	8-4-47
Paul Lyn	2-16-49

****

PETER, PAUL & MARY

Stookey Paul	12-30-37
Travers Mary	11-7-37
Yarrow Peter	5-31-38

SEEKERS

Durham Judith	7-7-43
Guy Athol	1-5-40
Potger Keith	3-2-41
Woodley Bruce	7-25-42

WEAVERS

Darling Erik	9-25-33
Gilbert Ronnie	9-7-27
Hays Lee	1914
Hellerman Fred	5-13-27
Krause Bernie	12-8-38
Seeger Pete	5-3-19

* * * * * * * * * * * * * * * *

GOSPEL & CHRISTIAN

Akers Doris	5-21-23
Andrews Inez	10-19-35
Armstrong Vanessa Bell	10-2-53
Barrett Delois	12-3-26
Baylor Helen	1-8-53
Becker Margaret	1960
Benson Jodi	10-10-61
Boone Debby	9-22-56
Bowman Sister Thea	12-29-37
Bradford Alex	1-23-27
Bradley J Robert	9-11-20
Brewster William H	7-2-1897
Caesar Shirley	10-13-38
Card Michael	4-11-57
Carr Sister Wynona	8-23-29
Chapman Steven Curtis	11-21-62
Cheeks Julius 'June'	8-7-29
Cleveland James	12-5-31
Coates Dorothy Love	1-30-28
Cooney Rory	5-29-52
Crosse Clay	2-11-67
Crouch Andrae	7-1-42
Crouch Sandra	6-1-50
Dixon Jessy	3-12-38
English Michael	1962
Evans Clay	6-23-25
Fountain Clarence	11-28-29
Gaither Bill	3-28-36

JAZZ MUSICIANS

Gaither Gloria	3-4-42
Grant Amy	11-25-60
Hawkins Edwin	8-18-43
Hawkins Tremaine	10-11-56
Hawkins Walter	5-18-49
Houston Cissy	1933
Jackson Mahalia	10-26-11
LeFlore Mylon	10-6-45
Ligon Willie Joe	9-11-42
Nicholas Philip	2-18-45
Pace Charles Henry	8-4-1886
Paris Twila	1958
Patti Sandi	7-12-56
Rambo Dottie	3-2-34
Robinson Cleophus	3-18-32
Shea George Beverly	2-1-09
Smallwood Richard	11-30-48
Smith Michael W	1958
Smith Harold	1935
Staples Cleotha	1934
Staples Mavis	1940
Staples Roebuck 'Pop'	12-28-15
Staples Yvonne	1939
Talbot John Michael	5-8-54
Tharpe Sister Rosetta	3-20-15
Troccoli Kathy	1958
Walker Albertina	8-28-29
Ward Clara	4-21-24
Watson Wayne	10-5-54
Williams Marion	8-29-27
Winans Marvin & Carvin	1958
Winans Michael	6-5-59

* * * * * * * * * * * * * * * *

JAZZ MUSICIANS

Abdullah Ahmed	5-10-46
Abercrombie John	12-16-44
Abrams Muhal Richard	9-19-30
Adderley Cannonball	9-9-28
Adderley Nat	11-25-31
Addison Bernard	4-15-05
Akiyoshi Toshiko	12-12-29
Albany Joe	1-24-24
Ali Rashied	7-1-35
Allen Geri	6-12-57
Allen Henry 'Red'	1-7-08
Allison Mose	11-11-27

Almeida Laurindo	9-2-17
Ammons Gene 'Jug'	4-14-25
Anderson Ray	10-16-52
Armstrong Lillian	2-3-02
Armstrong Louis	7-4-00
Ashby Irving	12-29-20
Ayler Albert	7-13-36
Bacsik Elek	5-22-26
Bailey Buster	7-19-02
Bailey Derek	1-29-32
Baker Chet	12-23-29
Baker Shorty	5-26-14
Barbarin Paul	5-5-1899
Barbieri Gato	11-28-34
Barbour Dave	5-28-12
Barker Danny	1-13-09
Barksdale Everett	4-28-10
Barnes George	7-17-21
Bauer Billy	11-14-15
Bean Billy	12-26-33
Bechet Sidney	5-14-1897
Beiderbecke Bix	3-10-03
Bellson Louis	7-26-24
Benson George	3-22-43
Berry Chu	9-13-10
Bertoncini Gene	4-6-37
Best Skeeter	11-20-14
Bickert Ed	11-29-32
Bigard Barney	3-3-06
Blackman Cindy	11-18-59
Blackwell Ed	10-10-29
Blake Eubie	2-7-1883
Blake Ran	4-20-35
Blakey Art	10-11-19
Blanchard Terence	3-13-62
Bley Carla	5-11-38
Bley Paul	11-10-32
Bluiett Hamiet	9-16-40
Bolden Bunny	9-6-1877
Bonfa Luiz	10-17-22
Bostic Earl	4-25-13
Boulou (Ferre)	4-24-51
Bowie Lester	10-11-41
Bown Patti	7-26-31
Brackeen JoAnne	7-26-38
Bradford Bobby	7-19-34

Braff Ruby	3-16-27
Braxton Anthony	6-4-45
Breau Lenny	8-5-41
Brookmeyer Bob	12-19-29
Brooks Hadda	10-29-16
Brown Clifford	10-30-30
Brown Marion	9-8-35
Brown Pete	11-9-06
Brubeck Dave	12-6-20
Bruford Bill	5-17-49
Brunis Georg	2-6-02
Budimir Dennis	6-20-38
Bunn Teddy	1909
Burrell Kenny	7-31-31
Burton Gary	1-23-43
Bushkin Joe	11-6-16
Butler Billy	12-15-25
Butterfield Billy	1-14-17
Byard Jaki	6-15-22
Byas Don	10-21-12
Byrd Charlie	9-16-25
Byrd Donald	12-9-32
Candoli Conte	7-12-27
Carr Joe 'Fingers'	7-18-10
Carroll Baikida	1-15-47
Carroll Barbara	1-25-25
Carver Wayman	12-25-05
Casey Al	9-15-15
Catherine Philip	10-27-42
Catlett Big Sid	1-17-10
Cavalli Pierre	7-12-28
Chaloff Serge	11-24-23
Chambers Joe	6-25-42
Cheatham Doc	6-13-05
Cherry Don	11-18-36
Chisholm George	3-29-15
Christian Charlie	7-29-16
Clarke Kenny	1-9-14
Clarke Stanley	6-30-51
Clayton Buck	11-12-11
Cless Rod	5-20-07
Cobb Arnett	8-10-18
Cobham Billy	5-16-44
Cohn Al	11-24-25
Cole Cozy	10-17-09
Coleman Bill	8-4-04

Coleman Ornette	3-19-30
Coleman Steve	9-20-56
Collins John	9-20-13
Collins Lee	10-17-01
Coltrane Alice	8-27-37
Coltrane John	9-26-26
Condon Eddie	11-16-05
Corea Chick	6-12-41
Coryell Larry	4-2-43
Counce Curtis	1-23-26
Crawford Jimmie	1-14-10
Crispell Marilyn	3-30-47
Crosby Israel	1-19-19
Curson Ted	6-3-35
Dameron Tadd	2-21-17
Dankworth John	9-20-27
Davern Kenny	1-7-35
Davis Eddie 'Lockjaw'	3-2-22
Davis Maxwell	1-14-16
Davis Miles	5-25-26
Davison Wild Bill	1-5-06
DeArango Bill	9-20-21
DeFranco Buddy	2-17-23
DeJohnette Jack	8-9-42
deParis Sidney	5-30-05
deParis Wilbur	9-20-00
Desmond Paul	11-25-24
DiMeola Al	7-22-54
Diorio Joe	8-6-36
Distel Sacha	1-29-33
Dodds Baby	12-24-1898
Dodds Johnny	4-12-1892
Dolphy Eric	6-20-28
Dominuque Natty	8-2-1896
Donald Barbara	2-9-42
Donegan Dorothy	4-6-24
Dorham Kenny	8-30-24
Drew Kenny	8-28-28
Duke George	1-12-46
Duncan Hank	10-26-1894
Duran Eddie	9-6-25
Durham Eddie	8-19-06
Eager Allen	1-10-27
Eldridge Roy	1-29-11
Ellis Don	7-25-34
Ellis Herb	8-4-21

Ervin Booker	10-31-30
Etri Bus	1917
Eubanks Kevin	11-15-57
Evans Bill	8-16-29
Evans Frank	10-1-36
Evans Sue	7-7-51
Farlow Tal	6-7-21
Farmer Art	8-21-28
Fatool Nick	1-2-15
Ferguson Maynard	5-4-28
Flanagan Tommy	3-16-30
Fountain Pete	7-3-30
Gafa Al	4-9-41
Gaillard Slim	1-4-16
Galbraith Barry	12-18-19
Gale Eric	9-20-38
Galper Hal	4-18-38
Garcia Dick	5-11-31
Gardner Jumbo	8-14-03
Garland Red	5-13-23
Garner Erroll	6-15-21
Garrison Arv	8-17-22
Getz Stan	2-2-27
Gibbs Terry	10-13-24
Gillespie Dizzy	10-21-17
Giuffre Jimmy	4-26-21
Glenn Tyree	11-23-12
Gonsalves Paul	7-12-20
Gordon Dexter	2-27-23
Gourley Jimmy	6-9-26
Grappelli Stephane	1-26-08
Graves Milford	8-20-41
Gray Wardell	2-13-21
Green Freddie	3-31-11
Green Grant	6-6-31
Greer Sonny	12-13-03
Griffin Johnny	4-24-28
Grosz Marty	2-28-30
Guarnieri Johnny	3-23-17
Guy Fred	5-23-1899
Hackett Bobby	1-31-15
Haden Charlie	8-6-37
Hahn Jerry	9-21-40
Haig Al	7-22-24
Hall Edmond	5-15-01
Hall Jim	12-4-30

Hamilton Chico	9-21-21
Hamilton Jimmy	5-25-17
Hampton Lionel	4-12-13
Hancock Herbie	4-12-40
Harriott Joe	7-15-28
Harris Barry	12-15-29
Harris Beaver	4-20-36
Harris Bill	4-14-25
Harrison Jimmy	10-17-00
Hawes Hampton	11-13-28
Hawkins Coleman	11-21-04
Hayes Louis	5-31-37
Hayes Tubby	1-30-35
Haynes Roy	3-13-26
Heath Percy	4-30-23
Hemphill Julius	1-24-38
Henderson Horace	11-22-04
Henderson Joe	4-24-37
Hendrickson Al	5-10-20
Henry Ernie	9-3-26
Heywood Eddie	12-4-26
Higgins Billy	10-11-36
Hill Andrew	6-30-37
Hines Earl 'Fatha'	12-28-05
Hinton Milt	6-23-10
Hirt Al	11-7-22
Hodes Art	11-4-14
Holt Red	5-16-32
Hope Elmo	6-27-23
Horn Shirley	5-1-34
Howard Darnell	7-25-00
Howell Michael	10-8-43
Hubbard Freddie	4-7-38
Hucko Peanuts	4-7-18
Hutcherson Bobby	1-27-41
Isaacs Ike	12-1-19
Jackson Milt	1-1-23
Jackson Quentin	1-13-09
Jamal Ahmad	7-2-30
Jarman Joseph	9-14-37
Jarrett Keith	5-8-45
Jefferson Hilton	7-30-03
Jenkins Leroy	3-11-32
Johnson Bunk	12-27-1879
Johnson Gus	11-15-13
Johnson J J	1-22-24

Johnson James P	2-1-1891
Jones Elvin	9-9-27
Jones Hank	7-13-18
Jones Jo	10-7-11
Jones Jonah	12-31-09
Jordan Duke	4-1-22
Jordan Stanley	7-31-59
Jordan Steve	1-15-19
Kay Connie	4-27-27
Kessel Barney	10-17-23
Kirk Rahsaan Roland	8-7-36
Klugh Earl	9-16-53
Kress Carl	10-20-07
Krupa Gene	1-15-09
Kuhn Steve	3-24-38
Kyle Billy	7-14-14
Lacy Steve	7-23-34
Lake Oliver	9-14-42
Lamare Nappy	6-14-07
Land Harold	12-18-28
Lang Eddie	10-25-02
Larkins Ellis	5-15-23
LaRoca Pete	4-7-38
Lewis George	7-13-00
Lewis George	7-14-52
Lewis John	5-3-20
Lewis Meade Lux	9-4-05
Lewis Ramsey	5-27-35
Little Booker	4-2-38
Lloyd Charles	3-15-39
Lovano Joe	12-29-52
Lowe Frank	6-24-43
Lowe Mundell	4-21-22
Lyttelton Humphrey	5-23-21
Mairants Ivor	7-18-08
Mangione Chuck	11-29-40
Mangione Gap	7-31-38
Mann Herbie	4-16-30
Manne Shelly	6-11-20
Manone Wingy	2-13-04
Mantler Mike	8-10-43
Marmarosa Dodo	12-12-25
Marsalis Branford	8-26-60
Marsalis Ellis	11-14-34
Marsalis Wynton	10-18-61
Marsh Warne	10-26-27

Marshall Jack	11-23-21
Martino Pat	8-25-44
Mastren Carmen	10-6-13
Maxted Billy	1-21-17
McGregor Chris	12-24-36
McLean Jackie	5-17-32
McPartland Jimmy	3-15-07
McPartland Marian	3-20-18
McPhee Joe	1-3-39
Metheny Pat	8-12-54
Miley Bubber	4-3-03
Miller 'Kid Punch'	6-14-1894
Mingus Charles	4-22-22
Mitchell George	8-3-1899
Mitchell Roscoe	8-3-40
Mobley Hank	7-7-30
Mole Muff	3-11-1898
Moncur Grachan III	6-3-37
Monk Thelonius	10-10-20
Monterose J R	1-19-27
Montgomery Wes	3-6-23
Moody James	2-26-25
Moore Oscar	12-25-16
Morello Joe	7-17-28
Morgan Lee	7-10-38
Morton Jelly Roll	9-20-1885
Motian Paul	3-25-31
Mulligan Gerry	4-6-27
Murphy Turk	12-16-15
Murray David	2-19-55
Murray Sunny	9-21-37
Napoleon Marty	6-2-21
Napoleon Teddy	1-23-14
Navarro Fats	9-24-23
Nelson Oliver	6-4-32
Newton Frankie	1-4-06
Nicholas Albert	5-27-00
Nicholas Wooden Joe	9-23-1883
Nichols Herbie	12-3-19
Noone Jimmie	4-23-1895
Oliver King	5-11-1885
Ory Kid	12-25-1886
Osborne Mary	7-17-21
Osborne Mike	9-28-41
Page Hot Lips	1-27-08
Palmier Remo	3-29-23

Parenti Tony	8-6-00
Parker Charlie 'Bird'	8-29-20
Parker Evan	4-5-44
Parker Leo	4-18-25
Pass Joe	1-13-29
Pastorius Jaco	12-1-51
Paul Les	6-9-16
Pepper Art	9-1-25
Perkins Carl	8-16-28
Peterson Oscar	8-15-25
Pettiford Oscar	9-30-22
Pisano John	2-6-31
Pizzarelli Bucky	1-9-26
Ponty Jean-Luc	9-29-42
Powell Baden	8-6-37
Powell Bud	9-27-24
Powell Mel	2-13-23
Pullen Don	12-25-41
Puma Joe	8-13-27
Quinn Snoozer	10-18-06
Raney Jimmy	8-20-27
Ranglin Ernest	1933
Redman Dewey	5-17-31
Redman Joshua	2-1-69
Reinhardt Django	1-23-10
Remus Alfredo	11-9-38
Reuss Allan	6-15-15
Rich Buddy	6-30-17
Ritenour Lee	1-11-52
Rivers Sam	9-25-30
Rizzi Tony	4-16-23
Roach Max	1-10-24
Roberts Howard	10-2-29
Roberts Marcus	8-7-63
Robinson Jim	12-25-1890
Rodgers Nile	9-19-52
Rogers Shorty	4-14-24
Rollini Adrian	6-28-04
Rollins Sonny	9-7-29
Rosewoman Michele	3-19-53
Rosollino Frank	8-20-26
Rowles Jimmy	8-19-18
Rudd Roswell	11-17-35
Ruiz Hilton	5-29-52
Rushen Patrice	9-30-54
Russell George	6-23-23

Russell Luis	8-6-02	Stewart Slam	9-21-14
Russell Pee Wee	3-27-06	Stitt Sonny	2-2-24
Rypdal Terje	8-23-47	Strayhorn Billy	11-29-15
Salvador Sal	11-21-25	Sullivan Joe	11-4-06
Sample Joe	2-1-39	Sun Ra	5-22-14
Sanders Pharoah	10-13-40	Surman John	4-30-44
Schuller Gunther	11-22-25	Sutton Ralph	11-4-22
Schuur Diane	12-10-53	Szabo Gabor	3-8-36
Scobey Bob	12-9-16	Tatum Art	10-13-10
Scofield John	12-26-51	Taylor Art	4-6-29
Scott Bud	1-11-1890	Taylor Billy	7-24-21
Scott Hazel	6-11-20	Taylor Cecil	3-15-33
Scott Ronnie	1-28-27	Teagarden Charlie	7-19-13
Scott-Heron Gil	4-1-49	Teagarden Jack	8-20-05
Seaman Phil	8-28-28	Templeton Alec	7-4-10
Sete Bola	7-16-28	Teschemacher Frank	3-14-06
Shank Bud	5-27-26	Themen Art	11-26-39
Sharrock Sonny	8-27-40	Thielemans Toots	4-29-22
Shearing George	8-13-19	Thomas Rene	2-25-27
Sheldon Jack	11-30-31	Threadgill Henry	2-15-44
Shepp Archie	5-24-37	Tjader Cal	7-16-25
Shirley Jimmy	5-31-13	Tolliver Charles	3-6-42
Shorter Wayne	8-25-33	Tough Davey	4-26-08
Silver Horace	9-28-28	Towner Ralph	3-1-40
Simeon Omer	7-21-02	Tracey Stan	12-30-26
Simmons Sonny	8-4-33	Trenner Donn	3-10-27
Sims Zoot	10-29-25	Tristano Lennie	3-19-19
Singleton Zutty	5-14-1898	Turner Bruce	7-5-22
Smeck Roy	2-6-00	Turrentine Stanley	4-5-34
Smith Floyd	1-25-17	Tyner McCoy	12-11-38
Smith Jabbo	12-24-08	Upchurch Phil	7-19-41
Smith Joe	6-28-02	VanEps George	8-7-13
Smith Johnny	6-25-22	Ventura Charlie	12-2-16
Smith Stuff	8-14-09	Venuti Joe	9-16-03
Smith Willie 'The Lion'	11-23-1897	Viola Al	6-16-19
Solal Martial	8-23-27	Vitous Miroslav	12-6-47
South Eddie	11-27-04	Waldron Mal	8-16-26
Spanier Muggsy	11-9-06	Waller Fats	5-21-04
Spann Les	5-23-32	Wallington George	10-27-24
St Cyr Johnny	4-17-1890	Watson Leo	2-27-1898
Stacy Jess	8-11-04	Wayne Chuck	2-27-23
Steig Jeremy	9-23-42	Wells Dicky	6-10-07
Stevens John	6-10-40	Wellstood Dick	11-25-27
Stewart Jimmy	9-8-37	Westbrook Mike	3-21-36
Stewart Louis	1-5-44	Weston Randy	4-6-26
Stewart Rex	2-22-07	Whetsol Arthur	1905

White Hy	12-17-15	Brown Gatemouth	4-18-24
Wilber Bob	3-15-28	Brown Henry	7-25-06
Wilkins Jack	6-3-44	Butterfield Paul	12-17-42
Williams Clarence	10-8-1893	Byrd Roy 'Prof Longhair'	12-19-18
Williams Cootie	7-24-08	Cannon Gus	9-12-1883
Williams Mary Lou	5-8-10	Carr Leroy	3-27-05
Williams Tony	12-12-45	Carr Sam	4-17-26
Wilson Dick	11-11-11	Cephas John	9-4-30
Wilson Teddy	11-24-12	Collins Albert	10-1-32
Winding Kai	5-18-22	Copeland Johnny	3-27-37
Woods Phil	11-2-31	Cotton James	7-1-35
Wright Frank	7-9-35	Cray Robert	8-1-53
Wright Gene	5-29-23	Davis Blind John	12-7-13
Wyble Jimmy	1-25-22	Davis Larry	12-4-36
Young Eldee	1-7-36	Dawkins Jimmy	10-24-36
Young Lester	8-27-09	Diddley Bo	12-30-28
Zawinul Joe	7-7-32	Dixon Floyd	2-8-29
Zoller Attila	6-13-27	Dixon Willie	7-1-15
		Dupree Champion Jack	7-23-09
* * * * * * * * * * * * * * * *		Earl Ronnie	3-10-53
BLUES MUSICIANS		Edwards Honeyboy	6-28-15
Allison Luther	8-17-39	Frost Frank	4-15-36
Alexander Dave	3-10-38	Fuller Blind Boy	7-10-07
Ammons Albert	9-23-07	Fulson Lowell	3-31-21
Archibald (Gross)	9-14-12	Funderburgh Anson	11-14-54
Arnold Billy Boy	9-16-35	Geremia Paul	4-21-44
Arnold Kokomo	2-15-01	Grimes Tiny	7-7-16
Ball Marcia	3-20-49	Grossman Stefan	4-16-45
Barnes Booba	9-25-36	Guitar Slim	12-10-26
Bartholomew Dave	12-24-20	Guy Buddy	7-30-36
Bell Carey	11-14-36	Handy W C	11-16-1873
Bell Lurrie	12-13-58	Harpo Slim	1-11-24
Below Fred	9-16-26	Helfer Erwin	1-20-36
Bennett Wayne	12-13-33	Hite Bob	2-26-45
Bloomfield Mike	7-28-44	Hooker Earl	1-15-30
Blumenfeld Roy	5-11-44	Hooker John Lee	8-17-20
Bond Graham	10-28-37	Hopkins Lightnin'	3-15-12
Bonner Juke Boy	3-22-32	Horton Big Walter	4-6-17
Booker James	12-17-39	House Son	3-21-02
Boyd Eddie	11-25-14	Howlin' Wolf (Burnett)	6-10-10
Bradford Perry	2-14-1893	James Elmore	1-27-18
Bradshaw Tiny	9-23-05	Jeffery Robert	1-14-15
Branch Billy	10-3-53	Johnson Johnnie	7-8-24
Brenston Jackie	8-15-30	Johnson Lonnie	2-8-1889
Brooks Lonnie	12-18-33	Johnson Pete	3-25-04
Brown Andrew	2-25-37	Johnson Robert	5-8-11
Brown Charles	9-13-22		

Blues Musicians Joh-Rob

Johnson Tommy	1896
Jones Floyd	7-21-17
Kalb Danny	9-19-42
Katz Steve	5-9-45
Kooper Al	2-5-44
King Albert	4-25-23
King B B	9-16-25
King Curtis (Ousley)	2-7-34
King Freddie	9-3-34
Korner Alexis	4-19-28
Kulberg Andy	4-30-44
Ladnier Tommy	5-28-00
Lay Sam	3-20-35
Lazy Lester (Johnson)	6-20-33
Lenoir J B	3-5-29
Lewis Furry	3-6-1893
Lewis Noah	9-3-1895
Lightnin' Slim (Hicks)	3-13-13
Little Walter (Jacobs)	5-1-30
Lockwood Robert Jr	3-27-15
Love Willie	11-4-06
Luandrew Sunnyland Slim	9-5-07
Magic Sam (Maghett)	2-14-37
Magic Slim (Holt)	8-7-37
McClennan Tommy	4-8-08
McCoy Charlie	5-26-09
McCoy Joe	5-11-05
McCracklin Jimmy	8-13-21
McDowell Mississippi Fred	1-12-04
McGhee Brownie	11-30-15
McTell Blind Willie	5-5-01
Memphis Slim (Chapman)	9-3-15
Milburn Amos	4-1-27
Milton Roy	7-31-07
Montgomery Little Brother	4-18-06
Musselwhite Charlie	1-31-44
Nighthawk Robert	11-30-09
Nix Willie	8-6-22
Otis Johnny	12-28-21
Perkins Pinetop	7-7-13
Perryman Speckled Red	10-23-1892
Price Sammy	10-6-08
Ragusa Pete	3-8-49
Reed Jimmy	9-6-25
Robillard Duke	10-4-48
Robinson Fenton	9-23-35

Blues Musicians Rog-Z

Rogers Jimmy	6-3-24
Rush Otis	4-29-34
Seals Son	8-13-42
Shade Will	2-5-1898
Shines Johnny	4-15-15
Smith Harmonica	4-22-24
Smith Huey 'Piano'	1-26-34
Smith J T 'Funny Papa'	1885
Smith Jimmy	12-8-25
Smith Pinetop	1-11-04
Smith Moses 'Whispering'	1-25-32
Spann Otis	3-21-30
Stackhouse Houston	9-28-10
Sumlin Hubert	11-16-31
Sykes Roosevelt	1-31-06
Taylor Eddie	1-29-23
Taylor Hound Dog	4-12-17
Taylor Larry	6-26-42
Terry Sonny	10-24-12
Thackery Jimmy	5-19-53
Tucker Luther	1-20-36
Ulmer James Blood	2-2-42
Vaughan Jimmie	3-20-51
Vaughan Stevie Ray	10-3-54
Vestine Henry	12-24-44
Vinson Eddie 'Cleanhead'	12-18-17
Walker T-Bone	5-28-10
Waters Muddy	4-14-15
Watson Johnny 'Guitar'	2-3-35
Weaver Curley	3-25-06
Wells Junior	12-9-34
Wenner Mark	11-2-48
Wheatstraw Peetie	12-21-02
White Bukka	11-12-09
Whittaker Tampa Red	12-25-00
Wilkins Joe Willie	1-7-23
Williams Big Joe	10-16-03
Williams Paul 'Hucklebuck'	7-13-15
Williamson Homesick James	5-3-05
Williamson Sonny Boy	3-30-14
Wilson Alan	7-4-43
Wilson Kim	1-6-51
Witherspoon Jimmy	8-8-23
Yancey Jimmy	2-20-1898
Young Johnny	1-1-18
Zukowski Jan	7-10-50

****

BIG BAND MUSICIANS

Alpert Trigger	9-3-16
Anderson Cat	9-12-16
Bauduc Ray	6-18-09
Beneke Tex	2-12-14
Berman Sonny	4-21-25
Berry Emmett	7-23-15
Best Johnny	10-20-13
Bishop Joe	11-27-07
Blanton Jimmy	1918
Bose Sterling	2-23-06
Brooks Randy	3-28-17
Brown Lawrence	8-3-07
Brown Vernon	1-6-07
Caceres Ernie	11-22-11
Candoli Pete	6-23-23
Carney Harry	4-1-10
Carruthers Jock	5-27-10
Castle Lee	2-28-15
Cooper Bob	12-6-25
Corcoran Corky	7-28-24
Cornelius Corky	12-3-14
Covington Warren	8-7-21
Cutshall Cutty	12-29-11
Davis Pat	5-26-09
Dickenson Vic	8-6-06
Dixon Joe	4-21-17
Dunham Sonny	11-16-14
Edison Harry	10-10-15
Elman Ziggy	5-26-14
Erwin Peewee	5-30-13
Fazola Irving	12-10-10
Freeman Bud	4-13-06
Gentry Chuck	12-14-11
Gifford Gene	5-31-08
Gozzo Conrad	2-6-22
Griffin Chris	10-31-15
Hardwicke Toby	5-31-04
Harris Bill	10-28-16
Haymer Herbie	7-24-15
Herfurt Skeets	5-28-11
Higginbotham J C	5-11-06
Hill Teddy	12-7-09
Hite Les	2-13-03
Hodges Johnny	7-25-06
Hunt Peewee	5-10-07

****

Hutchenrider Clarence	6-13-08
Jackson Chubby	10-25-18
Jacquet Illinois	10-31-22
Jenney Jack	5-12-10
Jerome Jerry	6-19-12
Johnson Buddy	1-10-15
Jones Thad	3-28-23
Jordan Louis	7-8-08
Jurgens Dick	11-9-11
Kaminsky Max	9-7-08
Kazebier Nate	8-13-12
Killian Al	10-15-16
Kirby John	12-31-08
Kirk Andy	5-28-1898
Klein Manny	2-4-08
Klink Al	12-28-15
Lamond Don	8-18-20
Lawson Yank	5-3-11
Lee Sonny	8-26-04
Leonard Harlan	7-2-05
Lewis Ed	1-22-09
Lombardo Carmen	7-16-03
Marsala Joe	1-4-07
Matthews Dave	6-6-11
Maxwell Jimmy	1-9-17
McEachern Murray	8-16-15
McGarity Lou	7-22-17
McGhee Howard	3-6-18
McKusick Hal	6-1-24
Miller Eddie	6-23-11
Mince Johnny	7-8-12
Minor Dan	8-10-09
Mondello Toots	1912
Mooney Joe	3-14-11
Morton Benny	1-31-07
Mundy Jimmy	6-28-07
Musso Vido	1-13-13
Nance Ray	12-10-13
Nanton Joe	2-1-04
Page Walter	2-9-00
Peterson Chuck	1915
Phillips Flip	3-26-15
Privin Bernie	2-12-19
Procope Russell	8-11-08
Purtill Moe	5-4-16
Richman Boomie	4-2-21

****

Rodin Gil	12-9-06
Rodney Red	9-27-27
Rollini Arthur	2-13-12
Russin Babe	6-18-11
Safranski Eddie	12-25-18
Sampson Edgar	8-31-07
Sargent Kenny	3-3-06
Sears Al	2-21-10
Shavers Charlie	8-3-17
Sherock Shorty	11-17-15
Shertzer Hymie	4-2-09
Slack Freddy	8-7-10
Smith Howard	10-19-10
Smith Tab	1-11-09
Smith Warren	5-4-32
Smith Willie	11-25-10
Tanner Paul	10-15-17
Tate Buddy	2-22-15
Teagarden Charlie	7-19-13
Terry Clark	12-14-30
Thompson Lucky	6-16-24
Tizol Juan	1-22-00
Travis Nick	11-16-25
Trumbauer Frankie	5-30-01
Warren Earle	7-1-14
Washington Jack	7-17-10
Watts Grady	6-30-08
Webster Ben	3-27-09
Webster Freddie	1916
Webster Paul	8-24-09
Weiss Sid	4-30-14
Wells Henry	1906
Wess Frank	1-4-22
Wettling George	11-28-07
Young Snooky	2-3-19
Young Trummy	1-12-12
Zarchy Zeke	6-12-15
Zurke Bob	1-17-12

****

POPULAR MUSICIANS

Adler Larry	2-10-14
Alpert Herb	3-31-35
Bent Fabric	12-7-24
Bilk Acker	1-28-29
Black Bill	9-17-26
Borge Victor	1-3-09

Bryant Willie	8-30-08
Caiola Al	9-7-20
Case Peter	1952
Clayderman Richard	12-28-53
Clayton Adam	3-13-60
Connors Norman	3-1-48
Denny Martin	4-10-21
Doggett Bill	2-16-16
Dragon Daryl	8-27-42
Duchin Eddy	4-1-09
Duchin Peter	7-28-37
Feinstein Michael	9-7-56
Feliciano Jose	9-10-45
Ferrante Arthur	9-7-21
Fleck Bela	1953
Floren Myron	11-5-19
Hammer Jan	4-17-48
Hayman Richard	3-27-20
Howard Bart	6-1-15
Ingmann Jorgen	4-26-25
Jones Quincy	3-14-33
Justis Bill	10-14-26
Kaempfert Bert	10-16-23
Kottke Leo	9-11-45
Levant Oscar	12-27-06
Liberace	5-16-19
Liberace George	7-31-11
Masekela Hugh	4-4-39
McFerrin Bobby	3-11-50
Meco (Monardo)	11-29-39
Montenegro Hugo	1925
Morath Max	10-1-26
Mottola Tony	4-18-18
Nero Peter	5-22-34
Randolph Boots	6-3-25
Short Bobby	9-15-26
Smith Ethel	11-22-10
Teicher Louis	8-24-24
Toussaint Allen	1-14-38
Troup Bobby	10-18-18
Walter Cy	9-16-25
Washington Grover Jr	12-12-43
Williams Mason	8-24-38
Williams Roger	10-1-26
Yankovic Frankie	7-28-15
Zabach Florian	8-15-21

****

********************************* | *********************************

BANDLEADERS

Alexander Jeff	7-2-10	Flanagan Ralph	4-7-19
Anthony Ray	1-20-22	Garber Jan	11-5-1895
Arnheim Gus	9-11-1897	Goldkette Jean	3-18-1899
August Jan	1912	Goodman Al	8-12-1890
Auld Georgie	5-19-19	Goodman Benny	5-30-09
Ayres Mitchell	12-24-10	Gray Glen	6-7-06
Barnet Charlie	10-26-13	Hawkins Erskine	7-26-14
Barron Blue	3-22-11	Hayton Lennie	2-13-08
Basie Count	8-21-06	Heidt Horace	5-21-01
Baxter Les	3-14-22	Henderson Fletcher	12-18-1897
Berigan Bunny	11-2-09	Henderson Skitch	1-27-18
Bernie Ben	5-30-1891	Herman Woody	5-16-13
Bestor Don	9-23-1889	Holmes Leroy	9-22-13
Bleyer Archie	6-12-09	Hopkins Claude	8-3-03
Bloch Ray	8-3-02	Hutton Ina Ray	3-13-17
Bradley Will	7-12-12	Hyman Dick	3-8-27
Brown Les	3-12-12	James Harry	3-15-16
Busse Henry	5-19-1894	Jenkins Gordon	5-12-10
Byrne Bobby	10-10-18	Jones Isham	1-31-1894
Calloway Cab	12-25-07	Jones Spike	12-14-11
Carle Frankie	3-25-03	Kaye Sammy	3-13-10
Carter Benny	8-8-07	Kemp Hal	3-27-05
Carroll David	10-15-13	Kenton Stan	2-19-12
Cavallero Carmen	5-6-13	King Wayne	2-16-01
Chacksfield Frank	5-9-14	Kyser Kay	6-18-06
Clinton Larry	8-17-09	Lanin Lester	8-26-11
Conniff Ray	11-6-16	Lavalle Paul	9-6-08
Crosby Bob	8-23-13	Lawrence Elliot	2-14-25
Davis Meyer	1-10-1895	Lewis Ted	6-6-1892
DeLange Eddie	1-2-04	Light Enoch	8-18-07
DeLugg Milton	12-2-18	Little 'Little Jack'	5-28-00
DeVol Frank	9-20-11	Lombardo Guy	6-19-02
Donahue Sam	3-8-18	Lopez Vincent	12-30-1898
Dorsey Jimmy	2-29-04	Lunceford Jimmie	6-6-02
Dorsey Tommy	11-19-05	Lyman Abe	8-4-1897
Dragon Carmen	7-28-14	Mantovani (Annunzio)	11-5-05
Dunham Sonny	1914	Marterie Ralph	12-24-14
Elgart Larry	3-20-22	Martin Freddy	12-9-06
Elgart Les	8-3-18	Maupin Rex	11-25-1886
Ellington Duke	4-29-1899	McCoy Clyde	12-29-03
Ellington Mercer	3-11-19	McGriff Jimmy	4-3-36
Engel Lehman	9-12-10	McIntyre Hal	11-29-14
Faith Percy	4-7-08	McKinley Ray	6-18-10
Fields Shep	9-12-10	McKinney William	9-17-1895
FioRito Ted	12-20-00	McShann Jay	1-12-16
		Melachrino George	5-1-09

****

Miller Glenn	3-1-04	**ARRANGERS**	
Miller Mitch	7-4-11	Alexander Van	5-2-15
Millinder Lucky	8-8-00	Burke Sonny	3-22-14
Mooney Art	2-4-11	Burns Ralph	6-29-22
Morgan Russ	4-28-04	Camarata Tutti	5-11-13
Morrow Buddy	2-8-19	Challis Bill	7-8-04
Moten Bennie	11-13-1894	Evans Gil	5-13-12
Napoleon Phil	9-2-01	Finegan Bill	4-3-17
Newson Tommy	2-25-29	Fuller Gil	4-14-20
Nichols Red	5-8-05	Gray Jerry	7-3-15
Noble Ray	12-17-03	Haggart Bob	3-13-14
Norvo Red	3-31-08	Hefti Neal	10-29-22
Pastor Tony	10-26-07	Hudson Will	3-8-08
Pollack Ben	6-22-03	Johnson Budd	12-14-10
Powell Teddy	3-1-06	Jones Dick	5-1-06
Prima Louis	12-7-12	Kincaide Deane	3-18-11
Raeburn Boyd	10-27-13	Mandel Johnny	11-23-35
Petrillo Caesar	8-1-1898	Matlock Matty	4-27-07
Rey Alvino	7-1-11	May Billy	11-10-16
Rose David	6-15-10	Oliver Sy	12-17-10
Rubinoff Dave	9-3-1897	Redman Don	7-29-00
Savitt Jan	9-4-13	Riddle Nelson	6-1-21
Scott Raymond	9-10-09	Rugulo Pete	12-25-15
Severinsen Doc	7-7-27	Sauter Eddie	12-2-14
Shaffer Paul	11-28-49	Wagner Larry	9-15-07
Shaw Artie	5-23-10	**✶✶✶✶✶✶✶✶✶✶✶✶✶✶✶✶**	
Sissle Noble	7-10-1889	**JAZZ & BLUES SINGERS**	
Sosnik Harry	7-13-06	Ace Johnny	6-9-29
Spitalny Phil	11-7-1890	Adams Faye	1932
Spivak Charlie	2-17-06	Adams Johnny	1-5-32
Sylvern Henry	3-26-08	Agee Ray	4-10-30
Thornhill Claude	8-10-08	Alexandria Lorez	8-14-29
Trotter John Scott	6-14-08	Anderson Ernestine	11-11-28
Tucker Orrin	2-17-11	Anderson Ivie	7-10-05
Tucker Tommy	5-18-08	Babs Alice	1-26-24
VanSteeden Peter	4-13-04	Bailey Mildred	2-27-07
Vaughn Billy	4-12-19	Baldry Long John	1-12-41
Warnick Clay	12-14-15	Barton Lou Ann	2-17-54
Warnow Mark	4-10-02	Belle Regina	7-17-63
Webb Chick	2-10-02	Belvin Jesse	12-15-33
Weems Ted	9-26-01	Bennett Betty	10-23-21
Welk Lawrence	3-11-03	Boone Richard	2-23-30
Weston Paul	3-12-12	Bridgewater DeeDee	5-27-50
Whiteman Paul	3-28-1891	Broonzy Big Bill	6-26-1893
Winterhalter Hugo	8-15-09	Brown Nappy	10-12-29
Zentner Si	6-13-17	Brown Olive	8-30-22

Brown Roy	9-10-25
Bryant Beulah	2-20-18
Carlisle Una Mae	12-26-15
Carroll Jeanne	1-15-31
Carter Betty	5-16-29
Christy June	11-20-25
Clay Otis	2-11-42
Connor Chris	11-8-27
Cox Ida	2-25-1896
Crudup Arthur 'Big Boy'	8-24-05
Davis Kay	12-5-20
Eckstine Billy	7-8-14
Estes Sleepy John	1-25-04
Fitzgerald Ella	4-25-18
Gonzales Babs	10-27-19
Green Lillian	12-22-19
Harris Wynonie	8-24-15
Hibbler Al	8-16-15
Hill Bertha 'Chippie'	3-15-05
Hill Z Z	9-30-35
Holiday Billie	4-7-15
Horne Lena	6-30-17
Humes Helen	6-23-13
Hunter Alberta	4-1-1895
Hurt Mississippi John	7-3-1893
James Skip	6-9-02
Jarreau Al	3-12-40
Johnson Ella	6-22-23
Jones Etta	11-25-28
Jordan Sheila	11-18-28
Kelly Jo-Ann	1-5-44
King Morgana	6-4-30
Kittrell Jean	6-27-27
Krog Karin	5-15-37
Laine Cleo	10-28-27
LaSalle Denise	7-16-39
Lee Julia	10-31-02
Lincoln Abbey	8-6-30
Mayfield Percy	8-12-20
McCorkle Susannah	1-1-49
McRae Carmen	4-8-22
Memphis Minnie (Douglas)	6-3-1897
Merrill Helen	7-21-29
Murphy Mark	3-14-32
Myers Amina Claudine	3-21-43
O'Day Anita	12-18-19

Olay Ruth	7-1-27
Parker Junior	3-27-32
Patterson Ottilie	1-31-32
Price Kerry	3-6-39
Rainey Gertrude 'Ma'	4-26-1886
Redd Vi	9-20-28
Richards Ann	10-1-35
Ross Annie	7-25-30
Rushing Jimmy	8-26-03
Scott Little Jimmy	7-17-25
Simone Nina	2-21-33
Smith 'Big Maybelle'	5-1-24
Smith Bessie	4-15-1894
Smith Carrie	8-25-41
Smith Mamie	5-26-1883
Spann Lucille	6-23-38
Spivey Victoria	10-15-06
Staton Dakota	6-3-32
Strehli Angela	11-22-45
Sullivan Maxine	5-13-11
Taylor Koko	9-28-35
Taylor Little Johnny	2-11-43
Thomas Rufus	3-26-17
Thornton Willie Mae	12-11-26
Turner Big Joe	5-18-11
Vaughan Sarah	3-27-24
Vinson Walter	2-2-01
Wallace Sippie	11-11-1898
Washington Dinah	8-29-24
Webster Katie	9-1-39
Waters Ethel	10-31-1897
Wiley Lee	10-9-15
Williams Joe	12-12-18
Wilson Cassandra	12-4-55
Wilson Edith	9-2-06
Winstone Norma	9-23-41
Wright Marva	3-20-48
Wright O V	10-9-39

****

TORCH SINGERS

Etting Ruth	11-23-1897
Holman Libby	5-23-06
Morgan Helen	8-2-00
Morse Lee	1900
Piaf Edith	12-19-15
Roth Lillian	12-13-10

BIG BAND SINGERS

Arnell Amy	1918
Babbitt Harry	11-2-13
Baker Bonnie	1918
Bowlly Al	1-7-1899
Brito Phil	9-15-15
Carroll Bob	6-18-18
Carroll Georgia	11-18-19
Carson Mindy	7-16-27
Clark Buddy	7-26-12
Clooney Rosemary	5-23-28
Como Perry	5-18-13
Copeland Alan	10-6-26
Cornell Don	4-21-19
Davis Johnny 'Scat'	1910
Dawn Dolly	2-3-19
Desmond Johnny	11-14-21
Dickinson Hal	12-12-13
Eberle Ray	1-19-19
Eberly Bob	7-24-16
Ennis Skinnay	8-13-09
Forrest Helen	4-12-18
Gibbs Georgia	8-26-23
Grayco Helen	1924
Haines Connie	1-20-22
Haymes Dick	9-13-16
Howard Eddy	9-12-09
Hutton Marion	3-10-19
Jeffries Herb	9-24-16
Kallen Kitty	5-25-23
Lane Abbe	12-14-32
Lee Peggy	5-26-20
Leonard Jack	1915
Lon Alice	1926
Martin Tony	12-25-12
McAfee Johnny	7-24-13
McCall Mary Ann	5-4-19
Morgan Marion	12-14-24
O'Connell Helen	5-23-20
Richmond June	7-9-15
Roche Betty	1-9-20
Russell Andy	9-16-20
Sherrill Joya	8-20-27
Shore Dinah	3-1-17
Simms Ginny	5-25-16
Sinatra Frank	12-12-15

Smith Keely	3-9-32
Stafford Jo	11-12-18
Starr Kay	7-21-22
Tilton Martha	11-14-15
Tomlin Pinky	9-9-07
Wain Bea	4-30-17
Ward Helen	9-19-16
Warren Fran	3-4-28
Wayne Frances	8-26-24

RADIO SINGERS

Antoine Josephine	10-27-08
Austin Gene	6-24-00
Baker Kenny	9-30-12
Crumit Frank	9-26-1889
Davis Janette	1924
Day Dennis	5-21-17
deLeath Vaughn	9-26-1896
DellaChiesa Vivian	10-9-15
Downey Morton	11-14-02
Dragonette Jessica	2-14-10
Edwards Joan	2-13-19
Ellis Anita	4-12-26
Gillham Art	1-1-1895
Hanshaw Annette	10-18-10
Hildegarde (Sell)	2-1-06
Jepson Helen	11-28-05
Kay Beatrice	1910
Langford Frances	4-4-13
Marvin Johnny	7-11-1897
Massey Curt	5-3-10
Melton James	1-2-04
Novis Donald	1906
Parker Frank	4-29-03
Pickens Jane	8-10-09
Ross Lanny	1-19-06
Sanderson Julia	8-20-1887
Smith Jack	11-16-18
Smith Kate	5-1-09
Thomas John Charles	9-6-1891
Todd Dick	1914
Tracy Arthur	6-3-03
Vallee Rudy	7-28-01

HAPPINESS BOYS

Hare Ernest	3-16-1883
Jones Billy	3-15-1889

CABARET SINGERS	
Akers Karen	10-13-45
Allyn David	7-19-23
Ames Nancy	9-30-37
Barnes Mae	1-23-07
Carpenter Thelma	1-15-22
Dardanelle (Breckenridge)	12-27-17
Dearie Blossom	4-28-26
deLuce Virginia	3-25-21
Dennis Matt	2-11-14
Frishberg Dave	3-23-33
Jackie (Cain)	5-22-28
Jones T C	10-26-20
King Teddi	9-18-29
Kirkwood James Jr	8-22-30
Kral Irene	1-18-32
Laurence Paula	1-25-16
London Julie	9-26-26
Loudon Dorothy	9-17-33
Mercer Mabel	2-3-00
Nelson Portia	5-27-20
Paris Jackie	9-20-26
Premice Josephine	7-21-26
Roy (Kral)	10-10-21
Sanders Felicia	1921
Scott Bobby	1-29-37
Southern Jeri	8-5-26
Syms Sylvia	1-6-34
Todd Art	3-11-20
Todd Dotty	6-22-23
Wilson Julie	10-21-24

POP SINGERS	
Adams Edie	4-16-29
Alberghetti Anna Maria	5-15-36
Alberts Al	8-10-22
Allen Peter	2-10-44
Ames Ed	7-9-27
Ames Gene	2-13-25
Ames Joe	5-3-24
Ames Vic	5-20-26
Andrews LaVerne	7-6-15
Andrews Maxene	1-3-18
Andrews Patti	2-16-20
Anton Susan	10-12-50
Arms Russell	2-3-29

Aznavour Charles	5-22-24
Bailey Pearl	3-29-18
Barton Eileen	11-24-29
Basil Toni	1950
Bassey Shirley	1-8-37
Belafonte Harry	3-1-27
Belland Bruce	10-26-36
Bennett Tony	8-3-26
Black Cilla	5-27-43
Bofill Angela	5-2-54
Boswell Connee	12-3-07
Branigan Laura	7-3-57
Brewer Teresa	5-7-31
Bryant Anita	3-25-40
Cantrell Lana	8-7-43
Cara Irene	3-18-59
Carpenter Karen	3-2-50
Carpenter Richard	10-15-46
Carr Vikki	7-19-40
Carroll Diahann	7-17-35
Chapin Harry	12-7-42
Chapman Tracy	3-30-64
Charo	1-15-41
Cherry Don	1-11-24
Clark Petula	11-15-32
Cole Nat King	3-17-19
Collins Dorothy	11-18-26
Columbo Russ	1-4-08
Connick Harry Jr	9-11-67
Corey Jill	9-30-35
Crewe Bob	11-12-31
Croce Jim	1-10-43
Dale Alan	7-9-26
Damone Vic	6-12-28
Dana Vic	8-26-42
Daniels Billy	9-12-15
Davidson John	12-13-41
Davis Sammy Jr	12-8-25
DeJohn Dux	1-21-33
DeJohn Julie	3-18-31
Dinning Ginger & Jean	3-29-24
Dinning Lou	9-29-22
Donegan Lonnie	4-29-31
Elliman Yvonne	12-29-51
Falana Lola	9-11-42
Finn Mickie	6-16-38

Pop Singers Fis-Luf

Fisher Eddie	8-10-28
Ford Mary	7-7-24
Fox Inez	9-9-42
Froman Jane	11-10-07
Gary John	11-29-32
Genevieve	4-17-30
Gilberto Astrud	3-30-40
Gorme Eydie	8-16-32
Grant Gogi	9-20-24
Gray Dobie	7-26-42
Greco Buddy	8-14-26
Heatherton Joey	9-14-44
Hill Dan	6-3-54
Ho Don	8-13-30
Houston Whitney	8-9-63
Hudson Bill	10-17-49
Hudson Brett	1-18-53
Hudson Mark	8-23-51
Humperdinck Engelbert	5-3-36
James Joni	9-22-30
Jeffries Fran	1939
Johansen David	1-8-50
Johnson Betty	3-16-32
Johnston Johnny	12-1-15
Jones Jack	1-14-38
Kane Helen	8-4-03
Kazan Lainie	5-16-40
King Peggy	2-16-30
Kitt Eartha	1-26-28
Laine Frankie	3-30-13
Lanson Snooky	4-27-14
LaRosa Julius	1-2-30
Lawrence Carol	9-5-32
Lawrence Steve	7-8-35
Lennon Dianne	12-1-39
Lennon Janet	6-15-46
Lennon Kathy	8-2-43
Lennon Peggy	4-8-41
Leonetti Tommy	9-10-29
Lewis Monica	5-5-25
Lind Bob	11-25-44
Longet Claudine	1-29-42
Lopez Trini	5-15-37
Lor Denise	5-3-29
Lowe Jim	5-7-27
Luft Lorna	11-21-52

Pop Singers Lyn-Sev

Lynn Vera	3-20-17
MacKenzie Gisele	1-10-27
Manchester Melissa	2-15-51
Manilow Barry	6-17-46
March Peggy	3-8-48
Marlowe Marion	3-7-29
Martin Dean	6-17-17
Martino Al	10-7-27
Mathis Johnny	9-30-35
McGovern Maureen	7-27-49
McGuire Christine	7-30-28
McGuire Dorothy	2-13-30
McGuire Phyllis	2-14-31
McKenzie Scott	10-1-44
McNair Barbara	3-4-34
Melanie (Safka)	2-3-47
Midler Bette	12-1-45
Mills Donald	4-29-15
Mills Harry	8-19-13
Mills Herbert	4-2-12
Mills John	2-11-1889
Mitchell Guy	2-22-25
Monroe Vaughn	10-7-11
Monte Lou	4-2-17
Moore Melba	10-29-45
Morgan Jane	1920
Morgan Jaye P	12-3-32
Mouskouri Nana	10-10-36
Near Holly	6-6-49
Newton Wayne	4-3-42
Nilsson Harry	6-15-41
Nixon Marni	2-22-29
O'Sullivan Gilbert	12-1-46
Oliver (Swofford)	2-22-45
Orlando Tony	4-3-44
Page Patti	11-8-27
Purim Flora	3-6-42
Quinn Carmel	1931
Ray Johnnie	1-10-27
Reddy Helen	10-25-41
Riperton Minnie	11-8-48
Rodgers Jimmie	9-18-33
Sadler Barry	11-5-41
Scarbury Joey	6-7-55
Secombe Harry	9-8-21
Seville David	1-27-19

Sherwood Roberta	7-1-12
Shocked Michelle	1963
Simms Lu Ann	1932
Sinatra Frank Jr	1-10-44
Sinatra Nancy	6-8-40
Small Millie	10-6-46
Sommers Joanie	2-24-41
Stevens April	4-29-36
Stevens Connie	8-8-38
Streisand Barbra	4-24-42
Sumac Yma	9-10-22
Taylor James	3-12-48
Taylor Livingston	11-21-50
Tempo Nino	1-6-37
Tennille Toni	5-8-43
Thompson Kay	11-9-13
Thompson Sue	7-19-26
Tiny Tim	4-12-22
Torme Mel	9-13-25
Tyler Bonnie	6-8-53
Uggams Leslie	5-25-43
Vale Jerry	7-8-32
Valente Caterina	1-14-31
Valli June	6-30-30
Vannelli Gino	6-16-52
Vaughan Frankie	2-3-28
Warwick Dionne	12-12-40
Weldon Joan	8-5-33
Weston Kim	12-20-39
Whitfield David	2-2-26
Whiting Margaret	7-22-24
Whittaker Roger	3-22-36
Williams Andy	12-3-28
Williams Vanessa	3-18-63
Wilson Dolores	7-31-26
Wilson Eileen	1-15-25
Wilson Nancy	2-20-37
Wright Martha	3-23-26
Wrightson Earl	1-1-16
Yankovic Weird Al	10-23-59
Yuro Timi	8-4-40
FOUR FRESHMEN	
Barbour Don	4-19-29
Barbour Ross	12-31-28
Errair Ken	1-23-30
Flanigan Bob	8-22-26

FOUR SEASONS	
DeVito Tommy	6-19-36
Gaudio Bob	11-17-42
Massi Nick	9-19-35
Valli Frankie	5-3-37
HI-LO's	
Burroughs Clark	3-3-30
Morse Robert	7-27-27
Puerling Eugene	3-31-29
Strasen Robert	4-1-28
INK SPOTS	
Fuqua Charlie	1911
Jones Orville	2-17-05
Kenny Bill	1915
Watson Ivory	1909
LETTERMEN	
Butala Tony	11-20-40
Engemann Bob	2-19-36
Pike Jim	11-6-38
MANHATTAN TRANSFER	
Bentyne Cheryl	1954
Hauser Tim	12-12-41
Paul Alan	1949
Siegel Janis	7-23-52
***************	
RHYTHM & BLUES/SOUL	
Acklin Barbara	2-28-43
Ashford Nickolas	5-4-42
Austin Patti	8-10-48
Baker Anita	1-26-58
Baker LaVern	11-11-29
Ballard Hank	11-18-36
Bass Fontella	7-3-40
Bell Archie	9-1-44
Bell Ricky	9-18-67
Bell William	7-16-39
Benton Brook	9-19-31
Bivins Michael	10-10-68
Bland Bobby 'Blue'	1-27-30
Booker T (Jones)	11-12-44
Brickley Shirley	12-9-44
Brown Bobby	2-5-69
Brown James	5-3-28
Brown Ruth	1-30-28
Bryson Peabo	4-13-51
Burke Solomon	1936

Burton Jenny	11-18-57
Butler Jerry	12-8-39
Campbell Tevin	11-19-78
Carey Jake	9-9-26
Carey Zeke	1-24-33
Carter Clarence	1-4-36
Carter Mel	4-22-43
Chandler Gene	7-6-37
Charles Ray	9-23-30
Cherry Neneh	8-10-64
Clark Dee	11-7-38
Clinton George	7-22-40
Cole Natalie	2-6-50
Collins Bootsy	10-26-51
Conley Arthur	1-4-46
Cooke Sam	1-22-31
Cornelius Billie Jo	1946
Cornelius Carter	1948
Cornelius Edward	1943
Cornelius Sister Rose	1947
Crawford Randy	2-18-52
Crothers Scatman	5-23-10
Dash Sarah	8-18-43
Dave (Prater)	5-9-37
Davis Spencer	7-17-38
Davis Tyrone	5-4-38
DeBarge Bunny	3-10-55
DeBarge El	6-4-61
DeBarge James	8-22-63
DeBarge Mark	6-19-59
DeBarge Randy	8-6-58
DeVoe Ronald	11-17-67
Doe Ernie K	2-22-36
Dorsey Lee	12-24-26
Dyson Ronnie	6-5-50
Edwards Tommy	2-17-22
Everett Betty	11-23-39
Flack Roberta	2-10-39
Floyd Eddie	6-25-35
Franklin Aretha	3-25-42
Freeman Bobby	6-13-40
Gaye Marvin	4-2-39
Graham Larry	8-14-46
Grant Earl	1-20-33
Greaves R B	11-28-44
Green Al	4-13-46

Hamilton Roy	4-16-29
Harrison Wilbert	1-6-29
Hart Wilbert	10-19-47
Hart William	1-17-45
Hathaway Donny	10-1-45
Hawkins Screamin' Jay	7-18-29
Hayes Isaac	8-20-42
Hendryx Nona	8-18-45
Henry Clarence 'Frogman'	3-19-37
Hunt Tommy	6-18-33
Hunter Ivory Joe	10-10-11
Ingram James	2-16-56
Ingram Luther	11-30-44
Isley O'Kelly	12-25-37
Isley Ronald	5-21-41
Isley Rudolph	4-1-39
Jackson Chuck	7-22-37
Jackson Jackie	5-4-51
Jackson Janet	5-16-66
Jackson Jermaine	12-11-54
Jackson LaToya	5-29-56
Jackson Marlon	3-12-57
Jackson Michael	8-29-58
Jackson Millie	7-15-43
Jackson Rebbie	5-29-50
Jackson Tito	10-15-53
James Etta	1-25-38
James Rick	2-1-52
John Little Willie	11-15-37
Johnson Marv	10-15-38
Jones Jimmy	6-2-37
Khan Chaka	3-23-53
King Ben E	9-28-38
King Evelyn 'Champagne'	6-1-60
LaBelle Patti	5-24-44
Lance Major	4-4-41
Lattisaw Stacy	11-25-66
Laws Ronnie	10-3-50
Lester Ketty	8-16-34
Levert Gerald	7-13-66
Levert Sean	9-28-68
Lewis Barbara	2-9-43
Lewis Bobby	2-17-33
Little Eva (Boyd)	6-29-45
Little Milton (Campbell)	9-7-34
Lovett Winfred 'Blue'	11-16-43

* *

Lutcher Nellie	10-15-15
Lymon Frankie	9-30-42
Mahal Taj	5-17-42
Mason Barbara	8-9-47
Mayfield Curtis	6-3-42
McCoy Van	1-6-44
McDaniels Gene	2-12-35
McPhatter Clyde	11-15-33
Melvin Harold	6-25-39
Miles Buddy	9-5-46
Morse Ella Mae	9-12-24
Nash Johnny	8-19-40
Nelson Nate	4-10-32
Neville Aaron	1-24-41
Ocean Billy	1-21-50
Osborne Jeffrey	3-9-48
Parker Ray Jr	5-1-54
Payne Freda	9-19-45
Peebles Ann	4-27-47
Pendergrass Teddy	3-26-50
Phillips Esther	12-23-35
Phillips Phil	3-14-31
Pickett Wilson	3-18-41
Pointer Anita	1-23-48
Pointer Bonnie	7-11-50
Pointer June	11-20-53
Pointer Ruth	3-19-46
Preston Billy	9-9-46
Price Lloyd	3-9-32
Prince	6-7-58
Prysock Arthur	1-2-29
Rawls Lou	12-1-36
Redding Otis	9-9-41
Reese Della	7-6-32
Reeves Martha	7-18-41
Richie Lionel	6-20-49
Ruffin Jimmy	5-7-39
Sade	1-16-59
Sam (Moore)	10-12-35
Scott Wallace & Walter	9-23-43
Sheila E (Escovedo)	12-12-59
Simon Joe	9-2-43
Simpson Valerie	8-26-46
Sledge Debbie	7-9-54
Sledge Joni	9-13-56
Sledge Kathy	1-6-59

Sledge Kim	8-21-57
Sledge Percy	11-25-41
Smith O C	6-21-32
Starr Edwin	1-21-42
Stone Sly	3-15-44
Swann Betty	10-24-44
Syreeta (Wright)	8-13-46
Tavares Butch	5-18-53
Tavares Chubby	6-2-50
Tavares Pooch	11-12-49
Tavares Ralph	12-10-48
Tavares Tiny	10-24-54
Taylor Johnnie	5-5-38
Taylor Sam the Man	10-25-34
Terrell Tammi	4-29-45
Tex Joe	8-8-33
Thomas Carla	12-21-42
Thomas Irma	2-18-41
Til Sonny	8-18-28
Troy Doris	1-6-37
Turner Ike	11-5-31
Turner Tina	11-26-39
Vandross Luther	4-20-51
Vega Tata	10-7-51
Wade Adam	3-17-37
Ward Billy	9-19-21
Watley Jody	1-30-59
Welch Lenny	5-15-38
Wells Mary	5-13-43
White Barry	9-12-44
Williams Billy	12-28-16
Williams Deniece	6-3-51
Williams Larry	5-10-35
Williams Tony	4-5-28
Willis Chuck	1-31-28
Wilson Al	6-19-39
Wilson Jackie	6-9-34
Wilson Paul	1-6-35
Winfield William	8-24-29
Withers Bill	7-4-38
Womack Bobby	3-4-44
Wonder Stevie	5-13-50
Wright Betty	12-21-53
Wright Norman	10-21-37
Wynne Philippe	4-3-41
Zulema	1-3-47

* *

COASTERS
Bright Ronnie	10-18-38
Carroll Earl 'Speedo'	11-2-37
Gardner Carl	4-29-28
Guy Billy	6-20-36

EARTH, WIND & FIRE
Bailey Phillip	5-8-51
Cleaves Jessica	1948
Dunn Larry	6-19-53
Graham Johnny	8-3-51
Johnson Ralph	7-4-51
McKay Alan	2-2-48
White Fred	1-13-55
White Maurice	12-19-41
White Verdine	7-25-51
Woolfolk Andrew	10-11-50

FIFTH DIMENSION
Davis Billy Jr	6-26-40
LaRue Florence	2-4-44
McCoo Marilyn	9-30-43
McLemore Lamonte	9-17-40
Townson Ron	1-20-41

FOUR TOPS
Benson Renaldo	1937
Fakir Duke	1938
Payton Lawrence	1938
Stubbs Levi	6-6-38

GLADYS KNIGHT & THE PIPS
Guest William	6-2-41
Knight Gladys	5-28-44
Knight Merald	9-4-42
Patten Edward	8-2-39

MIRACLES
Moore Warren 'Pete'	11-19-39
Robinson Smokey	2-19-40
Rogers Bobby	2-19-40
White Ronnie	4-5-39

O'JAYS
Levert Eddie	6-16-42
Strain Sam	12-9-41
Williams Walt	8-25-42

SHIRELLES
Alston Shirley	6-10-41
Harris Micky	1-22-40
Kenner Doris	8-2-41
Lee Beverly	8-3-41

SUPREMES
Ballard Florence	6-30-43
Birdsong Cindy	12-15-39
Ross Diana	3-26-44
Wilson Mary	3-7-44

TEMPTATIONS
Edwards Dennis	2-3-43
Franklin Melvin	10-12-42
Kendricks Eddie	12-17-40
Ruffin David	1-18-41
Williams Otis	10-30-39
Williams Paul	7-2-39

WAR
Allen Thomas 'Papa Dee'	7-18-31
Brown Harold	3-17-46
Dickerson Morris 'B B'	8-3-49
Jordan Lonnie	11-21-48
Miller Charles	6-2-39
Oskar Lee	3-24-46
Scott Howard	3-15-46

REGGAE
Buster Prince	5-24-38
Cliff Jimmy	1948
Dekker Desmond	7-16-42
Grant Eddie	3-5-48
Livingston Bunny	4-23-47
Marley Bob	2-6-45
Marley Ziggy	1968
Patra	11-22-72
Tosh Peter	10-19-44
Wailer Bunny	4-23-47

DISCO
Bell Robert 'Kool'	10-8-50
Bridges Alicia	7-15-53
Brown Peter	12-25-40
Casey Harry 'K C'	1-31-51
Gaynor Gloria	9-7-49
Gibb Barry	9-1-46
Gibb Maurice & Robin	12-22-49
Jones Grace	5-19-52
Lomas Barbara Joyce	5-19-52
Nightingale Maxine	11-2-52
Rock Monti III	5-29-42
Summer Donna	12-31-48

****

BONEY M
Barrett Marcia	10-14-48
Farrell Bobby	10-6-49
Mitchell Liz	7-12-52
Williams Maizie	3-25-51

VILLAGE PEOPLE
Briley Alexander	4-12-56
Hodo David	7-7-50
Huges Glenn	7-18-50
Jones Randy	9-13-52

****

RAP
Afrika Bambaataa	10-4-60
Blow Kurtis	8-9-59
Campbell Luther	1961
Davis Q-Tip	11-20-70
DJ Red Alert	11-27-56
Dr Dre	2-18-65
Elam Guru	7-18-66
Gerardo (Mejia)	4-16-67
Grandmaster Flash	1-1-58
Hammer	3-30-62
Ice Cube	6-15-69
Kane Big Daddy	9-10-68
LL Cool J	1-14-68
Lyte MC	1971
Markie Biz	4-8-64
Martin DJ Premier	5-3-69
Muhammad Ali	8-11-70
Queen Latifah	3-18-70
Snoop Doggy Dog	1971
Starski Lovebug	7-13-61
Taylor Phife-Dawg	4-10-70
Tone-Loc	1966
Vanilla Ice	10-31-67

DAS EFX
Krazy Dayz	9-8-71
Skoob	1972

DE LA SOUL
Jolicoeur Dave	9-21-68
Mason Mase	3-27-70
Mercer Pos	8-17-69

NAUGHTY BY NATURE
Brown Vinnie	9-17-70
Criss Treach	12-27-70
Gist Kay Gee	9-15-59

****

****

SALT N PEPA
Pepa (Denton)	11-9-69
Salt (James)	3-8-64

TONY TONI TONE
Riley Timothy Christian	12-10-65
Wiggins D'Wayne	2-14-63
Wiggins Raphael	5-14-66

****

TEEN IDOLS
Anka Paul	7-30-41
Avalon Frankie	9-18-40
Boone Pat	6-1-34
Cassidy David	4-12-50
Cassidy Shaun	9-27-58
Cochran Eddie	10-3-38
Cowsill Barry	9-14-55
Cowsill Bill	1-9-48
Cowsill Bob	8-26-49
Cowsill John	3-2-56
Cowsill Paul	11-11-50
Cowsill Susan	5-20-60
Danny (Rapp)	5-10-41
Dinning Mark	8-17-33
Dion (DiMucci)	7-18-39
Fabian	2-6-43
Ford Frankie	8-4-40
Gibson Debbie	8-31-70
Hyland Brian	11-12-43
Marky Mark (Wahlberg)	6-5-71
Noone Peter	11-5-47
Osmond Alan	6-22-49
Osmond Donny	12-9-57
Osmond Jay	3-2-55
Osmond Jimmy	4-16-63
Osmond Marie	10-13-59
Osmond Merrill	4-30-53
Osmond Wayne	8-28-51
Rydell Bobby	4-26-42
Sands Tommy	8-27-37
Scott Jack	1-24-36
Scott Linda	6-1-45
Sherman Bobby	7-22-45
Stevens Dodie	2-17-47
Tiffany (Darwish)	10-2-71
Zappa Dweezel	9-5-69
Zappa Moon	9-28-67

****

BAY CITY ROLLERS

Faulkner Eric	10-21-54
Longmuir Derek	3-19-52
McKeown Leslie	11-12-55
Mitchell Ian	8-22-58
Wood Stuart 'Woody'	2-25-57

BOYZ II MEN

McCary Michael	12-16-71
Morris Nate	6-18-71
Morris Wanya	7-29-73
Stockman Shawn	9-26-71

DINO, DESI & BILLY

Arnaz Desi Jr	1-19-53
Hinsche Billy	6-29-51
Martin Dean Paul	11-12-51

MONKEES

Dolenz Mickey	3-8-45
Jones Davy	12-30-46
Nesmith Mike	12-30-42
Tork Peter	2-13-44

NEW KIDS ON THE BLOCK

Knight Jonathan	11-29-68
Knight Jordan	5-17-70
McIntyre Joe	12-31-72
Wahlberg Donnie	8-17-69
Wood Danny	5-14-69

****

ROCK

Abdul Paula	6-19-62
Adams Bryan	11-5-59
Albrecht Bernard (Dicken)	1-4-56
Allen Verden 'Phally'	5-26-44
Allman Duane	11-20-46
Allman Gregg	12-8-47
Amos Tori	8-22-63
Anderson Ian	8-10-47
Anderson Jon	10-25-44
Anger Mick	7-2-57
Ant Adam	11-3-54
Appice Carmine	12-15-46
Arm Mark	2-21-62
Armatrading Joan	12-9-50
Astley Rick	2-6-66
Auger Brian	7-18-39
Bach Sebastian	4-3-68
Bachman Randy	9-27-43

Bailey Tom	1-18-56
Baker Ginger	8-19-39
Barrett Syd	1-6-46
Barron Chris	2-5-68
Barry Len	6-12-42
Bauman Jon 'Bowser'	9-14-47
Beck (Hansen)	7-8-70
Beck Jeff	6-24-44
Beckenstein Jay	5-14-51
Becker Walter	2-20-50
Beckley Gerry	9-12-52
Benatar Pat	1-10-53
Bender Ariel	12-23-49
Berry Chuck	10-18-26
Best Pete	11-24-41
Big Bopper	10-24-30
Bishop Elvin	10-21-40
Bishop Stephen	11-14-51
Bjelland Kat	12-9-63
Bjork (Gudmundsdottir)	11-12-65
Black Jay	11-2-38
Blackmore Ritchie	4-14-45
Blane Marcie	5-21-44
Bloom Eric	12-1-44
Blunstone Colin	6-24-45
Bogert Tim	8-27-44
Bolan Marc	7-30-47
Bolton Michael	2-26-53
Bonds Gary U S	6-6-39
Bonham John	5-31-47
BonJovi Jon	3-2-62
Bono (Hewson)	5-10-60
Bono Sonny	2-16-35
Bonoff Karla	12-27-52
Bouchard Joe	11-9-48
Bowen Jimmy	11-30-37
Bowie David	1-8-47
Boy George	6-14-61
Boyce Tommy	9-29-44
Bozzio Dale	3-2-55
Bragg Billy	12-20-57
Bramlett Bonnie	11-8-44
Bramlett Delaney	7-1-39
Brant Jon	2-20-54
Bratton Creed	2-8-43
Brill Rob	1-21-56

Britton Chris	6-21-45
Browne Jackson	10-9-48
Bruce Jack	5-14-43
Buckley Jeff	11-17-66
Buckley Tim	2-17-47
Buffett Jimmy	12-25-46
Bunnell Dewey	1-19-51
Burdon Eric	4-5-41
Burnette Billy	5-8-53
Burnette Dorsey	12-28-32
Burnette Johnny	3-25-34
Burnette Rocky	6-12-53
Bush Kate	7-30-58
Butler Terry 'Geezer'	7-17-49
Byrne David	5-14-52
Byrne Pete	6-9-54
Byron David	1-29-47
Caffey Charlotte	10-21-53
Cale John	12-3-40
Calver Bernard	9-16-42
Campbell JoAnn	7-20-38
Cannon Freddy	12-4-40
Cantrell Jerry	3-18-66
Carey Mariah	3-22-69
Carlisle Belinda	8-17-58
Carlos Bun E	6-12-53
Carmen Eric	8-11-49
Carnes Kim	7-20-46
Carr Cathy	6-28-38
Catherall Joanne	9-18-62
Cavalera Max	8-4-69
Cavaliere Felix	11-29-43
Cave Nick	9-22-57
Cetera Peter	9-13-44
Chad (Stuart)	12-10-43
Chamberlin Jimmy	6-10-64
Chance Larry	10-19-40
Channel Bruce	11-28-40
Checker Chubby	10-3-41
Cher	5-20-46
Chilton Alex	12-28-50
Christie Lou	2-19-43
Clanton Jimmy	9-2-40
Clapton Eric	3-30-45
Clark Dave	12-15-42
Clark Steve	4-23-60

Clarke Allan	4-5-42
Clayton-Thomas David	9-13-41
Clemons Clarence	1-11-42
Cobain Kurt	2-10-67
Cocker Joe	5-20-44
Coley John Ford	10-13-51
Collen Phil	12-8-57
Collins Phil	1-31-51
Coltrane Chi	11-16-48
Cooder Ry	3-15-47
Coonce Rick	8-1-47
Cooper Alice	2-4-48
Copeland Stewart	7-16-52
Corgan Billy	3-17-67
Cornell Chris	7-20-64
Cortez Dave 'Baby'	8-13-38
Costello Elvis	8-25-54
Coverdale David	9-22-51
Cracolici Phil	9-17-37
Crawford John	1-17-60
Creme Lol	9-17-47
Crofts Dash	8-14-40
Cronin Kevin	10-6-51
Cropper Steve	10-21-41
Cross Christopher	5-3-51
Crow Sheryl	2-11-63
Cummings Burton	12-31-47
Curnin Cy	12-12-57
Curtis Ian	7-15-56
D'Arby Terence Trent	3-15-62
Dale Clamma Churita	7-4-48
Dando Evan	3-4-67
Danko Rick	12-9-43
Danoff Bill	5-7-46
Danoff Taffy	10-25-44
Dante Ron	8-22-45
Danzig Glenn	6-23-59
Darin Bobby	5-14-36
Davies Ray	6-21-44
Davies Rick	7-22-44
Davis Martha	1-19-51
Day Bobby	7-1-32
Daye Cory	4-25-52
Dayne Taylor	3-7-63
Deal Kelley & Kim	7-10-61
Dean (Torrence)	3-10-41

****

Dean Paul	2-19-46
DeBurgh Chris	10-15-48
Dee Joey	6-11-40
Dee Kiki	3-6-47
DeGarmo Chris	6-14-63
DeLeo Dean	8-23-61
Delp Brad	6-12-51
Derringer Rick	8-5-47
DeShannon Jackie	8-21-44
DeYoung Dennis	2-18-47
Dharma Buck (Don Roeser)	11-12-47
Diamond Neil	1-24-41
Dickinson Bruce	8-7-58
Dio Ronnie James	7-10-49
Dion Celine	3-30-68
Dolby Thomas	10-14-58
Domino Fats	2-26-28
Donaldson Bo	6-13-54
Donner Ral	2-10-43
Donovan (Leitch)	5-10-46
Doo Dickey	6-17-39
Dove Ronnie	9-7-40
Downey Rick	8-29-53
Downing K K	10-27-51
Dr John (Rebennack)	11-21-40
Dryden Spencer	4-7-43
Dulli Greg	5-11-65
Dury Ian	5-12-42
Easton Sheena	4-27-59
Eddy Duane	4-26-38
Edge Graeme	3-30-44
Edmunds Dave	4-15-44
Edwards Jonathan	7-28-46
Edwards Nokie	5-9-39
Egan Walter	7-12-48
Eitzel Mark	1-30-59
Elfman Danny	5-29-53
Elliott Dennis	8-18-50
Elliott Joe	8-1-59
Elliott Robert	12-8-42
Elliott Ron	10-21-43
Emerson Keith	11-1-44
Ennis Ethel	11-28-34
Eno Brian	5-15-48
Entner Warren	7-7-44
Essex David	7-23-47

****

Etheridge Melissa	5-29-61
Evans Rod	1-19-45
Everly Don	2-1-37
Everly Phil	1-19-39
Fagen Donald	1-10-48
Faith Adam	6-23-40
Faithfull Marianne	12-29-46
Fame Georgie	6-26-43
Farner Mark	9-29-48
Farrar Jimmy	8-24-51
Farrell Perry	3-29-59
Fender Freddy	6-4-37
Ferry Bryan	9-26-45
Fisher Morgan	1-1-50
Fogelberg Dan	8-13-51
Fogerty John	5-28-45
Fontana Wayne	10-28-45
Foster Malcolm	1-13-56
Frampton Peter	4-22-50
Francis Connie	12-12-38
Furay Richie	5-9-44
Gabriel Peter	5-13-50
Gagliardi Ed	2-13-52
Gallagher Rory	3-2-48
Gardner Suzi	8-1-60
Garfunkel Art	10-13-42
Garrity Freddie	11-14-40
Gates David	12-11-40
Geils J(erome)	2-20-46
Geldof Bob	10-5-54
Gibb Andy	3-5-58
Gift Roland	5-28-62
Gilder Nick	11-7-51
Gillis Brad	6-15-57
Gilmer Jimmy	9-15-40
Gilmour Dave	3-6-44
Glitter Gary	5-8-40
Glover Corey	11-6-64
Gold Andrew	8-2-51
Gordon (Waller)	6-4-45
Gore Lesley	5-2-46
Goudreau Barry	11-29-51
Gracie Charlie	1-12-36
Gramm Lou	5-2-50
Green Peter	10-29-46
Greenwood Al	10-20-51

****

Rock Gri-Ido

Griffin Dale	10-24-50
Grill Rob	11-30-44
Hackett Steve	2-12-50
Hagar Sammy	10-13-47
Haley Bill	7-6-25
Halford Rob	8-25-51
Hall Daryl	10-11-48
Ham Peter	4-26-47
Hamilton Page	5-18-60
Hammett Kirk	11-18-62
Hardin Tim	12-23-41
Harding John Wesley	10-22-65
Harris Steve	3-12-56
Harvey Polly Jean	10-9-69
Hashian Sib	8-17-49
Hatfield Bobby	8-10-40
Hatfield Juliana	7-2-67
Hawkins Dale	8-30-38
Hawkins Ronnie	1-10-35
Hayward Justin	10-14-46
Hell Richard	10-2-49
Helm Levon	5-26-43
Helms Bobby	8-15-33
Hendrix Jimi	11-27-42
Hensley Ken	8-24-45
Hicks Tony	12-16-45
Hill Dusty	5-19-49
Hitchcock Russell	6-15-49
Hite Robert	2-26-45
Hogan Mike	4-29-73
Hogan Noel	12-25-71
Holly Buddy	9-7-36
Holmes Rupert	2-24-47
Hook Peter	2-13-56
Honeyman-Scott James	11-4-56
Hopkin Mary	5-3-50
Hopkins Telma	10-28-48
Hornsby Bruce	11-23-54
Howard 'Dr Robert'	5-2-61
Howe Steve	4-8-47
Hudson Garth	8-2-42
Hunter Ian	6-3-46
Hutton Danny	9-10-42
Hynde Chrissie	9-7-51
Ian Janis	4-7-51
Idol Billy	11-30-55

Rock Iha-Lea

Iha James	3-6-68
Iommi Tony	2-19-48
Isaak Chris	6-26-56
Iyall Debora	4-29-54
Jackson Eddie	1-29-61
Jackson Joe	8-11-54
James Tommy	4-29-47
Jan (Berry)	4-3-41
Jeremy (Clyde)	3-22-44
Jett Joan	9-22-60
Joel Billy	5-9-49
John Elton	3-25-47
Johnny (Farina)	4-30-41
Johnson Holly	2-19-60
Jones Howard	2-23-55
Jones John Paul	1-3-46
Jones Mick	12-27-44
Jones Rickie Lee	11-8-54
Jones Steve	5-3-55
Jones Tom	6-7-40
Joplin Janis	1-19-43
Kale James	8-11-43
Kalin Harold & Herbie	2-16-39
Kay John	4-12-44
Kaylan Howard	6-22-47
Kiley Tony	2-16-62
Kimball Bobby	3-29-47
Kimble Paul	9-24-60
King Carole	2-9-41
King Jonathan	12-6-44
Kirkwood Cris	10-22-60
Kirkwood Curt	1-10-59
Knopfler Mark	8-12-49
Knox Buddy	4-14-33
Koda Cub	10-1-48
Kramer Billy J	8-19-43
Kravitz Lenny	5-26-64
Kupferberg Tuli	9-28-23
Lake Greg	10-10-48
Lamm Robert	10-13-44
Lanegan Mark	11-25-64
Lanier Allen	6-25-46
Larson Nicolette	7-17-52
Lauper Cyndi	6-20-53
Lawler Feargal	3-4-71
Leadon Bernie	7-19-47

LeBon Simon	10-27-58
Lee Geddy	7-29-53
Lennon Julian	4-8-63
Lennox Annie	12-25-54
Lewis Gary	7-31-46
Lewis Huey	7-5-50
Lewis Jerry Lee	9-29-35
Lifeson Alex	8-27-53
Lindsay Mark	3-9-42
Liozzo Gary	8-16-45
Little Anthony (Gourdine)	1-8-40
Little Richard (Penniman)	12-5-32
Lobo (Lavoie)	7-31-43
Lodge John	7-20-45
Lofgren Nils	6-21-51
Loggins Kenny	1-7-48
Love Courtney	7-9-64
Love Darlene	7-26-41
Lowe Nick	3-25-49
Lowery Dave	10-10-60
Lulu (Marie Lawrie)	11-3-48
Luman Bob	4-15-37
Lwin Annabella	10-31-65
Lynne Jeff	12-30-47
MacColl Kirsty	10-10-59
MacIntosh Rob	10-25-57
Mackay Andy	7-23-46
Madonna (Ciccone)	8-16-58
Maestro Johnny	5-7-39
Major Ray	7-16-49
Mangrum Jim Dandy	3-30-48
Mann Manfred	10-21-40
Manuel Richard	4-3-44
Manzanera Phil	1-31-51
Marriott Steve	1-30-47
Marsden Gerry	9-24-42
Martell Vincent	11-11-45
Marx Richard	9-16-63
Mascis J	12-10-65
Mason Dave	5-10-46
Mason Nick	1-27-45
Matlock Glenn	8-27-56
May Brian	7-19-47
Mayall John	11-29-33
McCartney Linda	9-24-42
McDonald Country Joe	1-1-42

McDonald Ian	6-25-46
McDonald Michael	12-2-52
McIntire Onnie	9-25-45
McLachlan Sarah	1-28-68
McLaughlin John	1-4-42
McLean Don	10-2-45
McMurtry James	3-18-62
Meagher Ron	10-2-41
Meat Loaf	9-27-47
Medley Bill	9-19-40
Mellencamp John	10-7-51
Merchant Natalie	10-26-63
Mercury Freddie	9-8-46
Messina Jim	12-5-47
Michael George	6-25-63
Michaels Bret	3-15-62
Mickey (Baker)	10-15-25
Miller Steve	10-5-43
Moby (Richard Hall)	9-11-65
Money Eddie	3-2-49
Montez Chris	1-17-44
Moore Thurston	7-25-58
Morrison Van	8-31-45
Morrissey	5-22-59
Mould Bob	10-16-60
Moyet Alison 'Alf'	6-18-61
Muldaur Maria	9-12-43
Nash Graham	2-2-42
NdegeOcello Me'Shell	8-29-69
Neely Sam	8-22-48
Negron Chuck	6-8-42
Nelson Gunnar & Matthew	9-20-67
Nelson Sandy	12-1-38
Newton-John Olivia	9-26-47
Nico (Christa Paffgen)	10-16-38
Nielsen Rick	12-22-50
Nugent Ted	12-13-48
Numan Gary	3-8-58
Nunn Terri	6-6-51
Nyro Laura	10-18-47
O'Connor Sinead	12-8-67
O'Day Alan	10-3-40
O'Riordan Dolores	9-6-71
Oates John	4-7-48
Ocasek Rick	3-23-49
Orbison Roy	4-23-36

Osbourne Ozzy	12-3-48
Page Jimmy	1-9-44
Page Richard	5-16-53
Palmer Carl	3-20-47
Palmer Robert	1-19-49
Parker Graham	11-18-50
Parsons Gram	11-5-46
Paul (Ray Hildebrand)	12-21-40
Paula (Jill Jackson)	5-20-42
Pearcy Stephen	7-3-59
Peart Neil	9-12-52
Perkins John	8-28-31
Perry Joe	9-10-50
Perry Steve	1-22-49
Peter (Asher)	6-22-44
Peterson Garry	5-26-45
Peterson John	1-8-42
Peterson Ray	4-23-39
Petty Tom	10-20-50
Phair Liz	4-17-67
Phillips Chynna	2-12-68
Phillips Grant Lee	9-1-63
Phillips Sam	6-28-62
Pinder Mike	12-27-41
Pitney Gene	2-17-41
Plant Robert	8-20-48
Poole Brian	11-3-41
Pop Iggy	4-21-47
Presley Elvis	1-8-35
Presley Reg	6-16-44
Preston Johnny	8-18-39
Proby P J	11-6-38
Puckett Gary	10-17-42
Quatro Suzi	6-3-50
Rafferty Gerry	4-16-47
Raitt Bonnie	11-8-49
Ralphs Mick	3-31-44
Ranaldo Lee	2-3-56
Randazzo Teddy	5-20-37
Rashbaum David	2-7-62
Ray Amy	4-12-64
Reed Lou	3-2-43
Relf Keith	3-22-44
Reno Mike	1-8-55
Revere Paul	1-7-38
Reynolds Jody	12-3-38

Reznor Trent	5-17-65
Rhodes Nick	6-8-62
Richard Cliff	10-14-40
Richman Jonathan	5-16-51
Richrath Gary	10-18-49
Ridgeley Andrew	1-26-63
Robertson Robbie	7-5-44
Robinson Chris	12-20-66
Rodgers Paul	12-12-49
Roe Tommy	5-9-42
Rollins Henry	2-13-61
Ronstadt Linda	7-15-46
Rose Axl	2-6-62
Ross Rindy	6-26-51
Roth David Lee	10-10-55
Rotten Johnny	1-30-56
Rowland Kevin	8-17-53
Rundgren Todd	6-22-48
Russell Graham	6-1-50
Russell Leon	4-2-41
Rutherford Mike	10-2-50
Ryder Mitch	2-26-45
Saliers Emily	7-22-63
Sambora Richie	7-11-59
Sang Samantha	8-5-53
Santo (Farina)	10-24-37
Savage Rick	12-2-60
Sawyer Ray	2-1-37
Sayer Leo	5-21-48
Scaggs Boz	6-8-44
Schock Gina	8-31-57
Scholl Bob	7-14-38
Scholz Tom	3-10-47
Scialfa Patty	7-29-56
Score Mike	11-5-56
Scott Freddy	4-24-33
Seal (Sealhenry Samuel)	2-19-63
Seals Dan	2-8-50
Seals Jim	10-17-41
Sebastian John	3-17-44
Sedaka Neil	3-13-39
Seger Bob	5-6-45
Sembello Michael	4-17-54
Setzer Brian	4-10-60
Shannon Del	12-30-39
Sharp Dee Dee	9-9-45

Rock She-Tho

Name	Date
Sheehan Fran	3-26-49
Shelley Pete	4-17-55
Shondell Troy	5-14-44
Shorrock Glenn	6-30-44
Siegal Jay	10-20-39
Simmons Pat	1-23-50
Simon Carly	6-25-45
Simon Paul	10-13-41
Siouxsie Sioux (Susan Dallion)	5-27-57
Slash (Saul Hudson)	7-23-65
Smith Arlene	10-5-41
Smith Patti	12-31-46
Smyth Patty	6-26-57
Snider Dee	3-15-55
Snow Phoebe	7-17-52
Sohns Jim	8-23-49
South Joe	2-28-42
Southside Johnny (Lyon)	12-4-48
Spanky (McFarlane)	6-19-42
Spector Ronnie	8-10-47
Spencer Jeremy	7-4-48
Springfield Dusty	4-16-39
Springfield Rick	8-23-49
Springsteen Bruce	9-23-49
Squier Billy	5-12-50
Staley Layne	8-22-67
Stanley Michael	3-25-48
Stansfield Lisa	4-11-66
Stevens Cat	7-21-48
Stewart David	9-9-52
Stewart Rod	1-10-45
Stills Stephen	1-3-45
Sting (Gordon Sumner)	10-2-51
Strummer Joe	8-21-52
Such Alec	11-14-56
Summers Andy	12-31-42
Sweet Matthew	10-6-64
Sweet Rachel	7-28-62
Sylvia (Robinson)	5-6-36
Taylor Andy	2-16-61
Taylor John	6-20-60
Taylor Roger	4-26-60
Templeman Ted	10-24-44
Thomas Ray	12-29-41
Thompson Paul	5-13-51
Thompson Richard	4-3-49

Rock Tib-Wil

Name	Date
Tibbs Gary	1-25-58
Tikaram Tanita	8-12-69
Torres Tico	10-7-53
Tyler Steve	3-26-48
Tyner Rob	12-12-44
Ulrich Lars	12-26-63
Vai Steve	6-6-60
Valens Richie	5-13-41
Valenti Dino	10-7-43
Valentine Kathy	1-7-59
Valentino Sal	9-8-42
VanHalen Alex	5-8-55
VanHalen Eddie	1-26-57
Vann Joe	4-3-43
VanVliet Don	1-15-41
VanZandt Steve	11-22-50
VanZant Donnie	6-11-52
VanZant Ronnie	1-15-49
Vee Bobby	4-30-43
Vega Suzanne	7-11-59
Vera Billy	5-28-44
Vincent Gene	2-11-35
Vinton Bobby	4-16-35
Vicious Sid	5-10-57
Waite John	7-4-55
Waits Tom	12-7-49
Wakeman Rick	5-18-49
Wallinger Karl	10-19-57
Waters Roger	9-6-44
Watts Peter 'Overend'	5-13-49
Waybill Fee	9-17-50
Webb Jimmy	8-15-46
Weiland Scott	10-27-67
Welch Bob	7-31-46
Wells Cory	2-5-42
Westerberg Paul	12-31-59
Wetton John	7-12-49
Whitford Brad	2-23-52
Wilde Kim	11-18-60
Williams Wendy O	10-16-46
Wilson Ann	6-19-51
Wilson Carnie	4-29-68
Wilson Joyce	12-14-46
Wilson Nancy	3-16-54
Wilson Wendy	10-16-69
Wilton Michael	2-22-62

****

Winchester Jesse	5-17-48
Winter Edgar	12-28-46
Winter Johnny	2-23-44
Winwood Steve	5-12-48
Wolf Peter	3-7-46
Wood Brenton	7-26-41
Wray Link	5-2-35
Wretzky D'Arcy	5-1-68
Wright Gary	4-26-43
Wright Rick	7-28-45
Young Neil	11-12-45
Young Paul	1-17-56
Zander Robin	1-23-55
Zappa Frank	12-21-40
Zevon Warren	1-24-47
ABBA	
Andersson Benny	12-16-46
Faltskog Agnetha	4-5-50
Lyngstad Anni-Frid	11-15-45
Ulvaeus Bjorn	4-25-45
AC/DC	
Scott Bon	7-9-46
Young Angus	3-31-59
Young Malcolm	1-6-53
Williams Cliff	12-14-49
B-52s	
Pierson Kate	4-27-48
Schneider Fred III	7-1-51
Stickland Julian Keith	10-26-53
Wilson Cindy	2-28-57
Wilson Ricky	3-19-53
BANANARAMA	
Dallin Sarah	12-17-61
Fahey Siobhan	9-10-60
Woodard Keren	4-2-63
BEACH BOYS	
Jardine Al	9-3-42
Johnson Bruce	6-27-42
Love Mike	3-15-41
Wilson Brian	6-20-42
Wilson Carl	12-21-46
Wilson Dennis	12-1-44
BEASTIE BOYS	
Diamond Mike	11-20-65
Horowitz Adam	10-31-66
Yauch Adam	8-5-64

****

BEATLES	
Harrison George	2-25-43
Lennon John	10-9-40
McCartney Paul	6-18-42
Starr Ringo	7-7-40
BLONDIE	
Burke Clem	11-24-55
Destri Jimmy	4-13-54
Harry Deborah	7-1-45
Stein Chris	1-5-50
BYRDS	
Clark Mike	6-3-44
Clarke Gene	11-17-44
Crosby David	8-14-41
Hillman Chris	12-4-42
McGuinn Roger	7-13-42
DOORS	
Densmore John	12-1-45
Krieger Robby	1-8-46
Manzarek Ray	2-12-45
Morrison Jim	12-8-43
EAGLES	
Felder Don	9-21-47
Frey Glenn	11-6-48
Henley Don	7-22-47
Meisner Randy	3-8-46
Schmidt Tim	10-30-47
Walsh Joe	11-20-47
FLEETWOOD MAC	
Buckingham Lindsey	10-3-47
Fleetwood Mick	6-24-42
McVie Christine	7-12-43
McVie John	11-26-46
Nicks Stevie	5-26-48
GRATEFUL DEAD	
Garcia Jerry	8-1-42
Godchaux Donna	8-22-47
Godchaux Keith	7-19-48
Kreutzmann Bill	6-7-46
Lesh Phil	3-15-40
McKernan Ron 'Pigpen'	9-8-46
Weir Bob	10-16-47
GREEN DAY	
Armstrong Billie Joe	2-17-72
Cool Tre	12-9-72
Dirnt Mike	5-4-72

****

****

JEFFERSON AIRPLANE
Balin Marty	1-30-43
Kantner Paul	3-12-42
Slick Grace	10-30-39

KISS
Criss Peter	12-20-47
Frehley Ace	4-27-51
Simmons Gene	8-25-49
Stanley Paul	1-20-52

MAMAS & PAPAS
Doherty Dennis	11-29-41
Elliott Mama Cass	9-19-43
Phillips John	8-30-35
Phillips Michelle	4-6-44

MOTLEY CRUE
Lee Tommy	10-3-62
Mars Mick	4-4-55
Neil Vince	2-8-61
Sixx Nikki	12-11-58

PEARL JAM
Ament Jeff	3-10-63
Gossard Stone	7-20-66
McCready Mike	4-5-65
Vedder Eddie	12-23-64

RED HOT CHILI PEPPERS
Balzary Flea	10-16-62
Kiedis Anthony	11-1-62
Navarro Dave	6-7-67
Smith Chad	10-25-62

REM
Berry Bill	7-31-58
Buck Peter	12-6-56
Mills Mike	12-17-58
Stipe Michael	1-4-60

ROLLING STONES
Jagger Mick	7-26-43
Jones Brian	2-28-42
Richards Keith	12-18-43
Watts Charlie	6-2-41
Wood Ron	6-1-47
Wyman Bill	10-24-36

SOUL ASYLUM
Mueller Karl	7-27-63
Murphy Dan	7-12-62
Pirner Dave	4-16-64
Young Grant	1-5-64

****

****

URGE OVERKILL
Kato Nash	12-31-65
Onassis Blackie	8-27-67
Roesser 'Eddie' King	6-17-69

WHO
Daltrey Roger	3-1-44
Entwistle John	10-9-44
Moon Keith	8-23-46
Townshend Peter	5-19-45

****

LATIN
Alberto Jose	12-22-58
Barretto Ray	4-29-29
Bauza Mario	4-28-11
Blades Ruben	7-16-48
Bobo Willie	2-28-34
Colon Willie	4-28-50
Cruz Celia	10-21-28
Cuba Joe	4-22-31
Cugat Xavier	1-1-00
D'Leon Oscar	7-11-43
D'Rivera Paquito	6-4-48
Estefan Gloria	9-1-57
Guizar Tito	4-8-08
Hinojosa Tish	12-6-55
Iglesias Julio	9-23-43
Jimenez Flaco	3-11-39
Lopez Israel 'Cachao'	9-14-18
Melis Jose	2-27-20
Mendes Sergio	2-11-41
Mendoza Lydia	5-31-16
Morales Noro	1-4-11
Moreira Airto	8-5-41
Nieves Tito	6-4-58
O'Farrill Chico	10-28-21
Oquendo Manny	1-1-31
Pacheco Johnny	3-25-35
Palmieri Charlie	11-21-27
Palmieri Eddie	12-15-36
Perez Lou	6-21-28
Prado Perez	12-11-16
Puente Tito	4-20-23
Ramirez Louie	2-24-38
Rodriquez Lalo	5-16-58
Rodriquez Tito	1-4-23
Ros Edmundo	12-7-10

****

Rosario Willie	5-6-30
Sanchez Poncho	10-30-51
Sandoval Arturo	11-6-49
Santa-Rosa Gilberto	8-21-50
Santamaria Mongo	4-7-22
Santana Carlos	7-20-47
Santiago Eddie	1961
Secada Jon	1962
Selena (Quintanilla)	4-16-71
Torres Roberto	2-10-40
Valentin Bobby	6-9-41
Vega Tony	7-13-57

****
NEW AGE

Aaberg Philip	4-8-49
Ackerman Will	1949
Adams John	2-15-47
Anderson Ruth	3-21-28
Bardens Peter	6-19-45
Budd Harold	5-24-36
Ciani Suzanne	6-4-46
Curran Alvin	12-13-38
Davis Chip	1947
deGrassi Alex	2-13-52
Deodata	6-22-42
Dresher Paul	1-8-51
Egan Mark	1-14-51
Enya	5-17-61
Feldman Morton	1-12-26
Franke Christophe	4-4-42
Froese Edgar	6-6-44
Hassell Jon	3-22-37
Hedges Michael	12-31-53
Hoenig Michael	1-4-52
Horn Paul	3-17-30
Hykes David	3-2-53
Isham Mark	9-7-51
Jarre Jean-Michel	8-24-48
Johannson Sven	2-5-43
Kenny G	6-5-56
Kitaro	2-4-53
Kramer Jonathan	12-7-42
Lateef Yusef	10-9-20
Oldfield Mike	5-15-53
Reich Steve	10-3-36
Riley Terry	6-24-35

Rzewski Frederic	4-13-38
Sanborn David	7-30-45
Schulze Klaus	8-4-47
Scott Tony	6-17-21
Story Liz	10-28-56
Teitelbaum Richard	5-19-39
Vangelis (Papathanassiou)	3-29-43
Van Tiegham David	4-21-55
Winston George	1949
Winter Paul	8-31-39
Yanni	11-14-54
Zeitlin Denny	4-10-38

****
CHILDREN'S MUSIC

Bartels Joanie	5-21-53
Bram (Morrison)	1941
Cappelli Frank	8-17-52
Chapin Tom	3-13-45
Glazer Tom	9-3-14
Harley Bill	1954
Lois (Lilienstein)	1937
Luther Frank	8-5-05
Palmer Hap	10-28-42
Penner Fred	11-6-46
Polisar Barry Louis	11-18-54
Raffi (Cavoukian)	7-8-48
Rosen Gary	3-24-47
Sharon (Hampson)	1943

****
OPERA

Albanese Licia	7-22-13
Alexander Roberta	3-30-49
Amara Lucine	3-1-27
Ameling Elly	2-8-38
Anderson June	12-30-52
Anderson Marian	2-17-02
Angeles Victoria de los	11-1-23
Arroyo Martina	2-2-37
Auger Arleen	9-13-39
Baccaloni Salvatore	4-14-00
Baker Janet	8-21-33
Bampton Rose	11-28-09
Barbieri Fedora	6-4-20
Bartoli Cecilia	6-4-66
Battle Kathleen	8-13-48
Beardslee Bethany	12-25-27

Opera Ben-Hay

Benzell Mimi	4-6-24
Berberian Cathy	7-4-25
Berganza Teresa	3-16-35
Bjoerling Jussi	2-2-11
Blegen Judith	4-27-41
Bori Lucrezia	12-24-1887
Branzell Karin	9-24-1891
Brice Carol	4-16-18
Brooks Patricia	11-7-37
Brownlee John	1-7-01
Bumbry Grace	1-4-37
Caballe Montserrat	4-12-33
Callas Maria	12-3-23
Carreras Jose	12-5-46
Caruso Enrico	2-5-1873
Castagna Bruna	10-15-08
Corelli Franco	4-8-23
Costa Mary	4-5-30
Cotrubas Ileana	6-9-39
Crespin Regine	3-23-27
Crooks Richard	6-26-00
Curtin Phyllis	12-3-27
DellaCasa Lisa	2-1-19
DelMonaco Mario	7-27-15
Dobbs Mattiwilda	7-11-25
Domingo Placido	1-21-41
Elias Rosalind	3-13-31
Estes Simon	2-2-38
Farrar Geraldine	2-28-1882
Farrell Eileen	2-13-20
Fassbaender Brigitte	7-3-39
Ferrier Kathleen	4-22-12
Fischer-Dieskau Dietrich	5-28-25
Flagstad Kirsten	7-12-1895
Forrester Maureen	7-25-30
Freni Mirella	2-27-35
Galli-Curci Amelita	11-18-1889
Garden Mary	2-20-1877
Gauthier Eva	9-20-1885
Gigli Beniamino	3-20-1890
Gobbi Tito	10-24-15
Gorin Igor	10-26-08
Grist Reri	2-29-32
Hadley Jerry	6-16-52
Hampson Thomas	6-28-55
Hayes Roland	6-3-1887

Opera Hen-Sar

Hendricks Barbara	11-20-48
Hicks Peggy Glanville	12-29-12
Hines Jerome	11-8-21
Horne Marilyn	1-16-43
Jones Gwyneth	11-7-36
Kipnis Alexander	2-1-1896
Kirsten Dorothy	7-6-17
Korjus Miliza	8-18-09
Lawrence Marjorie	2-17-09
Lear Evelyn	1-18-31
Lehmann Lotte	7-2-1885
Lipton Martha	4-6-15
London George	5-30-20
Ludwig Christa	3-16-28
Madeira Jean	11-14-18
Malbin Elaine	5-24-32
Martini Nino	7-8-04
Melchior Lauritz	3-20-1890
Merrill Robert	6-4-19
Merriman Nan	4-28-20
Milanov Zinka	5-17-06
Milnes Sherrill	1-10-35
Moffo Anna	6-27-34
Morris James	1-10-49
Munsel Patrice	5-14-25
Nilsson Birgit	5-17-18
Norman Jessye	9-15-45
Novotna Jarmila	9-23-07
Olivero Magda	3-25-14
Pavarotti Luciano	10-12-35
Peerce Jan	6-3-04
Peters Roberta	5-4-30
Piazza Marguerite	5-6-26
Pinza Ezio	5-18-1892
Pons Lily	4-12-04
Ponselle Rosa	1-22-1897
Price Leontyne	2-10-27
Putnam Ashley	8-10-52
Ramey Samuel	3-28-42
Raskin Judith	6-21-28
Resnik Regina	8-30-24
Robeson Paul	4-9-1898
Robinson Faye	11-2-43
Rounseville Robert	3-25-14
Rysanek Leonie	11-12-26
Sarnoff Dorothy	5-25-17

Scheff Fritzi	8-30-1879
Schipa Tito	1-2-1890
Schwarzkopf Elisabeth	12-9-15
Scott Norman	11-30-28
Scotto Renata	2-24-34
Seefried Irmgard	10-9-19
Siepi Cesare	2-10-23
Sills Beverly	5-25-29
Steber Eleanor	7-17-16
Stevens Rise	6-11-13
Stratas Teresa	5-26-38
Stuarti Enzo	3-3-25
Studer Cheryl	10-24-55
Sutherland Joan	11-7-26
Swarthout Gladys	12-25-04
Te Kanawa Kiri	3-6-44
Tebaldi Renata	2-1-22
Thebom Blanche	9-19-19
Thomas Jess	4-8-27
Tibbett Lawrence	11-16-1896
Tozzi Giorgio	1-8-23
Traubel Helen	6-20-1899
Troyanos Tatiana	9-12-38
Tucker Richard	8-28-13
Upshaw Dawn	7-17-60
Varnay Astrid	4-25-18
Verrett Shirley	5-31-33
Vickers Jon	10-29-26
VonStade Frederica	6-1-45
Vyvyan Jennifer	3-13-25
Warfield William	1-22-20
Warren Leonard	4-21-11
Weathers Felicia	8-13-37
Weede Robert	2-22-03
Zylis-Gara Teresa	1-23-37

CONDUCTORS

Abbado Claudio	6-23-33
Anderson Gillian Bunshaft	11-28-43
Atherton David	1-3-44
Barbirolli John	12-2-1899
Baudo Serge	7-16-27
Barlow Howard	5-1-1892
Beecham Thomas	4-29-1879
Beinum Eduard van	9-3-00
Bernstein Leonard	8-25-18

Black Frank	11-28-1894
Bond Victoria	5-6-45
Boulez Pierre	3-26-25
Boult Adrian	4-8-1889
Caldwell Sarah	3-6-24
Ceccato Aldo	2-18-34
Craft Robert	10-20-23
Crosby John	7-12-26
Davies Dennis Russell	4-16-44
Davis Andrew	2-2-44
Davis Colin	9-25-27
DePreist James	11-21-36
deWaart Edo	6-1-41
Dohnanyi Christoph von	9-8-29
Dorati Antal	4-9-06
Fennell Frederick	7-2-14
Fiedler Arthur	12-17-1894
Freeman Paul	1-2-36
Giulini Carlo Maria	5-9-14
Goldman Edwin Franko	1-1-1878
Goldovsky Boris	6-7-08
Golschmann Vladimir	12-26-1893
Goossens Eugene	5-26-1893
Hanson Howard	10-28-1896
Harris Margaret	9-15-43
Harvey Raymond	12-9-50
Hendl Walter	1-12-17
Hillis Margaret	10-1-21
Hoffman Irwin	11-26-24
Irving Robert	8-28-13
Jackson Isaiah	1-22-45
Janssen Werner	6-1-00
Jarvi Neeme	6-7-37
Karajan Herbert von	4-5-08
Kertesz Istvan	8-29-29
Kleiber Carlos	7-3-30
Kleiber Erich	8-5-1890
Klemperer Otto	5-14-1885
Kondrashin Kiril	2-21-14
Kostelanetz Andre	12-22-01
Koussevitzky Serge	7-26-1874
Kubelik Rafael	6-29-14
Leinsdorf Erich	2-4-12
Levine James	6-23-43
Lewenthal Raymond	8-29-26
Lewis Henry Jay	10-16-32

Conductors	
Lockhart Keith	1959
Maazel Lorin	3-5-30
Mathieson Muir	1-24-11
Mehta Zubin	4-29-36
Mengelberg Willem	3-28-1871
Mitropoulos Dimitri	2-18-1896
Monteux Pierre	4-4-1875
Munch Charles	9-26-1891
Muti Riccardo	7-28-41
Ormandy Eugene	11-18-1899
Ozawa Seiji	9-1-35
Paray Paul	5-24-1886
Pelletier Wilfred	6-20-1896
Previn Andre	4-6-29
Queler Eve	1-1-36
Rattle Simon	1-19-55
Reiner Fritz	12-10-1888
Rodzinski Artur	1-2-1894
Rostropovich Mstislav	8-12-27
Saidenberg Daniel	10-12-06
Sargent Malcolm	4-29-1895
Schippers Thomas	3-9-30
Segal Uri	3-7-44
Sevitzky Fabien	9-30-1893
Slatkin Felix	12-22-15
Slatkin Leonard	9-1-44
Smallens Alexander	1-1-1889
Solti Georg	10-21-12
Steinberg William	8-1-1899
Stokowski Leopold	4-18-1882
Szell George	6-7-1897
Thomas Michael Tilson	12-21-44
Toscanini Arturo	3-25-1867
Voorhees Donald	7-26-03
Wallenstein Alfred	10-7-1898
Walter Bruno	9-15-1876
Wulstan David	1-18-37

****

CLASSICAL MUSICIANS

Accardo Salvatore	9-26-41
Aitken Webster	6-17-08
Amram David	11-17-30
Anda Geza	11-19-21
Andre Maurice	5-24-33
Argerich Martha	6-5-41
Arrau Claudio	2-6-04

Classical Musicians	
Artzt Alice	3-16-43
Ashkenazy Vladimir	7-6-37
Ax Emanuel	6-8-49
Bachauer Gina	5-21-13
Badura-Skoka Paul	1-15-27
Bar-Illan David	2-7-30
Barenbaim Daniel	11-15-42
Bauer Harold	4-28-1873
Behrend Jeanne	5-11-11
Berezowsky Nicolas	5-17-00
Berman Lazar	2-26-30
Biggs E Power	3-29-06
Bishop-Kovacevich Stephen	10-17-40
Bolet Jorge	11-15-14
Brailowsky Alexander	2-16-1896
Brain Dennis	5-17-21
Branscombe Gena	11-4-1881
Bream Julian	7-15-33
Brendel Alfred	1-5-31
Brouwer Leo	3-1-39
Brown Eddy	7-15-1895
Browning John	5-23-33
Bustabo Guila	2-25-19
Buswell James Oliver	12-4-46
Casadesus Gaby	8-9-02
Casadesus Robert	4-7-1899
Casals Pablo	12-29-1876
Chang Sarah	1980
Chasins Abram	8-17-03
Cherassky Shura	10-7-11
Chung Kyung-Wha	3-26-48
Ciccolini Aldo	8-15-25
Cliburn Van	7-12-34
Coci Claire	3-15-12
Cohen Harriet	12-2-1895
Corigliano John	8-28-01
Curzon Clifford	5-18-07
Cziffru Gyorgy	9-5-21
Darre Jeanne-Marie	7-30-05
Davidovich Bella	7-16-28
Dichter Misha	9-27-45
Dicterow Glenn	12-23-48
Dohnanyi Erno von	7-27-1877
Doktor Paul	3-28-19
DuPre Jacqueline	1-26-45
Dushkin Samuel	12-13-1891

****

Elman Mischa	1-20-1891
Entremont Philippe	6-7-34
Eschenbach Christoph	2-20-40
Feltsman Vladimir	1-8-52
Ferras Christian	6-17-33
Feuermann Emanuel	11-22-02
Firkusny Rudolf	2-11-12
Fischer Annie	7-15-14
Fleisher Leon	7-23-28
Fodor Eugene	3-5-50
Fournier Pierre	6-24-06
Fox Virgil	5-3-12
Francescatti Zino	8-9-05
Friedman Erick	8-16-39
Fulkerson Gregory	5-9-50
Galway James	12-8-39
Ganz Rudolph	2-24-1877
Garbousova Raya	9-25-09
Gieseking Walter	11-5-1895
Gilels Emil	10-19-16
Gimpel Jakob	4-16-06
Glenn Carroll	10-28-18
Goldberg Szymon	6-1-09
Goossens Leon	6-12-1897
Gould Glenn	9-25-32
Graffman Gary	10-14-28
Grainger Percy	7-8-1882
Grumiaux Arthur	3-21-21
Haendl Ida	12-15-23
Harrell Lynn	1-30-44
Harth Sidney	10-5-29
Heifetz Jascha	2-2-01
Hess Myra	2-25-1890
Hinderas Natalie	6-15-27
Hollander Lorin	7-19-44
Holliger Heinz	5-21-39
Holmes Ralph	4-1-37
Horowitz Vladimir	10-1-04
Howe Mary	4-4-1882
Istomin Eugene	11-26-25
Iturbi Amparo	3-12-1898
Iturbi Jose	11-28-1895
Janis Byron	3-24-28
Jenson Dylana	5-14-61
Johannesen Grant	7-30-21
Johansen Gunnar	1-21-06

****

****

Jonas Maryla	5-31-11
Joyce Eileen	11-21-12
Kafanian Ani	1948
Kafanian Ida	1950
Kahane Jeffrey	9-12-56
Kapell William	9-20-22
Katchen Julius	8-15-26
Katims Milton	6-24-09
Kennedy Nigel	12-28-56
Kim Young-Uck	9-1-47
Kipnis Igor	9-27-30
Kirkpatrick Ralph	6-10-11
Kissin Evgeny	10-9-71
Kogan Leonid	11-14-24
Krasner Louis	6-21-03
Kraus Lili	3-4-08
Kreisler Fritz	2-2-1875
Kremer Gidon	2-27-47
Kroll William	1-30-01
Landowska Wanda	7-5-1877
Laredo Jaime	6-7-41
Laredo Ruth	11-20-37
Larrocha Alicia de	5-23-23
Lateiner Jacob	5-31-28
Lev Rae	5-8-12
Ling Jahja	10-25-51
Lipatti Dinu	4-1-17
List Eugene	7-6-18
Lowe Jack	12-25-17
Lupu Radu	11-30-45
Ma Yo-Yo	10-7-55
Marlowe Sylvia	9-26-08
Menuhin Hephzibah	5-20-20
Menuhin Yehudi	4-22-16
Michelangeli Arturo Benedetti	1-6-20
Midori (Goto)	10-25-71
Milstein Nathan	12-31-04
Mischakoff Mischa	4-3-1895
Moiseivitch Benno	2-22-1890
Montoya Carlos	12-13-03
Morini Erika	1-5-06
Mutter Anne-Sophie	6-29-63
Novaes Guiomar	2-28-1895
Ohlsson Garrick	4-3-48
Oistrakh David	9-30-08
Oistrakh Igor	4-27-31

****

Oliveira Elmar	6-28-50
Ousset Cecile	3-3-36
Parkening Christopher	12-14-47
Pennario Leonard	7-9-24
Perahia Murray	4-19-47
Perlemuter Vlado	5-26-04
Perlman Itzhak	8-31-45
Piatigorsky Gregor	4-17-03
Pogorelich Ivo	10-20-58
Pollini Maurizio	1-5-42
Primrose William	8-23-04
Rabin Michael	5-2-36
Rabinof Benno	10-11-10
Rampal Jean-Pierre	1-7-22
Reisenberg Nadia	7-14-04
Ricci Ruggiero	7-24-18
Richter Sviatoslav	3-20-14
Robison Paula	6-8-41
Rosand Aaron	3-15-27
Rose Leonard	7-27-18
Rosen Charles	5-5-27
Rosen Max	4-11-00
Rosen Nathaniel	6-9-48
Rubinstein Artur	1-28-1889
Salerno-Sonnenberg Nadja	1-10-61
Salzedo Carlos	4-6-1885
Sandor Arpad	6-5-1896
Sandor Gyorgy	9-21-12
Sanroma Jesus Maria	11-7-02
Schiff Andras	12-21-53
Schneider Alexander	12-21-08
Segovia Andres	2-18-1894
Senofsky Berl	4-15-25
Serkin Peter	7-24-47
Serkin Rudolf	3-28-03
Shankar Ravi	4-7-20
Shumsky Oscar	3-23-17
Silverstein Joseph	3-21-32
Starker Janos	7-5-24
Stern Isaac	7-21-20
Suzuki Hidetaro	6-1-37
Tortelier Paul	3-21-14
Totenberg Roman	1-1-11
Treger Charles	5-13-35
Tureck Rosalyn	12-14-14
Uchida Mitsuko	12-20-48

Vasary Tamas	8-11-33
Watts Andre	6-20-46
Webster Beveridge	5-30-08
Weissenberg Alexis	7-26-29
Whittemore Arthur	10-23-16
Wild Earl	11-26-15
Williams John	4-24-41
Wilson Ransom	1951
Zimbalist Efrem	4-9-1889
Zimerman Krystian	12-5-56
Zukerman Eugenia	9-25-44
Zukerman Pinchas	7-16-48
Zukofsky Paul	10-22-43

BEAUX ARTS TRIO

Cohen Isidore	12-16-22
Greenhouse Bernard	1-3-16
Pressler Menahem	12-16-23

GUARNIERI STRING QUARTET

Dalley John	6-1-35
Soyer David	2-24-23
Steinhardt Arnold	4-1-37
Tree Michael	2-19-34

JUILLIARD STRING QUARTET

Adam Claus	11-5-17
Krosnick Joel	4-3-41
Mann Robert	7-19-20
Rhodes Samuel	2-13-41
Smirnoff Joel	1950

LaSALLE QUARTET

Fiser Lee	4-26-47
Kamnitzer Peter	11-27-22
Levin Walter	12-6-24
Meyer Henry	6-29-23

CHORAL DIRECTORS

Charles Ray	9-13-18
Darby Ken	5-13-09
Jessye Eva	1-20-1895
Johnson Hall	3-12-1888
Kerr Anita	10-13-27
Luboff Norman	4-14-17
Mann Johnny	8-30-28
Shaw Robert	4-30-16
Simeone Harry	5-9-11
Wagner Roger	1-16-14
Waring Fred	6-9-00

RADIO/TV CHILDREN'S SHOWS

Aberlin Betty	12-30-42
Allison Fran	11-20-07
Block Larry	10-30-42
Herbert Don	7-10-17
Herman Pee Wee	8-27-52
Hodge Al	1913
Keeshan Bob	6-27-27
Kemmer Ed	10-29-23
Lee Pinky	1916
Lee Will	8-6-08
McConnell Smiling Ed	1892
Miss Frances (Horwich)	7-16-08
Osborn Lyn	1-23-22
Perkins Marlin	3-28-02
Reed Alaina	11-10-46
Rogers Fred	3-20-28
Sales Soupy	1-8-26
Smith Buffalo Bob	11-27-17
Taylor Clarice	9-20-27
Tripp Paul	2-20-16
Wicker Ireene	11-24-05
Zaloom Paul	12-14-51

* * * * * * * * * * * * * * * *

RADIO/TV HOSTS & ANNOUNCERS

Abram Norm	1949
Adams Franklin P	11-15-1881
Adams Marcia	1938
Allen Steve	12-26-21
Anthony John J	9-1-1898
Attenborough David	5-8-26
Bailey Jack	9-15-07
Baker Art	1-7-1898
Baker Phil	8-24-1898
Baker Russell	8-14-25
Baldwin Bill	1913
Banghart Kenneth	1910
Barker Bob	12-12-23
Barris Chuck	6-3-28
Barry Jack	3-20-18
Bartlett Tommy	7-11-14
Baruch Andre	1906
Berry Bertice	1960
Bond Ford	1905
Bowes Major (Edward)	6-14-1874
Bradley Truman	1905

Bradshaw John	6-29-33
Breneman Tom	1902
Brokenshire Norman	6-10-1898
Brown Les	2-17-45
Brown Tony	4-11-33
Burrud Bill	1-12-25
Buscaglia Leo	3-31-24
Carpenter Ken	8-21-00
Carson Johnny	10-23-25
Cavett Dick	11-19-36
Cerf Bennett	5-25-1898
Child Julia	8-15-12
Clark Dick	11-30-29
Cobb Buff	10-19-28
Codrescu Andre	12-20-46
Convy Bert	7-23-33
Cooke Alistair	11-20-08
Cornelius Don	9-27-36
Cott Ted	1-1-17
Cross Milton	4-16-1897
Cullen Bill	2-18-20
Daly John	2-20-14
Dawson Richard	11-30-32
Dees Rick	3-14-50
Donahue Phil	12-21-35
Douglas Mike	8-11-25
Downey Morton Jr	12-9-33
Dunne Steve	1-13-16
Edwards Ralph	6-13-13
Elliot Win	5-7-15
Elliott Gordon	1956
Elvira (Cassandra Peterson)	9-17-51
Everage Lady Edith	2-17-34
Fadiman Clifton	5-15-04
Falkenburg Jinx	10-13-10
Faulk John Henry	8-21-13
Felton Happy	11-30-07
Fenneman George	11-10-19
Fitzgerald Ed	1893
Fitzgerald Pegeen	11-24-10
Fleming Art	5-1-20
Ford 'Senator' Ed	1887
Fox Sonny	6-17-25
Francis Arlene	10-20-08
Franklin Joe	1929
Frost David	4-7-39

Funt Allen	9-16-14
Gambling John B	4-9-1897
Garroway Dave	7-13-13
Gibson Charles	3-9-43
Gifford Kathie Lee	8-16-53
Gilbert Johnny	7-13-30
Glass Nancy	8-8-57
Gnagy Jon	1907
Godfrey Arthur	8-31-03
Goodwin Bill	7-28-10
Graham Virginia	7-4-12
Grauer Ben	6-2-08
Gray Barry	7-2-16
Griffin Merv	7-6-25
Gumbel Bryant	9-29-48
Hall Arsenio	2-12-59
Hall Monty	8-25-23
Hart Mary	11-8-50
Hart Dorothy	4-4-23
Hartman David	5-19-35
Hawk Bob	12-15-07
Hayes Peter Lind	6-25-15
Healy Mary	4-14-18
Hershfield Harry	10-13-1885
Hightower Jim Allen	1-11-43
Horowitz David	6-30-37
Hull Warren	1-17-03
James Dennis	8-24-17
Kelly Joe	5-31-01
Kennedy Tom	2-26-27
Kerr Graham	1-22-34
Keighley William	8-4-1889
Keillor Garrison	8-7-42
Kieran John	8-2-1892
Kilgallen Dorothy	7-3-13
King John Reed	10-25-14
King Larry	11-19-33
Kirby Durward	8-24-12
Kollmar Richard	12-31-10
Kovel Ralph	8-20-20
Kovel Terry	10-27-28
Lake Ricki	9-21-68
Lawes Lewis E	9-13-1883
Lawrence Vicki	3-26-49
Leach Robin	8-29-41
Leno Jay	4-28-50

Lescoulie Jack	11-17-17
Letterman David	4-12-47
Lewis Robert Q	4-25-21
Limbaugh Rush	1-12-51
Linkletter Art	7-17-12
Linkletter Jack	11-20-37
Ludden Allen	10-5-18
Mack Ted	2-12-04
Malone Ted	1910
March Hal	4-22-20
Marshall Peter	3-30-27
Marshall Rex	1919
Martindale Wink	12-4-34
McBride Mary Margaret	11-16-1899
McCarthy J P	3-22-34
McCrary Tex	1-21-19
McCullough David	7-7-33
McElhone Eloise	1921
McElroy Jack	10-21-13
McMahon Ed	3-6-23
McNamara Maggie	6-18-28
McNeill Don	12-3-07
McNellis Maggi	6-1-17
Miller Marvin	7-18-13
Moore Garry	1-31-15
Moore Tom	8-13-12
Murphy Terry	1949
Murray Arthur	4-4-1895
Murray Jan	10-4-17
Murray Kathryn	9-15-06
Narz Jack	11-13-22
Nash Ogden	8-19-02
Nesbitt John	8-23-10
Niles Ken	12-9-06
Niles Wendell	12-29-04
O'Brien Conan	4-18-63
O'Keefe Walter	8-18-00
Olsen Johnny	1910
Owens Gary	5-10-36
Paar Jack	5-1-18
Parks Bert	12-30-14
Peeples Nia	12-10-61
Pepin Jacques	12-18-35
Peters Tom	11-7-42
Petrie Howard	1907
Philbin Regis	8-25-33

****

Posner Vladimir	4-1-34
Povich Maury	1-17-39
Powter Susan	12-22-57
Prudhomme Paul	7-13-40
Purcell Sarah	10-8-48
Quinn Sally	7-1-41
Quivers Robin	1953
Raphael Sally Jessy	2-25-43
Rayburn Gene	12-22-17
Ripley Robert L	12-25-1893
Rivera Geraldo	7-3-43
Rose Charlie	1-5-42
Ross Bob	1942
Rukeyser Louis	1-30-33
Sagan Carl	11-9-34
Sajak Pat	10-26-47
Saralegui Cristina	1-29-48
Scourby Alexander	11-13-13
Serling Rod	12-25-24
Seymour Dan	6-28-14
Simmons Richard	7-12-48
Smith Jeff	1-22-39
Smith Verne	1914
Snyder Tom	5-12-36
Stern Howard	1-12-54
Stevens Shaddoe	1947
Stewart Martha	8-3-41
Story Ralph	1920
Sullivan Ed	9-28-02
Taylor Deems	12-22-1885
Taylor Marion Sayle	8-16-1889
Tesh John	7-9-52
Thomas Steve	1952
Tinney Cal	2-2-08
Trebek Alex	7-22-40
Valentine Lew	3-19-1882
Vampira	12-11-21
VanHorne Harriet	5-17-20
VanVoorhis Westbrook	9-21-03
Vila Bob	6-20-46
VonZell Harry	7-11-06
Wallington Jimmy	9-15-07
Wapner Joseph A	11-15-19
Watts Rolonda	7-12-59
Wendell Bill	3-22-24
White Vanna	2-18-57

****

****

Wilcox Harlow	1900
Williams Montel	1956
Williamson Marianne	7-8-52
Wilson Don	9-1-00
Winfrey Oprah	1-29-54
Woodhouse Barbara	5-9-10
Zacherley (John)	9-26-18

****

RADIO/TV NEWS

Aaron Betsy	11-11-38
Abel Elie	10-17-20
Abernethy Bob	11-5-27
Adams Cedric	5-27-02
Agronsky Martin	1-12-15
Albert Marv	6-12-43
Allen Mel	2-14-13
Archerd Army	1-13-19
Arledge Roone	7-8-31
Arnett Peter	11-13-34
Arnot Bob	2-23-48
Aug Stephen	1936
Barber Red	2-17-08
Barrett Rona	10-8-36
Bazell Robert	8-21-45
Beatty Bessie	1-27-1886
Beatty Morgan	9-6-02
Bell Steve	12-9-35
Berger Marilyn	8-23-35
Bergman Jules	3-21-27
Berman Chris	5-10-55
Beutel Bill	12-12-30
Blair Frank	5-30-15
Bourgholtzer Frank	10-26-19
Bradley Ed	6-22-41
Bradshaw Terry	9-2-48
Braver Rita	1949
Brazelton T Berry	5-10-18
Brickhouse Jack	1-24-16
Briggs Fred	5-31-32
Brinkley David	7-10-20
Brodie John	8-14-35
Brokaw Tom	2-6-40
Brown Hilary	1941
Bruno Hal	10-25-28
Buck Jack	8-21-24
Burdett Winston	12-12-13

****

Burrington David	3-11-31
Calmer Ned	7-16-07
Caray Harry	3-1-17
Carter Boake	9-28-1898
Carter Hodding	4-7-35
Castleberry Edward J	7-28-28
Chancellor John	7-14-27
Chase Rebecca	1949
Chase Sylvia	2-23-38
Christian Spencer	7-23-47
Chung Connie	8-20-46
Coleman John	11-15-35
Collingwood Charles	6-4-17
Collins Bud	6-17-29
Compton Ann	1-19-47
Considine Bob	11-4-06
Cordtz Dan	5-1-27
Corum Bill	7-20-1895
Cosell Howard	3-25-20
Costas Bob	3-22-52
Couric Katie	1-7-57
Cronkite Walter	11-4-16
Cross Irv	7-27-39
Culhane David	1930
Curry Ann	11-19-56
Davis Elmer	1-13-1890
Dean Morton	8-22-35
Deane Martha	11-21-09
Denny George V Jr	8-20-1899
Dickerson Nancy	1-19-30
Dierdorf Dan	6-29-49
Ditka Mike	10-18-39
Dobyns Lloyd	3-12-36
Donaldson Sam	3-11-34
Dotson Bob	10-3-46
Downs Hugh	2-14-21
Dreier Alex	6-26-16
Economaki Chris	10-15-20
Edwards Douglas	7-14-17
Eliot George Fielding	6-22-1894
Ellerbee Linda	8-15-44
Enberg Dick	1-9-35
Engberg Eric	9-18-41
Fenton Tom	4-8-30
Fernandez Giselle	5-15-61
Fidler Jimmy	8-26-1898

Flannery Harry W	3-13-00
Flemming Bill	9-3-26
Foss Joe	4-17-15
Frederick Pauline	2-13-08
Fuqua Stephen	12-25-1874
Garagiola Joe	2-12-26
Gergen David	5-9-42
Geyer Georgie Anne	4-2-35
Gibbons Floyd	7-16-1887
Gifford Frank	8-16-30
Gowdy Curt	7-31-19
Graham Fred	10-6-31
Greenfield Jeff	6-10-43
Gregory Bettina	6-4-46
Gumbel Greg	5-3-46
Harkness Richard C	9-29-07
Harsch Joseph C	5-25-05
Harvey Paul	9-4-18
Harwell Ernie	1-25-18
Heatter Gabriel	9-17-1890
Henry Bill	8-21-1890
Herman George	1-14-20
Hewitt Don	12-14-22
Hill Edwin C	4-23-1884
Hodges Russ	1909
Hopper Hedda	6-2-1890
Hottelot Richard C	9-22-17
Howar Barbara	9-27-34
Howe Quincy	8-17-00
Hughes Paul	5-1-16
Hume Brit	6-22-43
Hunter-Gault Charlayne	2-27-42
Huntley Chet	12-10-11
Husing Ted	11-27-01
Jackson Keith	10-18-28
Jamieson Bob	2-1-43
Jarriel Tom	12-29-34
Jennings Peter	7-29-38
Jones Charlie	11-9-30
Jones Phil	4-27-37
Kalb Bernard	2-5-22
Kalb Marvin	6-9-30
Kalber Floyd	12-23-24
Kaltenborn H V	7-9-1878
Kaplow Herb	2-2-27
Kashiwahara Ken	7-18-40

****

Kelly Dan	9-17-36
Keteyian Armen	3-6-53
Kiernan Walter	1-24-02
Kiker Douglas	1-7-30
Koppel Ted	2-8-40
Kroft Steve	8-22-45
Kuralt Charles	9-10-34
Kurtis Bill	9-21-40
Lehrer Jim	5-19-34
Leonard Bill	4-9-16
Lesueur Larry	6-10-09
Levine Irving R	8-26-22
Lewis Fulton Jr	4-30-03
Lindstrom Pia	9-20-38
Lisagor Peter	8-5-15
Lomax Stan	1899
Lunden Joan	9-19-50
Mackin Cassie	8-28-39
Madden John	4-10-36
Marash Dave	5-3-42
Martin John	12-3-31
McCarthy Clem	9-9-1882
McCarver Tim	10-16-41
McEwen Mark	9-16-54
McGee Frank	9-12-21
McGuire Al	9-7-31
McKay Jim	9-24-21
McLaughlin John	3-29-27
MacLeish Rod	1-15-26
McLendon Gordon	6-8-21
McNamee Graham	7-10-1888
MacNeil Robert	1-19-31
McWethy John	2-28-47
Meredith Don	4-10-38
Michaels Al	11-12-44
Morgan Edward P	6-23-10
Morton Bruce	10-28-30
Moyers Bill	6-5-34
Mudd Roger	2-9-28
Musburger Brent	5-26-39
Murray Joan	11-6-41
Murrow Edward R	4-25-08
Myers Lisa	1951
Nelson Lindsey	5-25-19
Newman Edwin	1-25-19
O'Brien Tim	7-11-43

****

O'Neil Roger	4-17-45
Osgood Charles	1-8-33
Oursler Fulton	1-22-1893
Palmer Bud	9-14-23
Pappas Ike	4-16-33
Parsons Louella	8-6-1881
Patrick Van	1916
Pauley Jane	10-31-50
Pearson Drew	12-13-1896
Pettit Tom	4-23-31
Phillips Stone	12-2-54
Plante Bill	1-14-38
Potter Mark	1953
Poussaint Renee	8-12-44
Quarles Norma	11-11-36
Quinones John	5-23-52
Quint Bert	9-22-30
Quirt John	6-26-39
Rashad Ahmad	11-19-49
Rather Dan	10-31-31
Reagan Ron	5-20-58
Reasoner Harry	4-17-23
Reynolds Frank	11-29-23
Reynolds Quentin	4-11-02
Rice Grantland	11-1-1880
Roberts Cokie	12-27-43
Roberts Steven V	2-11-43
Robinson Max	5-1-39
Roker Al	1955
Rollin Betty	1-3-36
Rooney Andy	1-14-19
Root Waverley	4-15-03
Ross Brian	10-23-48
Rowan Ford	5-31-43
Rudd Hughes	9-14-21
Rudolph Mendy	3-8-28
Russell Lynne	11-1-46
Russert Tim	5-7-50
Saerchinger Cesar	8-23-1889
Safer Morley	11-8-31
Salinger Pierre	6-14-25
Sanders Marlene	1-10-31
Savitch Jessica	2-2-47
Sawyer Diane	12-22-45
Sawyer Forrest	1949
Schaap Dick	9-27-34

****

****

Schell Tom	8-11-35
Schenkel Chris	8-21-23
Schieffer Bob	2-25-37
Schoenbrun David	3-15-15
Schorr Daniel	8-31-16
Score Herb	6-7-33
Scott Willard	3-7-34
Scully Vin	11-29-27
Serafin Barry	6-22-41
Sergio Lisa	3-17-05
Sevareid Eric	11-26-12
Shaw Bernard	5-22-40
Sherr Lynn	3-4-42
Shirer William L	2-23-04
Shriver Maria	11-6-55
Simpson Carole	12-7-40
Smith Harry	8-21-51
Smith Howard K	5-12-14
Smith Jack	4-25-45
Sokolsky George	9-5-1893
Stahl Lesley	12-16-41
Steel Johannes	8-3-06
Stern Bill	7-1-07
Stern Carl	8-7-37
Stookey Charley	5-4-00
Stossel John	3-6-47
Strait George	3-24-45
Strawser Neil	8-16-27
Streithorst Tom	1932
Sugrue Thomas	5-7-07
Sullivan Kathleen	5-17-53
Summerall Pat	5-10-30
Swayze John Cameron	4-4-06
Swing Raymond Gram	3-25-1887
Taylor Henry J	9-2-02
Thomas Lowell	4-6-1892
Thompson Dorothy	7-9-1894
Threlkeld Richard	11-30-37
Totenberg Nina	1-14-44
Trotta Liz	3-28-37
Trout Robert	10-15-08
Trumpy Bob	3-6-45
Tucker Lem	5-26-38
Uecker Bob	1-26-35
Utley Clifton	1904
Utley Garrick	11-19-39

****

****

Valeriani Richard	8-29-32
Vandercook John W	4-22-02
Vanocur Sander	1-8-28
Vitale Dick	6-9-40
VonFremd Mike	1952
Wallace Chris	10-12-47
Wallace Mike	5-9-18
Walters Barbara	9-25-31
Whitaker Jack	5-18-24
Wicker Tom	6-18-26
Williams Brian	1959
Williams Wythe	9-18-1881
Winchell Walter	4-7-1897
Wismer Harry	1913
Woodruff Judy	11-20-46
Wooten Jim	7-13-37
Zahn Paula	2-24-56

****

RADIO/TV RELIGION

Arthur Kay L	11-11-33
Bakker Jim	1-2-39
Bakker Tammy Faye	3-7-42
Burkett Larry	3-3-39
Dobson James	4-21-36
Elliot Elisabeth	12-21-26
Falwell Jerry	8-11-33
Graham Billy	11-7-18
Humbard Rex	8-13-19
Kennedy D James	11-3-30
Kinchlow Ben	12-27-36
Kuhlman Kathryn	5-9-07
MacArthur John F	6-19-39
Rev Ike (Eikerenkoetter)	6-1-35
Roberts Oral	1-24-18
Robertson Pat	3-22-30
Schuller Robert	9-16-26
Sheen Fulton J	5-8-1895
Swaggart Jimmy	3-15-35
Wildmon Don	1-18-38

****

TV FILM CRITICS

Ebert Roger	6-18-42
Maltin Leonard	12-18-50
Medved Michael	10-3-48
Shalit Gene	1932
Siskel Gene	1-26-46

****

CLASSICAL COMPOSERS

Addinsell Richard	1-13-04
Anderson Leroy	1-29-08
Arnold Malcolm	10-21-21
Barber Samuel	3-9-10
Barnes Billy	1-27-27
Bennett Robert Russell	6-15-1894
Blitzstein Marc	3-2-05
Bloch Ernest	7-24-1880
Bolcom William	5-26-38
Bowles Paul	12-30-10
Britain Radie	3-17-03
Britten Benjamin	11-22-13
Cage John	9-5-12
Coates Gloria	10-10-38
Corigliano John Jr	2-16-38
DelloJoio Norman	1-24-13
Foss Lukas	8-15-22
Francaix Jean	5-23-12
Glass Philip	1-31-37
Goldman Richard	12-7-10
Gould Morton	10-10-13
Grofe Ferde	3-27-1892
Harbison John	12-20-38
Harrison Lou	5-14-17
Hartke Stephen	7-6-52
Hindemith Paul	11-16-1895
Hoover Katherine	12-2-37
Hovhaness Alan	3-8-11
Joplin Scott	11-24-1868
Kay Ulysses	1-7-17
Khachaturian Aram	6-6-03
Kolb Barbara	2-10-39
LaBarbara Joan	6-8-47
Leon Tania	5-14-43
Maltby Richard	6-26-14
McDonald Harl	7-27-1899
Mennin Peter	5-17-23
Menotti Gian-Carlo	7-7-11
Musgrave Thea	5-27-28
Ran Shulamit	10-21-49
Rhodes Phillip	6-6-40
Richter Marga	10-21-26
Rorem Ned	10-23-23
Rosen Jerome	7-23-21
Schickele Peter	7-17-35

Schoenberg Arnold	9-2-1874
Schonthal Ruth	6-27-24
Shostakovich Dmitri	9-25-06
Sollberger Harvey	5-11-38
Suesse Dana	12-3-11
Swados Elizabeth	2-5-51
Tower Joan	9-6-38
Zaimont Judith Lang	11-8-45
Zwilich Ellen Taaffe	4-30-39

****

FILM & TV COMPOSERS

Addison John	3-16-20
Alcivar Bob	7-8-38
Amfitheatrof Daniele	10-29-01
Antheil George	6-8-00
Bacharach Burt	5-12-29
Bakaleinikoff Constantin	4-26-1898
Barry John	11-3-33
Bennett Richard Rodney	3-29-36
Bernstein Elmer	4-4-22
Bresler Jerry	5-29-12
Broughton Bruce	3-8-45
Bruns George	7-3-14
Buttolph David	8-3-02
Chang Gary	2-22-53
Conti Bill	4-13-42
Courage Alexander	12-10-19
Deutsch Adolph	10-20-1897
Duning George	2-25-08
Edelman Randy	6-10-47
Faltermeyer Harold	10-5-52
Fielding Jerry	6-17-22
Fox Charles	10-30-40
Friedhofer Hugo	5-3-02
Gold Ernest	7-13-21
Goldenberg Billy	2-10-36
Goldsmith Jerry	2-10-29
Gross Charles	5-13-14
Harline Leigh	3-26-07
Heindorf Ray	8-25-08
Herrmann Bernard	6-29-11
Hirschhorn Joel	12-18-37
Horner James	8-14-53
Jarre Maurice	9-13-24
Kamen Michael	4-15-48
Kaper Bronislau	2-5-02

Karlin Fred	6-16-36
Korngold Erich Wolfgang	5-29-1897
Lai Francis	4-26-32
Lava William	3-18-11
Legrand Michel	2-24-32
Levay Sylvester	5-16-45
Lindsey Mort	3-21-23
Mancini Henry	4-16-24
Matz Peter	11-6-28
Menken Alan	7-22-49
Moroder Giorgio	4-26-40
Morricone Ennio	10-11-28
Morris John	10-18-26
Newman Alfred	3-17-01
North Alex	12-4-10
Poledouris Basil	8-21-45
Post Mike	9-29-44
Raksin David	8-4-12
Raposo Joe	2-8-37
Ronnell Ann	12-25-10
Rose Earl	9-5-46
Rosenman Leonard	9-7-24
Rosenthal Laurence	11-4-26
Rota Nino	12-3-11
Rozsa Miklos	4-18-07
Rubinstein Arthur B	3-31-38
Salter Hans J	1-14-1896
Scharf Walter	8-1-10
Schifrin Lalo	6-21-32
Shaiman Marc	10-22-59
Shire David	7-3-37
Shore Howard	10-18-46
Silvestri Alan	3-26-50
Steiner Max	5-10-1888
Stevens Leith	9-13-09
Theodorakis Mikis	7-29-25
Tiomkin Dimitri	5-10-1899
Walker Shirley	4-10-45
Wallace Oliver	8-6-1887
Waxman Franz	12-24-06
Webb Roy	10-3-1888
Wilder Alec	2-17-07
Williams John	2-8-32
Williams Patrick	4-23-39
Young Victor	8-8-00
Zimmer Hans	9-12-57

BROADWAY COMPOSERS

Adler Richard	8-3-21
Bart Lionel	8-1-30
Berlin Irving	5-11-1888
Bock Jerry	11-23-28
Charig Philip	8-31-02
Coleman Cy	6-14-29
Edwards Sherman	4-3-19
Ford Nancy	10-1-35
Friml Rudolf	12-7-1879
Gaynor Charles	4-3-09
Gershwin George	9-26-1898
Gesner Clark	3-27-38
Grant Micki	6-30-41
Hague Albert	10-13-20
Hamlisch Marvin	6-2-44
Henderson Ray	12-1-1896
Heneker David	3-31-06
Herbert Victor	2-1-1859
Herman Jerry	7-10-32
Kander John	3-18-27
Kay Hershy	11-17-19
Kern Jerome	1-27-1885
Lane Burton	2-2-12
Leigh Mitch	1-30-28
Lewine Richard	7-28-10
Lewis Morgan 'Buddy'	12-26-06
Lloyd-Webber Andrew	3-22-48
Loesser Frank	6-29-10
Loewe Frederick	6-10-04
MacDermot Galt	12-19-28
Martin Hugh	8-11-14
McHugh Jimmy	7-10-1894
Moross Jerome	8-1-13
Porter Cole	6-9-1892
Rodgers Mary	1-11-31
Rodgers Richard	7-28-02
Romberg Sigmund	7-29-1887
Ruby Harry	1-27-1895
Schmidt Harvey	9-12-29
Schwartz Stephen	3-6-48
Sherwin Manning	1-4-02
Sondheim Stephen	3-22-30
Stothart Herbert	9-11-1885
Strouse Charles	6-7-28
Styne Jule	12-31-05

Swift Kay	4-19-05
Warren Harry	12-24-1893
Weill Kurt	3-2-00
Willson Meredith	5-18-02
Wilson Sandy	5-19-24
Youmans Vincent	9-27-1898

****

ELECTRONIC/COMPUTER COMPOSERS

Appleton Jon	1-4-39
Arel Bulent	5-23-19
Ashley Robert	3-28-30
Austin Larry	9-12-30
Babbitt Milton	5-10-16
Badings Henk	1-17-07
Behrman David	8-16-37
Berio Luciano	10-24-25
Brown Earle	12-26-26
Brun Herbert	7-9-18
Bussotti Sylvano	10-1-31
Cardero Cornelius	5-7-36
Carlos Walter/Wendy	11-14-39
Davidovsky Mario	3-4-34
Dockstadter Tod	3-20-32
Druckman Jacob	6-26-28
Eaton John C	3-30-35
El Dabh Halim	3-4-21
Erb Donald	1-17-27
Erickson Robert	3-7-17
Gaburo Kenneth	7-5-26
Ghent Emmanuel	5-15-25
Hiller Lejaren	2-23-24
Ichiyanagi Toshi	2-4-33
Ivey Jean Eichelberger	7-3-23
Johnston Ben	3-15-26
Kagel Mauricio	12-24-31
Kirchner Leon	1-24-19
Koening Gottfried Michael	10-5-26
Korte Karl	8-25-28
Kupferman Meyer	7-3-26
Lansky Paul	6-18-44
LeCaine Hugh	5-27-14
Leedy Douglas	3-3-38
Ligeti Gyorgy	5-28-23
Lucier Alvin	5-14-31
Luening Otto	6-15-00
Malovec Josef	3-24-33

Martirano Salvatore	1-12-27
Messiaen Olivier	12-10-08
Mimaroglu Ilhan	3-11-26
Oliveros Pauline	5-30-32
Penderecki Krzysztof	11-23-33
Pousseur Henri	6-23-29
Reynolds Roger	7-13-34
Risset Jean-Claude	3-13-38
Sahl Michael	9-2-34
Salzman Eric	9-8-33
Schwartz Elliott	1-19-36
Stockhausen Karlheinz	8-28-28
Subotnick Morton	4-14-33
Ussachevsky Vladimir	10-21-11
Varese Edgar	12-22-1883
Vercoe Barry L	1937
Whittenberg Charles	7-6-27
Wilson Olly	9-7-37
Wuorinen Charles	6-9-38
Xenakis Iannis	5-29-22

****

SONGWRITERS & LYRICISTS

Adams Lee	8-14-24
Arlen Harold	2-15-05
Ashman Howard	5-17-50
Barry Jeff	4-3-38
Bergman Alan	9-11-25
Bergman Marilyn	11-10-29
Bettis John	10-24-46
Blane Ralph	7-26-14
Brel Jacques	4-8-29
Brown Lew	12-10-1893
Brown Nacio Herb	2-22-1896
Bryant Boudleaux	2-13-20
Bryant Felice	8-7-25
Burke Johnny	10-3-08
Caesar Irving	7-4-1895
Cahn Sammy	6-18-13
Carmichael Hoagy	11-22-1899
Comden Betty	5-3-15
Coots J Fred	5-2-1897
Cryer Gretchen	10-17-35
Darion Joe	1-30-17
David Hal	5-25-21
DeSylva B G 'Buddy'	1-27-1895
Dietz Howard	9-8-1896

Donaldson Walter	2-15-1893
Donnelly Dorothy	1-28-1880
Dozier Lamont	6-16-41
Duke Vernon	10-10-03
Ebb Fred	4-8-33
Evans Ray	2-4-15
Fain Sammy	6-17-02
Fields Dorothy	7-15-04
Fields Herbert	7-26-1897
Fields Joseph	2-21-1895
Fine Sylvia	8-29-1893
Forrest George	7-31-15
Furber Douglas	5-13-1885
Gershwin Ira	12-6-1896
Green Adolph	12-2-15
Green Johnny	10-10-08
Greenwich Ellie	10-23-40
Hamilton Nancy	7-27-08
Hammerstein Oscar II	7-12-1895
Harbach Otto	8-18-1873
Harburg E Y 'Yip'	4-8-1898
Harnick Sheldon	4-30-24
Hart Charles	6-3-61
Hart Lorenz	5-2-1895
Hillebrand Fred	12-25-1893
Holland Brian	2-15-41
Holland Eddie	10-30-39
Hooker Brian	11-2-1880
Horwitt Arnold	7-21-18
Howard Harlan	9-8-29
Howard Joe	2-12-1878
Jacobs Jim	10-7-42
Jones Tom	2-17-28
Kahn Gus	11-6-1886
Kalmar Bert	2-16-1884
Latouche John	11-13-17
Leiber Jerry	4-25-33
Leigh Carolyn	8-21-26
Lerner Alan Jay	8-31-18
Maltby Richard Jr	10-6-37
Mandel Frank	5-31-1884
Mann Barry	2-9-39
McCarthy Joseph	9-27-1885
McGuire William	7-9-1885
McKuen Rod	4-29-33
Mercer Johnny	11-18-09

Merrill Bob	5-17-21
Meyer Joseph	3-12-1894
Newley Anthony	9-24-31
Newman Randy	11-28-43
Parish Mitchell	7-10-00
Previn Dory	10-22-25
Rado James	1-23-39
Ragni Gerome	9-11-42
Rice Tim	11-10-44
Robin Leo	4-6-00
Rome Harold	5-27-08
Ross Jerry	3-9-26
Ryskind Morrie	10-20-1895
Sager Carole Bayer	3-8-47
Saidy Fred	2-11-07
Schwartz Arthur	11-25-00
Schwartz Jean	11-4-1878
Sherman Richard	6-12-28
Sherman Robert	12-19-25
Shevelove Burt	9-19-15
Stein Joseph	5-30-12
Stewart Michael	8-1-29
Stoller Mike	3-13-33
Stone Peter	2-27-30
Taupin Bernie	5-22-50
Thompson Fred	1-24-1884
VanHeusen Jimmy	1-26-13
VanZandt Townes	3-7-44
Wayne Mabel	7-16-04
Webster Paul Francis	12-20-07
Weidman Jerome	4-4-13
Whiting Richard	11-12-1891
Williams Paul	9-19-40
Wright Robert	9-25-14
Young Rida Johnson	2-28-1869

DRAMATISTS

Akins Zoe	10-30-1886
Albee Edward	3-12-28
Anderson Maxwell	12-15-1888
Anderson Robert	4-28-17
Anouilh Jean	6-23-10
Arden John	10-26-30
Axelrod George	6-9-22
Ayckbourn Alan	4-12-39
Barry Philip	6-18-1896

Beck Julian	5-31-25
Beckett Samuel	4-13-06
Behan Brendan	2-9-23
Benedictus David	9-16-38
Bolt Robert	8-15-24
Bond Edward	7-18-34
Brecht Bertolt	2-10-1898
Breen Richard L	6-26-19
Bullins Ed	7-25-35
Burrows Abe	12-18-10
Busch Charles	8-23-54
Carlino Lewis John	1-1-32
Chase Mary	2-25-07
Chavez Denise	8-15-48
Childress Alice	10-12-20
Connelly Marc	12-13-1890
Coward Noel	12-16-1899
Crouse Russel	2-20-1893
Delaney Shelagh	11-25-39
Durang Christopher	1-2-49
Fierstein Harvey	6-6-54
Foster Paul	10-15-31
Frings Ketti	2-28-15
Fry Christopher	12-18-07
Fugard Athol	6-11-32
Fuller Charles	3-5-39
Genet Jean	12-19-10
Gibson William	11-13-14
Gilles D B	8-30-47
Gilroy Frank D	10-13-25
Goldman James	6-30-27
Gordone Charles	10-12-25
Gray Simon	9-21-36
Guare John	2-5-38
Gurney A R Jr	11-1-30
Hampton Christopher	1-26-46
Hanley William	10-22-31
Hansberry Lorraine	5-19-30
Hare David	6-5-47
Hart Moss	10-24-04
Hecht Ben	2-28-1894
Hellman Lillian	6-20-05
Henley Beth	5-8-52
Hochhuth Rolf	4-1-31
Horovitz Israel	3-31-39
Hwang David Henry	8-11-57

Inge William	5-3-13
Ionesco Eugene	11-26-12
Isherwood Christopher	8-26-04
Jellicoe Ann	7-17-27
Kanin Garson	11-24-12
Kaufman George S	11-14-1889
Kennedy Adrienne	9-13-31
Kingsley Sidney	10-18-06
Kopit Arthur	5-10-37
Kushner Tony	7-16-56
Laurents Arthur	7-14-18
Lawrence Jerome	7-14-15
Lee Robert E	10-15-18
Lindsay Howard	3-29-1889
MacArthur Charles	11-5-1895
Mamet David	11-30-47
McNally Terrence	11-3-39
Mercer David	6-27-28
Miller Arthur	10-17-15
Mosel Tad	5-1-22
Norman Marsha	9-21-47
O'Casey Sean	3-30-1880
O'Neill Eugene	10-16-1888
Odets Clifford	7-18-06
Orton Joe	1-1-33
Osborne John	12-12-29
Owens Rochelle	4-2-36
Patrick John	5-17-05
Pinter Harold	10-10-30
Rabe David	3-10-40
Randall Bob	8-20-37
Rattigan Terrence	6-10-11
Resnik Muriel	6-25-03
Rice Elmer	9-28-1892
Richards Stanley	4-23-18
Rudnick Paul	1957
Sackler Howard	12-19-27
Schisgal Murray	11-25-26
Shaffer Anthony & Peter	5-15-26
Shange Ntozake	10-18-48
Shawn Wallace	11-12-43
Shepard Sam	11-5-43
Sherwood Robert E	4-4-1896
Simon Neil	7-4-27
Spewack Bella	3-25-1899
Spewack Samuel	9-16-1899

Spiegelgass Leonard	11-26-08
Stoppard Tom	7-3-37
Storey David	7-13-33
Taylor Samuel	6-13-12
VanDruten John	6-1-01
VanItallie Jean-Claude	5-23-36
Wasserman Dale	11-2-17
Wasserstein Wendy	10-18-50
Weiss Peter	11-8-16
Wesker Arnold	5-24-32
Williams Emlyn	11-26-05
Williams Tennessee	3-26-11
Willingham Calder	12-23-22
Wilson August	4-27-45
Wilson Lanford	4-13-37

RADIO WRITERS

Barnouw Eric	6-23-08
Corwin Norman	5-3-10
Knight Ruth Adams	10-5-1898
Morse Carleton E	6-4-01
Oboler Arch	12-6-09

SCREENWRITERS

Allen Jay Presson	3-3-22
Anhalt Edward	3-28-14
Behrman S N	6-9-1893
Byrnes Jim	8-31-43
Chandler Raymond	7-22-1888
Chayefsky Paddy	1-29-23
Costigan James	3-31-28
Diamond I A L	6-27-20
Douglas Jack	7-17-20
Ephron Nora	5-19-41
Eszterhas Joe	11-23-44
Foreman Carl	7-23-14
Frank Harriet Jr	3-3-18
Gale Bob	5-25-51
Ganz Lowell	8-31-48
Hamner Earl	7-10-23
Jhabvala Ruth Prawer	5-7-27
Joffe Roland	11-17-45
Johnson Nunnally	12-5-1897
Kanter Hal	12-18-18
Kellogg Virginia	12-3-07
Kingsley Dorothy	10-14-09

Kinoy Ernest	4-1-25
Kleiner Harry	9-10-16
Krasna Norman	11-7-09
Lardner Ring Jr	8-19-15
Lasky Jesse Jr	9-19-10
Lehman Ernest	1920
Lemay Harding	3-16-22
Lennart Isobel	5-18-15
MacDougall Ranald	3-10-15
Maibaum Richard	5-26-09
Mainwaring Daniel	2-27-02
Mandel Babaloo	10-13-49
Mandel Loring	5-8-28
Mankowitz Wolf	11-7-24
Mann Abby	12-1-27
Markey Gene	12-11-1895
McGuire Don	2-28-19
Melchior Ib	9-17-17
Menken Robin	12-22-46
Miller Seton I	5-3-02
Mortimer John	4-21-23
Nichols Dudley	4-6-1895
Nugent Frank S	5-27-08
Perry Eleanor	1913
Poe James	10-4-21
Polonsky Abraham	12-5-10
Potter Dennis	5-15-35
Rackin Martin	7-31-18
Ravetch Irving	11-14-20
Rose Jack	11-4-11
Sale Richard	12-17-11
Salt Waldo	10-18-14
Sandler Barry	2-23-47
Sangster Jimmy	12-2-27
Silliphant Stirling	1-16-18
Singer Ray	10-24-16
Slesar Henry	6-12-27
Tesich Steve	9-29-42
Tewkesbury Joan	8-8-36
Thompson Caroline	4-23-56
Towne Robert	11-23-34
Trotti Lamar	10-18-00
Trumbo Dalton	12-9-05
Wilbur Crane	11-17-1889
Wincelberg Shimon	9-26-24
Wynn Tracy Keenan	2-28-45

FILM & TV DIRECTORS

Abrahams Jim	5-10-44
Aldrich Robert	8-9-18
Algar James	6-11-12
Allen Woody	12-1-35
Almodovar Pedro	9-25-51
Altman Robert	2-20-25
Amateau Rod	12-20-23
Anderson Lindsay	4-17-23
Anderson Michael	1-30-20
Anger Kenneth	2-3-30
Annakin Ken	8-10-14
Antonioni Michelangelo	9-29-12
Apted Michael	2-19-41
Armstrong Gillian	12-18-50
Arnold Jack	10-14-16
Arzner Dorothy	1-3-00
Attenborough Richard	8-29-23
Avildsen John G	12-21-35
Badiyi Reza S	4-17-30
Bartel Paul	8-6-38
Beaumont Gabrielle	7-4-42
Benton Robert	9-29-32
Beresford Bruce	8-16-40
Bergman Ingmar	7-14-18
Bertolucci Bernardo	3-16-41
Bogart Neil	2-3-43
Bogart Paul	11-21-19
Bogdanovich Peter	7-30-39
Boorman John	1-18-33
Borzage Frank	4-23-1893
Boulting Roy	11-21-13
Brakhage Stan	1-14-33
Brenon Herbert	1-13-1880
Brickman Marshall	8-25-41
Bridges James	2-3-36
Broca Philippe de	3-15-33
Brooks Mel	6-28-26
Brooks Richard	5-18-12
Burton Tim	8-25-58
Buzzell Edward	11-13-1897
Cacoyannis Michael	6-11-22
Cameron James	8-16-54
Campion Jane	4-30-54
Capra Frank	5-18-1897
Carpenter John	1-16-48

Cassavetes John	12-9-29
Castle Nick Jr	9-21-47
Chabrol Claude	6-24-30
Chomsky Marvin	5-23-29
Cimino Michael	2-3-39
Clair Rene	11-11-1898
Clayton Jack	3-1-21
Clement Rene	3-18-13
Coen Ethan	9-21-57
Coen Joel	11-29-54
Cohen Larry	4-20-38
Columbus Chris	9-10-58
Coolidge Martha	8-17-46
Coppola Francis Ford	4-7-39
Costa-Gavras	2-12-33
Craven Wes	8-2-39
Crichton Charles	8-6-10
Cronenberg David	3-15-43
Cruze James	3-27-1884
Cukor George	7-7-1899
Cummings Irving	10-9-1888
Curtiz Michael	12-24-1888
DaCosta Morton	3-7-14
Damski Mel	7-21-46
Dante Joe	11-28-46
Dassin Jules	12-18-11
DeMille Cecil B	8-12-1881
Demme Jonathan	2-22-44
Demy Jacques	6-5-31
DePalma Brian	9-11-40
Donen Stanley	4-13-24
Donohue Jack	11-3-08
Dwan Allan	4-3-1885
Edwards Blake	7-26-22
Eisenstein Sergei	1-23-1898
Farrow John	2-10-06
Fassbinder Rainer Werner	5-31-46
Fellini Federico	1-20-20
Flaherty Robert J	2-16-1884
Fleischer Richard	12-8-16
Flicker Theodore J	6-6-30
Florey Robert	9-14-00
Forbes Bryan	7-22-26
Ford John	2-1-1895
Forman Milos	2-18-32
Foster Norman	12-13-03

Frankenheimer John	2-19-30
Friedkin William	8-29-39
Fuller Samuel	8-12-11
Furie Sidney J	2-28-33
Gimbel Peter	2-14-28
Glenville Peter	10-28-13
Godard Jean Luc	12-3-30
Griffith D W	1-22-1875
Guitry Sacha	2-21-1885
Hackford Taylor	12-31-44
Hamilton Guy	9-24-22
Harlin Renny	3-15-59
Harvey Anthony	6-3-31
Heckerling Amy	5-7-54
Herzog Werner	9-6-42
Hill George Roy	12-20-22
Hill Walter	1-10-42
Hiller Arthur	11-22-23
Hitchcock Alfred	8-13-1899
Hooper Tobe	1-25-43
Hopper Jerry	7-29-07
Hughes John	2-18-50
Hunt Peter H	12-19-38
Hussein Waris	12-9-38
Huston John	8-5-06
Ichikawa Kon	11-20-15
Ingram Rex	1-15-1892
Ivory James	6-7-28
Jaglom Henry	1-26-43
Jarrott Charles	6-6-27
Jewison Norman	7-21-26
Johnson Lamont	9-20-22
Jones Harmon	6-3-11
Jordan Neil	2-25-50
Julian Rupert	1-25-1889
Kaplan Jonathan	11-25-47
Kasdan Lawrence	1-14-49
Kaufman Phil	10-23-36
Kazan Elia	9-7-09
Kennedy Burt	9-3-22
Kershner Irvin	4-29-23
King Henry	1-24-1896
Kirkwood James	2-22-1883
Kleiser Randal	7-20-46
Korty John	7-22-36
Kotcheff Ted	4-7-31

Krasny Paul	8-8-35
Kubrick Stanley	7-26-28
Kurosawa Akira	3-23-10
Landis John	8-3-50
Lang Fritz	12-5-1890
Leacock Philip	10-8-17
Lean David	3-25-08
Leder Mimi	1-26-52
Lee Spike	3-20-57
Lelouch Claude	10-30-37
Leonard Robert Z	10-7-1889
Leone Sergio	1-3-21
LeRoy Mervyn	10-15-00
Lester Richard	1-19-32
Levin Henry	6-5-09
Levinson Barry	6-2-32
Lewis Robert Michael	11-9-34
Lindsay-Hogg Michael	5-5-40
Losey Joseph	1-14-09
Lubitsch Ernst	1-28-1892
Lumet Sidney	6-25-24
Lynch David	1-20-46
MacKenzie Will	7-24-38
Malick Terence	11-30-43
Malle Louis	10-30-32
Mankiewicz Joseph L	2-11-09
Mann Anthony	6-30-06
Mann Daniel	8-8-12
Mann Delbert	1-30-20
Marton Andrew	1-26-04
Mazursky Paul	4-25-30
McCarey Leo	10-3-1898
McLaglen Andrew V	7-28-20
Menzel Jiri	2-23-38
Meyer Russ	3-21-22
Miller David	11-28-09
Milius John	4-11-44
Minnelli Vincente	2-28-10
Needham Hal	3-6-31
Negulesco Jean	2-26-00
Neilan Marshall	4-11-1891
Nelson Ralph	8-12-16
Niblo Fred	1-6-1874
Nichols Mike	11-6-31
Nigh William	10-12-1881
Ophuls Marcel	11-1-27

****

Ophuls Max	5-6-02
Oswald Gerd	6-9-16
Page Anthony	9-21-35
Pakula Alan	4-7-28
Parker Alan	2-14-44
Peckinpah Sam	2-21-25
Penn Arthur	9-27-22
Perry Frank	8-20-30
Polanski Roman	8-18-33
Pollack Sydney	7-1-34
Pollard Harry A	1-23-1879
Porter Edwin S	4-21-1869
Powell Michael	9-30-05
Preminger Otto	12-5-06
Pressburger Emeric	12-5-02
Rafelson Bob	2-21-33
Raimi Sam	10-23-59
Rawlins John	6-9-02
Ray Nicholas	8-7-11
Ray Satyajit	5-2-21
Reed Carol	12-30-06
Reitman Ivan	10-27-46
Renoir Jean	9-15-1894
Resnais Alain	6-3-22
Rich David Lowell	8-31-20
Richardson Tony	6-5-28
Riefenstahl Leni	8-22-02
Ritchie Michael	11-28-38
Ritt Martin	3-2-20
Robson Mark	12-4-13
Roeg Nicolas	8-15-28
Rohmer Eric	12-1-20
Romero George A	2-4-40
Ross Herbert	5-13-27
Rossellini Roberto	5-8-06
Rossen Robert	3-16-08
Rudolph Alan	12-18-43
Russell Ken	7-3-27
Sandrich Jay	2-24-32
Sarafian Richard C	4-28-32
Sayles John	9-28-50
Schaefer George	12-16-20
Schatzberg Jerry	6-26-27
Schepisi Fred	12-26-36
Schlesinger John	2-16-26
Schrader Paul	7-22-46

****

Scorsese Martin	11-17-42
Scott Ridley	11-30-39
Sedgwick Edward	11-7-1892
Segal Alex	7-1-15
Seidelman Susan	12-11-52
Shelton Ron	9-15-45
Sidney George	10-4-16
Siegel Don	10-26-12
Silver Joan Micklin	5-24-35
Silverstein Elliot	8-3-27
Simon S Sylvan	3-9-10
Singleton John	1-6-68
Smight Jack	3-9-26
Soderbergh Steven	1-14-63
Spheeris Penelope	12-2-45
Spielberg Steven	12-18-47
Spottiswoode Roger	1945
Springsteen R G	9-8-04
Stevens George	12-18-04
Stone Andrew L	7-16-02
Stone Oliver	9-15-46
Sturges John	1-3-11
Sturges Preston	8-29-1898
Sutherland Edward	1-5-1895
Tarantino Quentin	3-27-63
Tashlin Frank	2-19-13
Taurog Norman	2-23-1899
Taylor Jud	2-25-40
Tetzlaff Ted	6-3-03
Thomas Ralph	8-10-15
Thorpe Richard	2-24-1896
Tourneur Jacques	11-12-04
Tourneur Maurice	2-2-1876
Townsend Robert	2-6-57
Truffaut Francois	2-6-32
Tully Montgomery	5-6-04
Tuttle Frank	8-6-1892
Ulmer Edgar G	9-17-04
Vadim Roger	1-26-28
VanDyke W S	3-21-1890
VanPeebles Melvin	9-21-32
VanSant Gus	7-24-52
Verhoeven Paul	7-18-38
Vidor Charles	7-27-00
Vidor King	2-8-1894
vonStroheim Erich	9-22-1885

****

****

Wagner Jane	2-2-35
Walsh Raoul	3-11-1887
Walters Charles	11-17-11
Wang Wayne	1-12-49
Waters John	4-22-46
Weber Lois	6-13-1881
Weill Claudia	1947
Weinstein Paula	11-19-45
Weir Peter	8-8-44
Welles Orson	5-6-15
Wellman William A	2-29-1896
Wenders Wim	8-14-45
Wertmuller Lina	8-14-28
Whale James	7-22-1896
Wilder Billy	6-22-06
Wise Robert	9-10-14
Woo John	1945
Wood Edward Jr	10-10-24
Wyler William	7-1-02
Yates Peter	7-24-29
Yellen Linda	7-13-49
Zefferelli Franco	2-12-23
Zemeckis Robert	5-14-51
Zinnemann Fred	4-29-07
Zucker David	10-16-47
Zucker Jerry	3-11-50

****

STAGE DIRECTORS

Abbott George	6-25-1889
Ambush Benny	6-17-51
Anderson John Murray	9-20-1886
Bogart Anne	9-25-51
Bogdanov Michael	12-15-38
Boleslavsky Richard	2-4-1889
Brook Peter	3-21-25
Brown Arvin	5-24-40
Carroll Vinette	3-11-22
Chaikin Joseph	9-16-35
Chang Tisa	4-5-41
Charnin Martin	11-24-34
Chekhov Michael	8-16-1891
Cimber Matt	1-12-36
Clurman Harold	9-18-01
Coe Peter	4-18-29
Colon Miriam	8-20-35
Curiel Tony	9-2-54

****

Davidson Gordon	5-7-33
Dickerson Glenda	2-9-45
Dodson Owen	11-28-14
Donehue Vincent J	9-22-22
Dowling Vincent	9-7-29
Falls Robert	3-2-54
Feuer Cy	1-15-11
Foreman Richard	6-10-37
Galban Margarita	10-27-36
Gates Michael	1-9-44
Guthrie Tyrone	7-2-00
Hall Adrian	12-3-28
Hall Peter	11-22-30
Harris Jed	2-25-00
Henry Martha	2-17-38
Hirsch John	5-1-30
Hopkins Arthur	10-4-1878
Huerta Jorge	11-20-42
Hunt Peter	3-11-28
Jones Margo	12-12-11
Jory Jon V	6-1-38
Kahn Michael	9-9-40
King Woodie Jr	7-27-37
Lamos Mark	3-10-46
Leach Wilford	8-26-29
LeCompte Elizabeth	4-28-44
Leftwich Alexander	1884
Lewis Robert	3-16-09
Littlewood Joan	10-6-14
Logan Joshua	10-5-08
Ludlum Charles	4-12-43
MacGregor Edgar	1879
Mamoulian Rouben	10-8-1898
Mann Emily	4-12-52
Marre Albert	9-20-25
Mason Marshall	2-24-40
McAnuff Des	6-19-52
McClintic Guthrie	8-6-1893
Meadow Lynn	11-12-46
Moeller Philip	8-21880
Mosher Gregory	1-15-49
Nunn Trevor	1-14-40
O'Horgan Tom	5-3-26
Pemberton Brock	12-14-1885
Prince Harold	1-30-28
Purdy Claude	5-11-40

****

****

Quintero Jose	10-15-24
Reinhardt Max	9-9-1873
Saks Gene	11-8-21
Schechner Richard	8-23-34
Schneider Alan	12-12-17
Schumann Peter	6-11-34
Schwartz Maurice	6-18-1890
Scott Harold	9-6-35
Sellars Peter	9-27-57
Sierra Ruben	12-6-46
Sills Paul	11-18-27
Strasberg Lee	11-17-01
Teer Barbara Ann	6-18-37
Thompson Tazewell	5-27-54
Valdez Luis	6-26-40
Vance Nina	10-22-14
Vaughan Stuart	8-23-25
Ward Douglas Turner	5-5-30
Wilson John C	8-19-1899
Wilson Robert	10-4-41
Woodruff Robert	3-18-47
Wright Garland	4-18-46
Zaks Jerry	9-7-46

****

FILM PRODUCERS

Abrahams Mort	3-26-16
Adler Buddy	6-22-09
Allen Irving	11-24-05
Allen Irwin	6-12-16
Arkoff Samuel Z	6-12-18
Arnold Danny	1-23-25
Begelman David	8-26-21
Bender Lawrence	1958
Berman Pandro	3-28-05
Brisson Frederick	3-17-17
Broccoli Albert R	4-5-09
Bronston Samuel J	1909
Brown David	7-28-16
Brown Harry Joe	9-22-1890
Camp Joe	4-20-39
Carr Allan	5-27-41
Castle William	4-24-14
Chartoff Robert	8-26-33
Chow Raymond	5-17-27
Cooper Merian C	10-24-1893
Corman Roger	4-5-26

****

****

DeLaurentiis Dino	8-8-19
deRochemont Louis	1-13-1899
Diller Barry	2-2-42
Eisner Michael	3-7-42
Evans Robert	6-29-30
Frankovich Mike J	9-29-10
Golan Menahem	5-31-29
Goldwyn Samuel	8-27-1884
Goldwyn Samuel Jr	9-7-26
Grazer Brian	7-12-51
Haley Jack Jr	10-25-33
Hecht Harold	6-1-07
Henson Lisa	5-9-60
Hunter Ross	5-6-16
Hurd Gale Anne	10-25-55
Ince Thomas H	11-6-1882
Irving Jules	4-13-25
Jacobs Arthur P	3-7-22
Janni Joseph	5-12-16
Kastner Elliott	1-7-30
Katzenberg Jeff	1950
Kline Herbert	3-13-09
Koch Howard W	4-11-16
Kohlmar Fred	8-10-05
Korda Alexander	9-16-1893
Kramer Stanley	9-29-13
Ladd Alan Jr	10-22-37
Laemmle Carl	1-17-1867
Landau Ely	1-20-20
Lang Jennings	5-28-15
Lansing Sherry	7-31-44
Lasky Jesse L	9-13-1880
Lesser Sol	2-17-1890
Levine Joseph E	9-9-05
Lewis Claude	7-5-26
Lewton Val	5-7-04
Lucas George	5-14-44
Manulis Martin	5-30-15
Mayer Louis B	7-4-1885
Maysles Albert	11-26-26
Maysles David	1-10-32
Melcher Martin	8-1-15
Melnick Daniel	4-21-32
Merchant Ismail	12-25-36
Mirisch Walter	11-8-21
Obst Lynda	4-14-50

****

* *

Pal George	2-1-08
Panama Norman	4-21-14
Pasternak Joseph	9-19-01
Pennebaker D A	7-15-25
Peters Jon	1945
Phillips Julia	4-7-44
Pine William H	2-15-1896
Ponti Carlo	12-11-13
Rank J Arthur	12-23-1888
Ransohoff Martin	1927
Roach Hal	1-14-1892
Ruddy Albert	3-28-34
Saltzman Harry	10-27-15
Schary Dore	8-31-05
Selznick David O	5-10-02
Sennett Mack	1-17-1880
Shenson Walter	6-23-19
Siegel Sol C	3-30-03
Small Edward	2-1-1891
Smith Pete	9-4-1892
Sperling Milton	7-6-12
Spiegel Sam	11-11-03
Steel Dawn	8-19-46
Stigwood Robert	4-16-34
Thalberg Irving G	5-30-1899
Thomas William C	8-11-03
Todd Mike	6-22-07
Wald Jerry	9-16-11
Wallis Hal B	9-14-1899
Walsh Bill	9-30-14
Wanger Walter	7-11-1894
Warner Jack L	8-2-1892
Wayne Michael	11-23-34
Weintraub Jerry	9-26-37
Weisbart David	1-21-15
Winkler Irwin	5-28-31
Wiseman Frederick	1-1-30
Wurtzel Sol M	9-12-1881
Yates Herbert J	8-24-1880
Youngson Robert	11-27-17
Zanuck Darryl F	9-5-02
Zanuck Lili Fini	4-2-54
Zanuck Richard	12-13-34
Zimbalist Sam	3-31-04
Zugsmith Albert	4-24-10
Zukor Adolph	1-7-1873

* *

* *

STAGE PRODUCERS

Abady Josephine	8-21-49
Akalaitis JoAnne	6-29-37
Bloomgarden Kermit	12-15-04
Bufman Zev	10-11-30
Carroll Earl	9-16-1893
Cohen Alexander H	7-24-20
Crawford Cheryl	9-24-02
Dalrymple Jean	9-2-10
Drabinsky Garth	1948
Elkins Hillard	10-18-29
Freedley Vinton	11-5-1891
Fryer Robert	11-18-20
Hayward Leland	9-13-02
Houseman John	9-22-02
Levin Herman	12-1-07
Martin Ernest	8-28-19
Merrick David	11-27-12
Nederlander James	3-21-22
Papp Joseph	6-22-21
Rose Billy	9-6-1899
Saint-Subber Arnold	2-18-18
Schwab Laurence	12-17-1893
Sillman Leonard	5-9-08
Smith Oliver	2-13-18
Stewart Ellen	10-7-31
Ziegfeld Florenz	3-15-1867

* * * * * * * * * * * * * * * * *

RADIO PRODUCERS

Bower Roger	1-8-04
Lord Phillips H	7-15-02
Phillips Irna	7-1-01
Quinn Don	11-18-00
Rountree Martha	1916

* * * * * * * * * * * * * * * * *

TV PRODUCERS

Avnet Jon	11-17-49
Banner Bob	8-15-21
Bell William J	3-6-27
Benson Hugh	9-7-17
Bloodworth-Thomason Linda	4-15-47
Bochco Steven	12-16-43
Brand Joshua	11-29-50
Brooks James L	5-9-40
Brownlow Kevin	6-2-38
Burns Allan	5-18-35

* *

Burns Ken	7-29-53
Burrows James	12-30-40
Cannell Stephen J	2-5-42
Carsey Marcy	11-21-44
Chambers Everett	8-19-26
Chermak Cy	9-20-29
Coe Fred	12-23-14
Cook Fielder	3-9-23
Cooney Joan Ganz	11-30-29
Corday Barbara	10-15-44
Corea Nicholas	4-7-43
Cramer Douglas	8-22-31
Curtis Dan	8-12-28
English Diane	1948
Friendly Ed	4-8-22
Friendly Fred W	10-30-15
Fries Charles	9-30-28
Gelbart Larry	2-25-28
Geller Bruce	10-13-30
Goldberg Gary David	6-25-48
Goldberg Leonard	1-24-34
Goodson Mark	1-24-15
Grade Lew	12-25-06
Greenspan Bud	9-18-26
Grossbart Jack	4-18-48
Haggis Paul	3-10-53
Halmi Robert	1-22-24
Harrison Joan	6-20-08
Hawkesworth John	12-7-20
Hemion Dwight	3-14-26
Henning Paul	9-16-11
Herskovitz Marshall	2-23-52
Husky Rick	5-6-40
Johnson Kenneth	10-26-42
Kelley David E	1956
King Zalman	5-23-41
Kohan Buz	8-9-33
Komack James	8-3-30
Krantz Steve	5-20-23
Laird Jack	5-8-23
Landsburg Alan	5-10-33
Lansbury Bruce	1-12-30
Larson Glen A	1937
Lear Norman	7-27-22
Leibman Max	8-5-02
Leonard Herbert B	10-8-22

Levinson Richard	8-7-34
Link William	12-15-33
London Jerry	1-21-37
Mancuso Frank	7-25-33
Mancuso Frank Jr	10-9-58
Mann Michael	2-5-43
Marshall Garry	11-13-34
Martin Quinn	5-22-22
Michaels Lorne	11-17-44
Music Lorenzo	5-2-37
Monty Gloria	8-12-21
Nixon Agnes	12-10-27
Otte Ruth	6-28-49
Parriott James D	11-14-50
Reynolds Gene	4-4-25
Rich Lee	12-10-26
Roddenberry Gene	8-19-21
Rosemont Norman	12-12-24
Rosenzweig Barney	12-23-37
Ross Stanley Ralph	7-22-40
Rukeyser Merryle	4-15-31
Rushnell Squire	10-31-38
Saltzman Philip	9-19-28
Sheldon Sidney	2-11-17
Silverman Fred	9-13-37
Smith Jacqueline	5-24-33
Sohmer Steve	12-16-41
Spelling Aaron	4-22-25
Stoddard Brandon	3-31-37
Sugarman Burt	1-4-38
Susskind David	12-19-20
Tarses Jay	7-3-39
Tartikoff Brandon	1-13-49
Thomopoulos Tony	2-7-38
Tinker Grant	1-11-26
Tinker Mark	1952
Todman Bill	7-31-16
Tors Ivan	6-12-16
VanScoyk Robert	1-13-28
vonZerneck Frank	11-3-40
Werner Tom	1950
Winsor Roy	4-13-12
Witt Paul Junger	3-20-41
Wolf Dick	12-20-46
Wolper David L	1-11-28
Yorkin Bud	2-22-26

ANIMATORS

Avery Tex	2-26-08
Bakshi Ralph	10-26-38
Barbera Joseph	3-24-11
Bluth Don	9-13-38
Bray John Randolph	8-25-1879
Clampett Bob	5-8-10
Disney Walt	12-5-01
Fleischer Max	7-19-1883
Freleng Friz	8-21-06
Hanna William	7-14-10
Hubley John	5-21-14
Iwerks Ub	3-24-01
Jones Chuck	9-1-12
Judge Mike	1963
Lantz Walter	4-27-00
Melendez Bill	11-15-16
Mendelson Lee	3-24-33
Quimby Fred	1886
Sullivan Pat	1887
Terry Paul	2-19-1887
Trnka Jiri	2-24-12
Vinton Will	11-17-47
Ward Jay	9-21-20

CINEMATOGRAPHERS

Almendros Nestor	10-30-30
Alonzo John A	6-12-34
August Joseph H	4-26-1890
Bitzer Billy	4-21-1872
Chapman Michael	11-21-35
Freund Karl	1-16-1890
Garmes Lee	5-27-1898
Howe James Wong	8-28-1899
Imi Tony	3-27-37
Kemper Victor J	4-14-27
Koenekamp Fred	11-11-22
Lang Charles B	3-27-02
Laszlo Andy	1-12-26
Lathrop Philip H	1-12-16
Mate Rudolph	1-21-1898
Morgan Donald M	2-11-42
Murphy Brianne	4-1-38
Nykvist Sven	12-3-22
Shamroy Leon	7-16-01
Surtees Bruce	7-23-51

Surtees Robert L	8-9-06
Toland Greg	5-29-04
Waite Ric	7-10-33
Watkin David	3-23-25
Wexler Haskell	2-6-22
Willis Gordon	5-28-31
Zsigmond Vilmos	6-16-30

FILM EDITORS

Allen Dede	12-3-25
Booth Margaret	1-16-1898
Hornbeck William	8-23-01
Kress Harold F	6-26-13

SPECIAL EFFECTS

Baker Rick	12-8-50
Harryhausen Ray	6-29-20
O'Brien Willis	3-2-1886

COSTUME DESIGNERS

Adrian (Gilbert)	3-3-03
Aghayan Ray	7-29-34
Adredge Theoni V	8-22-32
Barcelo Randy	9-10-46
Brooks Donald	1-10-28
Campbell Patton	9-10-26
Fletcher Robert	8-29-23
Greenwood Jane	4-30-34
Head Edith	10-28-07
Jeakins Dorothy	1-11-14
Klotz Florence	10-28-20
Louis Jean	10-5-07
Orry-Kelly	12-31-1897
Plunkett Walter	6-5-02
Stewart Marlene	8-25-49
Travilla (William)	3-22-20
Zipprodt Patricia	2-24-25

STUNTMEN

Canutt Yakima	11-29-1895
Farnsworth Richard	9-1-20
Lyons Cliff	1902
Randall Glenn Jr	2-11-41
Sharpe Dave	1910
Steele Tom	1915
VanSickel Dale	1907

RECORD PRODUCERS

Ertegun Ahmet	7-31-23
Geffen David	2-21-43
Gordy Berry Jr	11-28-29
Grusin Dave	6-26-34
Hammond John	12-15-10
Iglauer Bruce	7-10-47
Miller Jay	5-5-22
Mottola Tommy	7-14-··
Phillips Sam	1-5-23
Robey Don	1903
Spector Phil	12-26-40
Stone Cliffie	3-1-17
Yetnikoff Walter	8-11-33

****

MAGICIANS

Blackstone Harry Jr	6-30-34
Copperfield David	9-16-56
Henning Doug	5-3-47
Houdini Harry	3-24-1874
Penn (Jillette)	3-5-55
Randi James	8-7-28
Roy (Horn)	1945
Siegfried (Fischbacker)	1943
Teller (Ray)	2-14-48

****

PERFORMANCE ARTISTS

Allen Terry	5-7-43
Anderson Laurie	6-5-47
Antin Eleanor	2-27-35
Graham Dan	3-31-42
Hellermann William	7-15-39
Knowles Alison	4-29-33
Mumma Gordon	3-30-35
Phillips Liz	6-13-51
Rosenthal Rachel	11-9-26

****

VENTRILOQUISTS

Bergen Edgar	2-16-03
Dinsdale Shirley	10-31-26
Flowers Wayland	11-··-39
Lewis Shari	1-17-34
Nelson Jimmy	12-15-28
Tyler Willie	9-8-40
Wences Senor	4-20-12
Winchell Paul	12-21-22

PUPPETEERS

Baird Bil	8-15-04
Baird Cora	1-26-12
Henson Brian	1963
Henson Jim	9-24-36
Krofft Sid	7-30-29
Oz Frank	5-24-44
Sarg Tony	4-24-1882
Tichenor Tom	2-10-23
Tillstrom Burr	10-13-17

****

MISS AMERICAS

Cornett Leanza	6-10-71
Cothran Shirley	1953
Dennison Jo-Carroll	12-16-23
George Phyllis	6-25-49
Howell Arlene	1940
LaPlanche Rosemary	1925
Meeuwson Terry	3-2-49
Meriwether Lee	5-27-35
Mobley Mary Ann	2-17-37
Myerson Bess	7-16-24
Shopp BeBe	8-17-30
VanDerbur Marilyn	6-16-37
Whitestone Heather	2-24-73

****

BURLESQUE DANCERS

Britton Sherry	7-23-24
Corio Ann	1914
Lee Gypsy Rose	2-9-14
Rand Sally	4-3-04
St Cyr Lili	6-3-17

****

RADIO/TV DISC JOCKEYS

Dr Demento	4-2-41
Edwards Tommy	3-27-23
Emery Ralph	3-10-33
Freed Alan	12-15-22
Fuentes Daisy	11-17-66
Kaufman Murray the K	2-14-22
Kasem Casey	4-27-32
Morrow 'Cousin Brucie'	1935
Nordine Ken	4-13-20
Quinn Martha	5-11-59
Williams William B	8-6-23
Wolfman Jack	1-21-38

ATHLETES

Alzado Lyle	4-3-49
Atwood Donna	2-14-23
Belita	10-25-23
Brown Jim	2-17-36
Casey Bernie	6-8-39
Dean Christopher	7-27-58
Dryer Fred	7-6-46
Dudikoff Michael	10-8-54
Ferrigno Lou	11-9-51
Fleming Peggy	7-27-48
Gorgeous George (Wagner)	1915
Graziano Rocky	12-31-21
Hamill Dorothy	7-26-56
Harding Tonya	11-12-70
Heiss Carol	1-20-40
Henie Sonja	4-8-12
Henry Mike	1941
Hogan Hulk	8-11-53
Johnson Lynn-Holly	1959
Karras Alex	7-15-35
Kerrigan Nancy	10-13-69
Kirkwood Joe Jr	5-30-20
Laughlin Tom	8-10-31
Lee Brandon	2-1-65
Lee Bruce	11-27-40
Lemon Meadowlark	4-25-32
Nielsen Brigitte	7-15-64
Norris Chuck	3-1-39
Olsen Merlin	9-15-40
Piper Rowdy Roddy	11-19-51
Ralston Vera Hruba	7-12-19
Reeves Steve	1-21-26
Rigby Cathy	12-12-52
Rocca Antonino	4-23-23
Savage Fred 'Macho Man'	11-15-52
Seagal Steven	4-10-51
Simpson O J	7-9-47
Smith Bubba	2-28-45
Torvill Jane	10-7-57
VanDamme Jean-Claude	10-18-60
Weathers Carl	1-14-48
Weissmuller Johnny	6-2-04
Williamson Fred	3-5-38
Witt Katarina	12-3-65
Yamaguchi Kristi	7-12-72

CIRCUS

Adler Felix	1898
Anthony Tony	2-13-15
Ayala Andrea	4-15-73
Bale Trevor	6-13-13
Beatty Clyde	6-10-03
Boas Charles 'Doc'	9-5-26
Burgess Hovey	9-8-40
Butler Roland	6-2-1887
Codona Alfredo	10-7-1883
Cole James M	1-11-06
Concello Antoinette	1912
Concello Art	3-26-12
Gaona Tito	1947
Gautier Axel	1942
Gebel-Williams Gunther	9-12-34
James Jimmy	8-25-40
Kelly Emmett	12-9-1898
Loyal Guistino	8-2-09
Miller Dory	7-27-16
North John Ringling	8-17-03
Petit Philippe	8-13-49
Vargas Cliff	12-7-24
Vazquez Miguel	12-6-64
Vazquez-Ayala Margarita	5-20-47
Wallenda Helen	12-11-10
Wallenda Karl	1905
Weber Herbie	5-17-14
White Patricia	1955
Zoppe Alberto	1-4-22

* * * * * * * * * * * * * * *

COMMERCIALS

Dietrich Dena	12-4-28
Fridell Squire	2-9-43
Furness Betty	1-3-16
Harmon Kelly	1947
Hutton Gunilla	5-15-44
Jordan Michael	2-17-63
Lasorda Tommy	9-22-27
Lenska Rula	9-30-46
Loren Donna	3-7-47
Namath Joe	5-31-43
Naughton David	2-13-51
Retton Mary Lou	1-24-68
Sedelmaier Joe	5-31-33
Thomas Dave	7-2-32

FASHION MODELS

Alexis Kim	7-15-60
Alt Carol	12-1-60
Avedon Doe	4-7-28
Brinkley Christie	2-2-53
Campbell Naomi	5-22-70
Crawford Cindy	2-20-66
Evangelista Linda	5-10-65
Fabio	3-15-61
Hall Jerry	7-2-56
Hansen Patti	1956
Hutton Lauren	11-17-43
Iman	7-25-56
Johnson Beverly	10-13-51
Jones Candy	12-31-25
Macpherson Elle	3-29-64
Moss Kate	1-16-74
Parker Suzy	10-28-33
Porizkova Paulina	4-9-65
Rice Donna	1-7-58
Schiffer Claudia	8-25-70
Shrimpton Jean	11-6-42
Sims Naomi	3-30-48
Stratten Dorothy	2-28-60
Tiegs Cheryl	9-25-47
Turlington Christy	1-2-69
Twiggy	9-19-49

****

ADULT FILMS

Chambers Marilyn	1952
Holmes John	1944
Lords Traci	5-7-68
Lovelace Linda	1952
Reems Harry	8-27-47
Spelvin Georgina	1937

****

MISCELLANY

Bass Saul	5-8-20
Blanc Mel	5-30-08
Buck Frank	3-17-1884
Butler Daws	11-16-16
Carol Sue	10-30-08
Clark Peggy	9-30-15
Dagmar (Jennie Lewis)	11-29-26
Divine (Harris Milstead)	10-19-45
Doll Bill	12-28-10

Dr Ruth (Westheimer)	6-4-28
Epstein Brian	9-19-34
Everson William K	4-8-29
Fisher Jules	11-12-37
Fox Carol	6-15-26
Geller Uri	12-20-46
Graham Bill	1-8-31
Gray Spaulding	6-5-41
Kirshner Don	4-17-34
Kirstein Lincoln	5-4-07
Knievel Evel	10-17-38
Knight Arthur	9-3-16
Kreskin	1-12-35
LaLanne Jack	9-26-14
Langlois Henri	11-13-14
Lazar Swifty	3-28-07
Lee Ming Cho	10-3-30
Marceau Marcel	3-22-23
Markle C Wilson	9-2-38
McCormack Mark	11-6-30
Meisner Sanford	8-31-05
Mengers Sue	9-2-38
Meredith Scott	11-24-23
Messick Don	9-7-26
Mielziner Jo	3-19-01
Morley Eric	9-26-18
Muller Romeo	8-7-28
Ovitz Michael	12-14-46
Parker Colonel Tom	6-26-10
Patterson Tom	6-11-20
Presley Lisa Marie	2-1-68
Preston Frances	8-27-34
Questal Mae	9-13-10
Regine (Zylberberg)	12-26-29
Russell Harold	1-14-14
Shields Robert	3-26-51
Shore Pauly	2-1-68
Smith Dick	6-26-22
Swift Allen	1-16-24
Trapp Maria von	1-26-05
Valenti Jack	9-5-21
VanDoren Charles	2-12-26
Wasserman Lew	3-15-13
Wayne Paula	11-3-37
Westmore Michael	3-22-38
Yarnell Lorene	3-21-48

****